Rastaman

Rastaman

The Rastafarian Movement in England

ERNEST CASHMORE

London
GEORGE ALLEN & UNWIN
Boston   Sydney

First published in 1979

GEORGE ALLEN & UNWIN LTD
40 Museum Street, London WC1A 1LU

© Ernest E. H. Cashmore, 1979

British Library Cataloguing in Publication Data

Cashmore, Ernest
    Rastaman.
    1. Ras Tafari movement
    2. West Indians in England
    I. Title
    301.45′29′96   BL2530.J3   79–40684

    ISBN 0–04–301108–X

Typeset in 10 on 11 point Plantin by Trade Linotype Ltd, Birmingham
and printed in Great Britain
by Biddles Ltd, Guildford and King's Lynn

At this moment methinks I see Ethiopia stretching forth her hands unto God and methinks I see the Angel of God taking up the standard of the Red, the Black and the Green, and saying, 'Men of the Negro Race, Men of Ethiopia, follow me.' Climb ye the heights of liberty and cease not in well doing until you have planted the banner of the Red, the Black and the Green on the hilltops of Africa.

Marcus Garvey (*Philosophy and Opinions*, Vol. 1, 1967)

And I saw a strong angel proclaiming with a great voice. Who is worthy to open the book, and to loose the seven seals thereof? And no one in heaven, or on earth, or under the earth, was able to open the book, or to look thereon: and one of the elders saith to me, Weep not: behold, the Lion that is of the tribe of Judah, the Root of David, hath overcome, to open the book and the seven seals thereof.

Revelation, 5 : 1–6

We're sick and tired of your easing kissing game
to die and go to heaven in Jesus name
we know and understand
almighty God is a living man

Bob Marley and Peter Tosh ('Get Up, Stand Up', 1973)

Preface

I became fascinated by the Rastafarian movement when a graduate student at the University of Toronto. Having noticed isolated groups of these somewhat bizarre-looking characters and heard of their uneasy relationship with the Toronto Metropolitan Police, I was intrigued to come across an article in *Rolling Stone* magazine which dealt with the contemporary movement in Jamaica (Michael Thomas, 1976).

In 1976 I left Canada to take up a position as a research student at the London School of Economics and had the chance to stop off at Jamaica *en route*. Here I took the opportunity to talk to locals and make observations on the movement. I found myself absorbed by their beliefs and lifestyle. On arrival in England I became very aware that the movement's relevance was not merely confined to Jamaica and Toronto, but to Birmingham, London and other urban areas of England. I had noticed the existence of tams (woolly hats) and peculiar hairstyles of black youths before leaving for Canada (in 1975) and was familiar with Dick Hebdige's then unpublished paper, 'Reggae, Rastas and Rudies' (1975), but the movement's growth in my absence was astonishing and I considered it worthy of serious attention.

Accordingly, I approached my supervisor, Professor Percy Cohen, with the idea of an empirical study to explore the origins, development and present state of the Rastafarian movement in England and, after a few false starts, the work got under way in November 1976.

My initial approaches were daunting, for the Rastas had recently suffered the embarrassment of being labelled a 'mafia organisation' (by the *Reading Evening Post*) – and were to suffer similar brandings in the months that followed. Complicating the issue further was the fact that its members regarded the movement as exclusive and not amenable to outsiders; for a white investigator like myself, I was informed 'it makes no sense'. On occasions I met with disinterest and even refusals to talk to me. Apart from chance encounters and casual conversations with individuals, I made little sustained contact. All the time I was piecing together the history of the movement and gaining what I later found out to be 'insight'.

The turning point came when Father M. Charles, an Anglican vicar, introduced me to members of the Ethiopian Orthodox Church in Birmingham to whom he loaned his church for services. I am indebted to these brothers for their co-operation and, indeed, encouragement. Armed with even deeper insight after reasoning at length with church members, I grew in confidence and was able to reason more effectively with other groups not affiliated to the church.

From here the situation 'snowballed', as well as attending the church, I frequented several Rastafarian haunts and engaged in protracted reasoning sessions (Rasta discourses); my reputation as a 'man of insight' grew and I gained what I felt to be acceptance. Having seen me in conversation with Rastas, other members had their initial doubts or fears assuaged and their suspicion or hostility dissolved, thus paving the way for open communication.

Periodic obstacles hindered the research: the publication of Brown's *Shades of Grey* in late 1977 aroused alarm about the nature of outsiders studying the movement and I came under scrutiny; my participation in the production of London Weekend Television's 'Credo' programme on the Rastas incurred the wrath of a great many, particularly those I had recruited for the interviews. Thankfully, I was able to convince them of my purity of intention and motivation and by the time of the work's completion (winter, 1978) my relationships were sounder and more amiable than ever.

To single out individuals from the hundreds of Rastas with whom I reasoned is an exercise to which Rastas themselves would object. I would, however, express a special thanks to Brothers Kinfe Gabriel and Claudius Haughton of the Ethiopian Orthodox Church, Birmingham, Ras Anthony Elliott of the Twelve Tribes of Israel, London, and Brother Dennis Deans for their unstinting co-operation in the provision of insight.

I would also like to acknowledge some intellectual debts. First, impersonal ones to Peter Berger and Thomas Luckmann whose book *The Social Construction of Reality* (1972) was inspirational to the whole exercise; but also to Bryan Wilson and Michael Barkun for their respective works *Magic and the Millennium* (1973) and *Disaster and the Millennium* (1974) both of which were treasure houses of concepts and themes; from these I have stolen many gems. Less visible, but still influential, was Roy Wallis's *The Road to Total Freedom* (1977). The chapter on 'Reality Maintenance in a. Deviant Belief System' was a direct spur to my Chapter 7.

On a more personal level I would like to thank Professor Abner Cohen of the School of Oriental and African Studies for reading and commenting on drafts of Chapters 7 and 8, Barry Troyna of the University of Leicester for his remarks on an earlier formulation of Chapter 6 and Claudius Haughton for reading a version of Chapter 4. I owe a particular debt of gratitude to my supervisor Percy Cohen who read through earlier drafts of the whole work and provided comment and criticism. His personal encouragement and support for the enterprise were indispensable assets.

The cover photograph was taken by my friend, Robin Coulthard, to whom I express my appreciation. My thanks also to Elaine Kirby and Maria Salmon for typing the original manuscript.

Lastly, I acknowledge a deep debt to all those Rastas who reasoned with me, argued against me and sometimes just tolerated me. Although they bear no responsibility for the final product, this is really their book.

Contents

Chapter 1

Introduction: The Sociological Interest in Rasta

Sociology takes its place in the company of sciences that deal with man *as* man; that it is, in that specific sense, a humanistic discipline. An important consequence of this conception is that sociology must be carried on in a continuous conversation with both history and philosophy or lose its proper object of inquiry. This object is society as part of a human world, made by men, inhabited by men, and, in turn making men, in an ongoing historical process. It is not the least fruit of a humanistic sociology that it re-awakens our wonder at this astonishing phenomenon.

Peter Berger and Thomas Luckmann, 1972

The British black power leader Obi Egbuna once reflected that during the 1960s it was 'the climax of absurdity to call a "West Indian" African' (1970, p. 17). During the middle and latter stages of the 1970s it was an outrage to tens of thousands of West Indians to call them anything but African. In 1978 I asked a young black in London his nationality; he replied: 'I'm from Ethiopia, but I was born in the West Indies.' Here in a nutshell lies the sociological problem behind this work.

The dramatic and comprehensive changes in consciousness occurring within the West Indian community of England during the 1970s was arguably the most important development in the history of the black presence. First-generation migrants from the West Indies were relatively accommodating, cultivating thoughts and postures conducive to their low visibility and repressed anxieties; few attempted to articulate their felt grievances and for the most part phrased their ambitions in terms of the institutional facilities available. Their sons and daughters totally and utterly rejected their parents' perspectives: they developed radically different stances *vis-à-vis* the wider society, nurtured and preserved new ways of thinking, fresh methods of expressing their anxieties; they created a new reality. For the sociologist this elicits two questions: why they did. it, and how they did it. My effort, therefore, was to advance on these two fronts, asking what were the motivations, dispositions and cognitive states impelling black youths to new modes of thought and action, and how it was possible for them to construct for themselves a conception of reality so divorced and distinct from that of their parents that it was breathtaking to imagine that only one generation separated them. The fruit of my inquiry was intended to be an understanding of the processes whereby a new definition of reality was achieved: how West Indian youth in the 1970s created a peculiarly Rastafarian reality.

But the sociologist is not interested merely in the internal pressures and processes at work in the creation of reality, the mechanisms social groups develop for constructing their conceptions and defusing challenges to their definition, important though they are. He must go further to investigate the historical situation from which that group grew, the material context out of which it emerged, the relationships sustained or terminated with other groups and the consequences it produces for insiders and outsiders. To crystallise these concerns into a single theme one might say that the impulse is to uncover the social foundations of a particular conception of reality. In order to satisfy adequately this impulse and lay bare the social bases of the English Rastafarian movement my investigations took me as far back as the seventeenth century and as far afield as Jamaica and Africa – albeit an Africa of the imagination; from the general area of British colonialism and the particular brand of racism it manifested and perpetuated to the specific area of West Indian attitude change, or shift in cognition.

The historical dimension is intended to anchor the English movement in its past; to unravel the complex processes and mechanisms which contributed to the production and transmission of a belief system so compelling in appeal that not only did it remain a dominant cultural force in its original context (Barrett, 1977, pp. 185–97), but transferred to North America most particularly to Toronto (where I noticed the movement in 1975–6 and was informed by the Inspector of the Intelligence Bureau, Metropolitan Toronto Police, that the Rastas' 'relationship with the Metropolitan Toronto Police Force is usually of a criminal nature'); to Hartford, Connecticut where the movement emerged around 1962 (Barrett, 2 June 1977, personal communication); and most strikingly to New York City where the cult was linked to trafficking in ganja (marihuana), extortion and murder after four Rastas were found murdered execution style (C. Gerald Fraser, June 1977, New York Times Service). In 1977 the movement surfaced in Paris. Though I am unqualified to comment on these, I observed that the British movement provoked similar patterns of reaction from the wider society, reaching a full pitch with the publication of the *Shades of Grey* report (1977) and the sense of panic it generated in Birmingham. Historical analysis reveals that the attribution of deviant status had been a feature of the movement since its inception in 1930. This in itself warranted investigation and I took care to focus on societal reactions to the cult and how they might have affected its overall development. It is important to realise how a volatile reaction from the wider society can impinge on the movement's ability to produce and sustain a version of reality at variance to 'conventional' conceptions.

To offer a synopsis, my attempt was to dig an exploratory shaft into the social foundations of the movement by tracing the development of religious thought in colonial and post-colonial Jamaica, noting the influences on and conditions underlying these developments and documenting the legacy they left in their wake. Particular attention was paid to Marcus Garvey, without question the most socially important precursory inspiration to the movement. He cut a path through extant traditions of thinking in Jamaica and presented building blocks on which to construct a totally fresh and exhilarating conception of reality. The Rastafarian interpretation of Garvey's concepts and categories was far more exotic and bizarre than the charismatic prophet's own; it constituted what Michael Barkun (1974, p. 37) calls a 'quantum leap' – that which separates millenarian movements from other forms of social protest. Unlike Garvey, who had worked pragmatically at achieving his central aim of repatriating all blacks to their 'native' Africa, the Rastas conceived the idea that the entire social universe would be totally transformed and they would be returned to Africa through the power of the then Ethiopian Emperor Haile Selassie I who was taken to be the living God. After repeated failures of the millennium to materialise in the late fifties and early sixties some factions of the movement reconceptualised the nature of the messianic consummation and encouraged its arrival through resort to violence; their efforts were severely consequential in prompting a societal reaction of such intensity that panic gripped the island for several years. To conclude Chapter 2 I summarise the contemporary situation in Jamaica and the routes along which it is likely to develop, paying particular attention to neo-Marxist interpretations of the cult.

To link the two movements I open Chapter 3 with a description of the post-war Jamaican migration to England, and a cursory glance at the type of reception the immigrants experienced. Some early patterns of black adaptation to the new environment are then outlined. Dealt with next is the emergence, development and contours of the English Rastafarian movement and the social origins of its members. From here I look at the two dynamics propelling the modern movement: the creation of a suggestible and receptive black populace; and the existence of a Rastafarian definition of reality and the social apparatus for its transmission. My efforts then turn to delineating the actual mechanisms which the movement operated to sustain and recreate its own particular version of reality. From here I inquire into how Rastas, despite their lack of material resources, were able to effect and consolidate the sense of belonging to an exclusive and in many ways élite groups, entry into which was restricted to only the 'enlightened ones'. Despite the Rastas' strain to perpetuate exclusivity, however, their very presence in urban–industrial centres necessitated contacts with outside groups, some of which were fraught with more tension than others. The movement's relationship with the police was the most conflict-riven and this gave rise to a panic of such proportions that the whole of the movement's membership was brought into severe disrepute. Finally, I conclude with an analysis of the African consciousness which has gripped the minds of West Indian youth in the 1970s and compare this with the *négritude* movement of the thirties and forties, which also sought to upgrade blacks by instilling in them pride and dignity in their African heritage.

CONCEPTUAL APPARATUS

During the course of my research it became apparent that the puzzle for the modern Rastas themselves was in discovering what in history made possible a forecast of an imminent and total transformation of the existing order and an entry into a realm of human perfection. In a peculiar way their problem was similar to mine for I, too, was trying to discover the social roots of the Rastaman. But while Rastas were looking to Africa, for them a continent of unlimited possibilities and the black man's Zion, I was focusing on Jamaica where the movement first emerged and on Africa only for the initial influences on thought which were elaborated, transmitted and rendered amenable to the fantastic synthesis which became known as Ras Tafari. From there my route was fairly clear: to follow the development of this mode of thought from its inception in the 1930s to its contemporary form and then to examine its transmission and growth in the new environment of England. In other words, while the Rastas were at work creating reality on the basis of their perceived African heritage, I was recreating the background, thought and actions of those responsible for the reality.

I anticipate the immediate and most serious set of objections to approaching the task in the manner I have and one of these is that my theorising tends to be over-impressionistic, sometimes unsubstantiated and occasionally too subjective in orientation. Unfortunately, I have little with which to counter such criticisms and can only concede that the nature of the work necessitated a heavy reliance on intuition and inference. No one who appreciates the craft of the sociologist would seriously expect a perfectly faithful and sympathetic reproduction of the actor's definition of reality (many sociologists would find this irrelevant anyway); the best I have achieved is a number of insights and understandings about the thoughts of the group about which I am concerned and their relationships with social settings. My conviction is simply that consciousness can be best expanded by analysing that of others in specific social contexts. This is a view of sociology as a humanistic enterprise.

A related exception to my approach might be that my indulgence takes me into the shadows of epistemological relativism, that because of my preparedness to adopt a stance of sociological agnosticism and not comment on the correctness, validity or truth of the beliefs with which I am dealing, my conclusions command no significantly higher level of theoretical awareness than those of the Rastas themselves and, therefore, are reduced to 'one amongst many' viewpoints. In my defence against this I marshall the support of Derek Phillips who contends: 'Objective knowledge exists in sociology in the sense that it is accredited by members of the sociological community' (1973, p. 143). The truth of a belief, then, lies in the agreement it elicits within a particular community. So, for example, what constitutes truth for a British sociologist may not be truth for a Brazilian Ubandist, nor for a Rastaman in Jamaica or England. Truth pertains to its specific social context so that a mature sociological analysis needs to examine varieties of truth; the analyst's own conclusions are never more than versions of reality for there is no way the sociologist can stand outside and analyse objectively (though he may endeavour to eliminate bias). Sociology is itself a socially organised activity and its results are received by a social community; they are converted into truth only by the application of canons of procedure which provide for the possibility of agreement. My aim is to proffer a version of the genesis and development of the particular consciousness informing the Rastafarian movement. Rastas themselves might well dispute its correctness and replace it with their own version; a Roman Catholic priest might contest the validity of both versions. I am not interested in the ultimate epistemological status of my version and feel that the inclusion of questions concerning the validity of knowledge within the sociological discipline is, as Berger and Luckmann express it, 'like trying to push a bus in which one is riding' (1972, p. 25).

Closely related to this issue is the question of choice of concepts used for the purposes of analysis. As an actor standing outside the movement, yet trying to comprehend what goes on inside, my task was complicated by my very social location. My analysis, therefore, is unavoidably coloured by my own conception of reality and phrased in concepts I find contributory to understanding. Given my general theoretical position I strenuously tried to eschew what I regarded to be impositional concepts, those constructs created and utilised by social scientists to analyse phenomena in terms not recognisable to the phenomena themselves. Whilst realising the necessity for some degree of imposition, I attempted to extract my concepts from the Rastas themselves, sometimes thematising them, often naming them differently, and sometimes linking them in ways with which Rastas would not agree.

To take an example, the 'Babylonian conspiracy' is not a phrase used by Rastas themselves but seems to capture the theoretical underpinnings of much Rastafarian thought. The process of 'mental erasure' is my own phrase but would be recognised by Rastas as a condition of membership. My research indicated that the concept of 'drift' (a term borrowed from David Matza) suggests the most fruitful method of analysing the process of progressive involvement with the movement; though Rastas might find this offensive and argue that they were always Rastafarian, it just being a matter of time before realising this: 'Jah passed over I' being an illustrative response.

Other concepts retain much more fidelity and so rely on Rastafarian world views, which are, of course, replete with their own analytic tools. 'Acceptance' of Ras Tafari as the living God, I discerned, was the critical moment in the career of becoming a Rastaman; this constituted the opening of new windows from which to look out at reality, or what I chose to call the acquisition of new 'conceptual maps' (*pace* Jarvie). At this point 'insight' is said to be achieved. The notion of a 'brotherhood' or 'brethren' to characterise the social organisation of the movement are terms derived from the Rastas themselves and give revealing glimpses into how Ras Tafari held together as a movement as opposed to a loose aggregation of individuals. This connected closely with what I considered to be the most enriching concept in the Rastafarian vocabulary, 'I and I'. Expressed through the words of a Rasta, this denotes, 'the oneness of two persons . . . that God is in all men'. In Rastafarian reality God is both a deity and inherent in all men, thus providing a tie or link between all brothers. The relevance of this important concept becomes apparent as the total picture unravels. So, while I am not specifically interested in the philosophy of the Rastafarian reality in itself, I had little hesitation in drawing upon Rastafarian analytic constructs to supplement my own analysis. Some sociologists might find such short cuts unacceptable and unscholarly: I make no apology.

In more detached moments I made use of terms which are the exclusive property of the analyst. The meaning of many of my borrowed concepts, such as Ian Jarvie's 'conceptual maps' and Stanley Cohen's 'folk devils' are clarified as the book unfolds, but others require elaboration at the outset. I characterise Ras Tafari as both 'cult' and 'movement'. Without indulging in a consideration of what exactly is to constitute a cult (as opposed to a sect or a church) let me simply state that I do not accept criteria which include the content of the belief system or their life-span. With Roy Wallis I agree that the central characteristic of the cult is 'epistemological individualism': 'By epistemological individualism I mean to suggest that the cult has no clear locus of final authority beyond the individual member' (1976, p. 14).

The belief system of Ras Tafari was so vague and loosely defined, even at its inception, due to its lack of a single authoritative voice, that what was to be acceptable doctrine was largely a matter of individual interpretation. Never in the history of the movement had there been a leader effective enough to impose an unambiguous interpretation and so make demands on members in such a way as to establish clear boundaries. Instead there existed few demands and no distinction between members and non-members (technically, at least). This introduced the problem of distinguishing what constituted the typical Rastaman; but if there was a solution to this it was an arbitrary one. As a cult, Ras Tafari had a very transient membership, usually an expanding one. In its English manifestation I preferred to see the membership as constantly in flux with members drifting towards the core of the belief system until they came to accept the divinity of Haile Selassie; but even this was not a spur-of-the-moment decision but a 'process' of acquiring insight. The belief system itself remained broadly based and amenable to differential interpretation, adaptation, supplementation and abridgement.

Lacking in centralised authority, the Rastas were never able to organise themselves on sectarian models and, therefore, faced problems of control which continually threatened to dissolve the membership and render it a loose aggregation instead of a warrantable movement. I take the term 'movement' to transcend particular types of religious manifestation, such as cult and sect, and refer more generically to a collective mode of response to specific interpretations of evil; and here I look to Bryan Wilson who contends that 'Men apprehend evil in many different ways and thus look for relief from it in different forms of supernatural action. The various responses to the world embrace different conceptions of the source of evil and the ways in which it will be overcome' (1973, p. 21).

Ras Tafari was a response to the perceived source of evil – the white colonial system of Babylon. Rastas collectively located the evil and responded to it in a relatively focused manner. Sharing this common focus and perceived ways of alleviating their anxieties united them into a movement. The Rastas' response was to reject dominant cultural goals by declaring that only the wholesale transformation of the social world, the destruction of Babylon, would suffice.

What made the Rastafarian a 'millenarian movement' was that the process of transformation was to be engineered and executed by a supernatural agency, in this case Haile Selassie (though it should be pointed out that some groups felt the need to participate in the process of transforming by assisting with violent measures). The movement conformed neatly to Norman Cohn's (1957) seminal definition of a millenarian movement, the five criteria of which were: that it will be a collective response; that salvation will be activated in this world; that the transformation will occur imminently; that it will be total, overturning the extant order; and it will be miraculously achieved with the help of a supernatural agency.

My work indicated that in the transition to England the movement lost little of the millenarian vitality which characterised its Jamaican predecessor. True, there were no congregation at London docks to await the arrival of Haile Selassie's ships, but this is not to concede that the contemporary Rastas lost their commitment to the supernaturally wrought destruction of Babylon and the ensuing world transformation: 'must come' was the oft-heard reply to the question of the inevitability of the holocause, 'these are the last days'. The mechanics behind the transformation were never revealed but at no time was any doubt shown about its ultimacy and inevitability and that it would be the consequence of divine action: 'God's will'.

My preference for 'movement' as opposed to 'cult' is simply a reflection of the Rastas' predilection to use this term. Ras Tafari was most assuredly a cult, but I feel no clarity is forsaken through my use of 'movement'.

I use the term 'Rastafarian movement' to denote the central phenomenon under study; 'Ras Tafari' is used synonymously and sometimes taken to refer to the actual belief system. 'Rasta' I take to be the individual member and more generally as the symbolic collective; a member once told me: 'The music was real Rasta.' The 'Rastaman' also refers to the individual member, though I use the word mostly to mean the 'typical' Rastafarian member, sometimes as addressed by outsiders: 'The attribution of deviant status to the Rastaman'. Rastas sometimes used the expression 'I man' interchangeably with Rastaman. My use of 'Rastafarian' as an adjective, contrary to its popular usage as a noun, is in line with Rastas' own terminology.

Words I have not included but which are often used to describe Rastas are 'the dreadlocks', 'the dreads' and the 'Natty Dreads' which I consider to be slightly derogatory in tone. I have also desisted employing the concept of 'Rastafarianism', a term I personally abhor which seems to be a source of confusion to outsiders and embarrassment to Rastas themselves. Almost every contemporary commentator on the movement has used this insensitive term without considering the discipline of doctrine and organisation it seems to connote. Even Garvey who did establish a rigorous ideological programme and formal organisation through which to articulate it was not keen on 'isms' (M. Garvey, 1967, Vol. 2, p. 334). Ras Tafari most certainly does not warrant the attachment of 'ism' to its name.

METHODOLOGICAL APPARATUS

The prime methodological problem of the study was that of impenetrability. Rastas regarded themselves as a very exclusive and élite body of people, entry into which was restricted to those with 'insight' enough to accept the divinity of Haile Selassie. My initial task, then, was to gain their confidence and 'get inside' the movement. I became fairly involved in the history of the cult and its antecedents before my initial approaches were made and, having briefly visited Jamaica in 1976, I was familiar with the contemporary situation there. I made no effort to conceal the purpose of my inquiry and sought to impress the brothers with my seriousness of purpose and purity of intention. Having made sets of contacts with various Rastafarian groups in London and Birmingham and satisfied them (I think) with my knowledge and ambition, I was able to generate data through what I regarded as interviews and then develop these into broad themes.

As my face became 'worn in', suspicions were diminished and my reputation as a 'man of insight' grew. This was tarnished slightly by the publication of the damning *Shades of Grey* report in December 1977, the author of which had allegedly interviewed a small number of Handsworth Rastas on the pretext of making a 'purely academic' inquiry. He failed to mention that the study was being carried out under the aegis of the West Midlands Police Force. Having already made clear my academic status, I found myself in the somewhat hazardous position of sharing the same occupational sphere as the man who had done so much to bring the name of Ras Tafari into disrepute. Fortunately, the majority of my contacts were perspicacious enough to realise my purposes were antithetical to those of the *Shades of Grey* author: mine were to clarify and develop understanding, not to obfuscate and obscure.

During the course of my research I acted as consultant to a London Weekend Television programme, 'Credo', which focused on the Rastafarian movement in Britain. I suggested to the Rastas that it might be a way to erase much of the harm done by the *Shades of Grey* report and that a more accurate picture could be portrayed. The programme was composed of a series of interviews with Rastas which I arranged and conducted. (Rastas specifically requested that I should be allowed to do the interviewing as it was suggested that the regular interviewer for the programme lacked the necessary insight – which I thought revealed their apprehensions about talking to outsiders who may have been unsympathetic.) Unfortunately, I was denied any control over the editing of the programme, which was aired on 26

February 1978, and the finished product did not match up to expectations; only one Rasta out of nearly a hundred I spoke to in the immediate aftermath of the show was happy with the portrayal. A few were so dissatisfied that they even entertained the idea that I had worked in cohort with LWT for the sixteen months prior to the showing (i.e. when I began my research). I was able to assuage these fears and managed to patch up relationships.

Overall, the methodology of the work was eclectic. My ambition was not to subject any prestructured hypothesis to a series of tests, but rather to generate information on a subject which previously commanded only fleeting attention from newspaper journalists and had formed part of the focus of only one article, by Dick Hebdige, with whom I spoke before commencing my own work. The methods fell into three zones: historical, formal interviews and informal interviews.

Historically, I looked to the existing literature on the Jamaican movement, beginning with the early works of George Eaton Simpson (1955a, 1955b, 1955c, 1962), then progressing to the contributions of Sheila Kitzinger (1966, 1969) and the definitive statement of Smith, Augier and Nettleford (1967); after this I turned to theses of Joseph Moore (1953) which dealt with African influences in Jamaican religion prior to Ras Tafari, Leonard Barrett (1968) and Anthony Williams (1974) which looked at the role of the prophet in Jamaican religion. By this stage I had created a voluminous enough bibliography to probe further, looking more deeply into the roots of the cult by using newspaper reports, transcripted radio interviews and the documents of commentators on the slavery system of the West Indies. Of the material available on the contemporary movement in Jamaica I found Rex Nettleford's chapter in *Mirror, Mirror* (1974a) invaluable and Errol Bowen's article written in 1971 interesting, though Barrett's updating of his 1968 thesis, which was released during my research period, is now regarded by many as the most complete account of the Jamaican movement. Also published in Jamaica during my research was Joseph Owens' *Dread* (1977). For those interested in more detail on the history and development of the Jamaican movement I recommend my comprehensive, unpublished thesis (Cashmore, 1978).

Although I distinguished between 'formal' and 'informal' interviews, neither would measure up to 'formal' by conventional social scientific criteria. My distinction was merely to suggest that I prepared themes to be discussed and taped for the 'formal' interviews, each lasting between one and four hours. Much more exciting, however, was the 'informal' variety which consisted of my participation in 'reasoning' sessions. Reasoning, as I point out later, was the name given to Rastafarian discourse, when members came together spontaneously on a regular basis to engage in often lengthy discussions about virtually any subject. During the course of these very fluid sessions members might leave and others join, and topics changed rapidly. My participation in these sessions gave me rich insights into Rastafarian thinking, how the brothers and sisters interpret their world and my comprehension of their world view broadened with each successive session.

I reasoned with countless numbers of Rastas in such settings as their homes, in shops and restaurants and even on streets. Initially, contacts were made casually with individual members who would reason with me; these contacts gave me leverage, with other members joining in the dialogue and over a period of time I came to know more and more on personal bases and therefore widened my net of contacts. My very presence at reasoning sessions tended to allay any suspicions which new additions might have held, the mechanism being something like: 'If this man has insight enough to reason with my brothers, then he must be trustworthy.'

Not that my presence at reasoning sessions was greeted with unanimous approval. On several occasions I underwent anxious experiences when being questioned about my intentions by suspicious and sometimes hostile Rastas: 'What you need to know about Rasta? Him don't care nothing about you, so why you interested in him?' My usual justification was that I was attempting to break down the obstacles to understanding and promote a greater appreciation of the movement in the most faithful and accurate way possible: by finding out from the brethren themselves. But not all Rastas were desirous of being understood: 'Me no want you to understand Rasta; it is I's faith; it is my life'; 'Man, Rasta don't want other to understand him. Just want to be left alone; leave the mystery.' And when I pointed out that this mystery and secrecy attributed to the movement might eventually prove detrimental to its development I was shot down: 'Suspicious of I? Hah! Them ras suspicious. Let them be. Rastaman, he no care. Him keep his dread'; 'Them see that Rasta knows the truth and soon must come, must take his place in the world soon. Fear I? I thinks they must 'cause that day is soon.' Even the co-operative ones were sometimes sceptical about the ultimate usefulness of my project: 'See (yes), your intentions are good, but this society can never accept I man. Racialism is too deep. I see this in my work, in each day I face racialism; too much so to wipe away.' Despite these obstacles I persevered and came to reason with these brethren on a fairly comfortable basis, the topics usually gravitating towards the quality and intensity of racism and racialism in various societies.

These research procedures were most unmethodical but very valuable, supplying clues to the subjective experiences of Rastas, which are pivotal in this book. During the course of my research I reasoned with literally hundreds of Rastas, sometimes at length plumbing depths, at other times only briefly, making the reasoning cursory. I strained to encompass the widest span of Rastas possible: across age groups;

both sexes (though this was complicated by the reluctance of many sisters to play active parts in reasoning): members of institutionalised bodies (the Ethiopian Orthodox Church and the Twelve Tribes of Israel) and non-members; those who talked with great alacrity and those who did so only when specifically questioned. My extracted representation of these sessions is therefore something of a *mélange* containing elements from the widest variety of Rastafarian affiliates I could manage – though I make no allusions to definitiveness.

If the quotations I have taken from Rastas seem sagacious and illuminating, it is not because my respondents were all of an 'intellectual stratum' of the movement nor because I was highly selective in my choice of quotations. It is because the nature of the Rastafarian enterprise demanded that the members read and reasoned perpetually and in so doing acquired an ability to articulate freely, albeit in a highly stylised manner. The lack of a literary tradition and a high level of formal education did not produce cultural poverty for the Rastas, for their engagement in the movement made sure they developed linguistic and conceptual skills. I do not attribute this to any kind of 'self-selection' process whereby only those with the higher capacities for conceptual learning became Rastas; such a view would divert attention from the education functions of the enterprise. Blacks drifting into Ras Tafari receive a great deal of verbal and intellectual stimulation: to participate in Rastafarian reasoning was to participate fully in a highly verbal culture, to learn to manipulate abstract symbols, to practise analysing and generalising; in their own words, to gain 'insight'.

A NOTE ON DIALECT

The Rastas I spoke to during the research employed a stylised Jamaican patois when reasoning and made few concessions. They drew on a Jamaican oral culture but refined it to Rastafarian requirements. It will be noticed, however, that the numerous quotations I use do not accurately reflect the language of the Rastaman; I was forced to distort (quite consciously) the exotic qualities of Rasta speech simply to reduce ambiguity. So, although I resisted completely standardising the language, I have not utilised such spellings as *dem* for 'them', *fe* for 'for', *dis* for 'this', or *troot* for 'truth'. I hope no sensitivity will have been lost by my recording of pronunciation in a different vernacular. Before continuing, however, there are three small points which should be clarified: first, the term 'ras' when used with a lower case 'r' is a Jamaican swear word ('fuck' being the nearest English equivalent); secondly the word 'see' can be used to denote agreement (as in 'I see' or 'Yes, I see'); lastly, the expression 'Selassie I' is read not as 'Selassie the first' but as 'Selassie I' (the first person) denoting the implicit nature of Haile Selassie in all men including the speaker.

Chapter 2

The Rastaman in Jamaica

Men apprehend evil in many different ways and thus look for
relief from it in different forms of supernatural action. The
various responses to the world embrace different conceptions
of the source of evil with the ways in which it will be overcome.

Bryan Wilson, 1973

FROM THE SLEEP OF COUNTLESS CENTURIES . . .

Like most other movements of protest Ras Tafari was predicated on
the identification of evil. The response it manifested was an attempt
to eliminate this evil. Since the English conquest of Jamaica in 1655
and the instigation of a system of slavery, the island exhibited a
veritable spectrum of responses to evil among slaves and their offspring. Some sought the recruitment of supernatural agencies, others
pursued more secular and pragmatic means, some accepted institutional facilities for the attainment of goals, others rejected them. In all
cases, the manner in which the source of evil was apprehended determined the mode in which it was responded to.

For example, the most formative patterns of collective protest
exhibited an urgent desire to sever physical links with present circumstances and to create new and separate existences. The Maroons were
runaway slaves who periodically conspired to escape the confines of
the plantation and flee to the hilly inner regions of Jamaica where
they joined small, autonomous communities. They perceived evil in
what I call an immediate idiom, apprehending the immediate environment and attributing to its personnel causal efficacy, rather than
analysing the structures and processes which held together and perpetuated their subordinate position. For the Maroons, the evil presence
in their lives was the white man rather than the régime he supported.
Their attempt was to rid themselves of this presence by escaping his
domination and establishing self-supporting enclaves of ex-slaves. For
over eighty years after the British takeover in Jamaica in 1655 the
Maroons resisted military attempts to re-enslave them and waged
what became known as Maroon Wars under the leadership of such
demagogic figures as Cudjoe, Quao the Invisible Hunter and Nanny,

around whom developed a myth involving her possession of supernatural powers and invulnerability to whites' bullets. These leaders
inspired Maroon groups to mount regular attacks on whites and
encouraged other slaves to break away and join them. By 1730, the
Maroon threat had become critical enough for the British to spend
£100,000 in a massive attempt to suppress the danger (H. O.
Patterson, 1967, p. 270). Eventually in 1739 a treaty was signed
which brought to an end the wild, independent existence enjoyed by
Maroons and effectively tied them to the British as agents of social
control. This became known as the Blood Treaty because, according
to J. J. Williams 'Each man cut his hand and held it over a basin and
let the blood drain over the basin . . . Rum was poured on top and
shaken together, and each party drank blood and rum, pledging that
there should be no more war between the Maroons and the English
(1938, pp. 159–60).

Some Maroon groups refused to endorse the treaty and continued in
their rebellious activities. The British solution to this was to offer
incentives to the legally recognised Maroons for the capture and
intimidation of runaway slaves, thus rendering them a most effective
counter-rebellious force. The Blood Treaty inverted their role and
transformed them into the enemies of freedom. Though numerically
small,* they possessed an intimate knowledge of the interior geography
of the island which was an invaluable asset to the machinery of social
control. Their first real contribution was in subduing an uprising of
1,000 slaves in 1760; it was a Maroon who captured Tacky, the
instigator of the outburst. (For more detailed reading on the Maroons,
see Robinson, 1969.)

Apart from an attempt by a Trelawny-based group to regain their
independence in 1795, the Maroons continued to serve as mercenary
puppets of the colonial authorities until they eventually outlived their
usefulness and were allowed to retreat into the hills where they could
forget their auxiliary militia duties. Their last performance in this
capacity, however, was a singularly important and consequential event
occuring in 1865 at the south-eastern town of Morant Bay.

Perceived injustices in the Jamaican legal system were the spurs
behind a protest organised by a landowner, George William Gordon,
and a black preacher, Paul Bogle. They saw that the criminal legisla-
tion, passed between 1839 and 1840 to bring Jamaican law into
alignment with British precedents, was weighted strongly against blacks
and sought to articulate their resentment of this by leading 400 blacks
to a St Thomas courthouse. Their arrival was received by a cordon

---

*R. C. Dallas (1803) estimates totals as: 1739 – 600; 1770 – 885;
1773 – 1,028; 1788 – 1,400 (excluding those who remained outside the
law).

of militia surrounding the courthouse following a violent confrontation, fifteen people were killed and thirty-one injured. After this, a split occurred between the more moderate Gordon, and Bogle who, Bernard Semmel contends: 'organized small, secret societies whose long-range purpose was to foment rebellion and drive the white man from Jamaica' (1962a, pp. 45–6).

Bogle's activities gained him the attention of the white authorities who recruited the support of the Maroons to assist in apprehending the troublesome preacher who had attracted a following of several hundred. Attacks on whites ensued and Bogle became more vehement in his condemnation of all whites: 'With fury he denounced the Governor, the Custos, the Queen and, soon, every white man' (Semmel, 1962a; p. 45). His efforts were eventually crushed by the militia with the aid of Maroon ancillaries, and both he and Gordon were publicly hanged. Their followers were either eliminated or they absolved themselves from the cause. Significantly, however, Bogle had directed attention towards grievances which transcended local, personal horizons and pointed towards possibilities for overcoming them; possibilities which involved collective thought and action. It was his location of evil in the white man that prompted an attempted solution implying action on a collective rather than an individual basis.

Let me elaborate: prior to Bogle, evil had been perceived, in the main, as lying in spiritual realms. Stemming primarily from the African-derived obeah-myal belief complex, black Jamaican religions oriented to a social cosmos cohabited by humans and spirits which were amenable to manipulation by those mortals holding the requisite secrets. Obeah men were those gifted with the ability to control the spirits of the dead, 'duppies', and use them in their own service. As such, they were influential men (or sometimes women) who were often called upon to cast spells, or put a 'hex' on others. Myal was a response to the bad medicine of obeah; it sought through ritual to neutralise the obeah man's power and reduce his victim's chances of suffering the consequences of his spells. But, crucially, both subscribed to a basic set of beliefs which held that evil lay not in the order of things in this world, but in the less tangible world of spirits. How this evil was addressed was largely determined by how it was apprehended in the first instance. As long as the source of malevolence was perceived in this manner, obeah-myal posed little threat to the social order. It was only when the spirits were used to sanction this worldly action, such as in 1760 when over 1,000 slaves under Tacky were inspired to insurrectionary action by an obeah man, that it became dangerous (Long, 1774, Vol. 2, pp. 447–62). Following the uprising, the Jamaican House of Assembly introduced draconian measures to deter the practice of obeah and myal.

Some features of the obeah-myal complex were found to be

intriguingly compatible with those of Christianity. Though plantation owners were active in their discouragement of religious instruction, believing some of the more muscular passages of the Bible to be potentially subversive, Baptist and Wesleyan missions began to filter into Jamaica after the turn of the eighteenth century. Moravian missionaries had introduced the Christian doctrine eighty years before this, but with little response from the slaves. Following the conclusion of the North American War of Independence in 1784 many Empire loyalists departed for the West Indies, often taking with them substantial numbers of slaves many of whom were familiar with, if not converted to, Christianity through their contact with missions in the Southern states of America.

Travelling with their masters were four blacks who were to figure prominently in the development of a new innovatory religious form, fusing elements of Christianity with the obeah-myal complex. George Lisle (sometimes spelt Leile), a lay Baptist preacher arrived in Jamaica in 1783 and recruited the support of Moses Baker and George Gibb. These along with George Lewis, an African-born slave from Virginia, erected four tent-poles on which the canopy of Native Baptism was to be hung. It was a movement based on Christianity which was fused with African-derived elements, but slavery played a catalytic point in the synthesis; for as Malcolm Calley has observed: 'Possibly the most important role of slavery in the West Indies was to hinder the diffusion of a detailed knowledge of Christianity to the slaves, thus stimulating them to invent their own interpretations and their own sects' (1965, p. 16). These four were indeed stimulated to their 'own interpretations' after being exposed to Christian teaching in America and their mixture of Christian concepts and African ritualism was met enthusiastically by the Jamaican slaves. The movement's success was predicated on its similarity with familiar forms of worship. For example, Melville Herskovits speculates that the most 'logical adaptation' for New World slaves to make was to give their adherence to a form of Christianity which in its ritualism most resembled the type of worship known to them:

The Baptist churches had an autonomous organization that was in line with the tradition of local self-direction congenial to African practice. In these churches the slaves were also permitted less restrained behaviour than in the more sedate denominations. And such factors only tended to reinforce the initial pre-disposition of these Africans towards a cult which in emphasizing baptism by total immersion made possible the worship of new supernatural power, in ways that at least contained elements not entirely unfamiliar. (1941, p. 233)

Though the movement provoked some suspicions from the land-owning whites, it caused no hostility until the period immediately preceding emancipation when a Native Baptist leader or 'Daddy', Samuel Sharpe, used his status to sanction a slave rebellion. In his capacity as a domestic slave to a Montego Bay solicitor, Sharpe was privy to some of the activities of the Abolitionist movement in England; in his role as a Native Baptist leader he was familiar with the central Biblical theme of the equality of all men before God. In fact Mary Reckord goes so far as to note: 'Christianity came to provide a positive justification for action. Sharpe and his aides proclaimed the natural equality of men and, on the authority of the Bible, denied the right of the white man to hold them to bondage' (1969, p. 28).

Sharpe informed his followers that they were all free men and that his former mentor, the Reverend Thomas Burchell to whom almost messianic power was attributed, had left for England and would return with documentary evidence of their freedom, the 'free paper'. In view of this, Sharpe told his followers to withdraw their labour from Christmas 1831 onwards. In punishment, the whites burned down some slaves' dwellings and the blacks retaliated instantly prompting a series of attacks on whites which spread throughout the island. Burning and looting ensued: bloodshed abounded and martial law was declared, as it was later to be at Bogle's uprising. The rebellion was brought under control by the end of January and Sharpe and other agitators were hanged. Further reaction came in the form of the whites' Colonial Church Union, whose members embarked on a programme of chapel-wrecking and intimidation of missionaries.

The next significant uprising of blacks was also inspired by a Native Baptist, for Bogle, like Sharpe, was a preacher who envisaged equality for the Island's negroes. In the interim, of course, significant changes came in the form of emancipation and the short-lived apprenticeship system which effectively tied ex-slaves to their former owners as wage labourers. The period following emancipation in 1834 saw a boom in popularity for the missions, as more and more slaves associated their new-found freedom with the missionary movements' abilities to dissolve the plantation owners' domination. But enthusiasm waned as disillusionment at the failure of emancipation to effect any real improvement in the material condition of blacks set in. By the 1840s the more conventional Christian doctrines had begun to lose plausibility for the ex-slaves and the missions gave way to a resurgence of Afro-elements.

1842 saw the reawakening of myalism, this time equipped with a millenarian promise. Writing at the time, the Reverend Thomas Banbury observed of its exponents: 'They went by the name "Mial People"; they were also called *Angel Men*. They declared that the world was to be at an end: Christ was coming and God had sent them' (1894, p. 20). An extraordinarily bright comet was sighted which the mial people interpreted as a presage of the second coming. This group constituted something of a qualitative break with other movements of dissidence, and it was, after all, a movement of dissidence in so far as it exhibited a divergence in agreement as to the desirability of present circumstances and an impulse to improve them – in the shape of the second coming. The mial people organised themselves around the vision of a new social order, changed not by themselves but by some supernatural agency. Prescribed, were courses of action totally at variance with those outlined by the Maroons, Sharpe and Bogle: decreased was the reliance on pragmatic measures; believers were merely exhorted to prepare for the future salvation.

And, crucially, this pattern of action was determined ultimately by the mial people's depiction of evil. Whereas the previous movements apprehended the evil perpetuating the blacks as immediate, tangible and susceptible to eradication through pragmatic procedures, the mial people perceived their ills as deriving from more transcendental sources. Accordingly, the measures chosen to deal with them were cast in terms of a preparation for the imminent salvation. In effect, the mial people saw evil as so omnipotent and all-pervasive that they sought to recruit supernatural assistance.

An important consequence of the way in which evil was interpreted was the vision of change it inspired. The Maroons and the rebellions of Sharpe and Bogle served to discharge hostility, express discontent, or seek the alleviation of specific grievances whilst leaving the society more or less as it was, changing only the positions of extant offices but leaving those positions intact. Bogle and Sharpe were both encrusted in a Christian tradition which accepted the legitimacy of the present social order. Their demands for change were phrased in terms of such an acceptance, for their seizures of initiative were unaccompanied by the expectation of a comprehensive social structural transformation. Although they broke away from the narrow and particularistic orientation of the obeah-myal complex, where concern was relief from specific ills by special dispensations, they were not fired by the vision of a coming cataclysm.

The mial people were the first evidenced group to manifest the vision of a transformed social cosmos, but a more celebrated vision was that of Alexander Bedward, a Native Baptist leader who turned his local following into a fully fledged millenarian movement. Bedward created his somewhat unexceptional Baptist Free Church in 1895, at August Town where he cultivated a reputation on the basis of his alleged healing powers. He conducted baptismal ceremonies in the celebrated Hope River which was thought to have prophylactic properties. At the turn of the century, however, the leader introduced a new and somewhat startling dimension into his hitherto conventional

Native Baptism. He told his followers of an impending holocaust in which all the whites would be destroyed and the blacks redeemed. In the Jamaican *Daily Gleaner* of 22 January 1895 he was quoted as saying 'we are the true people; the white men are hypocrites'. He went on: 'The Government passes laws which oppress the black people. They take their money out of their pockets, they rob them of their bread and they do nothing for it. Let them remember the Morant War.'

But, although he alluded to Bogle's 'Morant War', his challenge was founded on the premise that the evil whites were too powerful to be confronted and it was only through the intervention of supernatural agencies that their dominance could be smashed. Throughout the early 1900s Bedward used his reputation as a healer as a basis for credibility and gained the attention of hundreds of blacks. His message to them was simple and dramatic: Bedward asserted that he was the reincarnated Jesus Christ and that he would ascend to heaven like Elijah in a chariot of fire at 10.00 a.m. on 31 December 1920; after three days he would return and carry the elect with him to heaven. Following this, fire would ravage the world and pave the way for the perfect future.

Bedward attended the scene dressed in white robes and turban and sat patiently in his 'chariot' (a decorated chair) for the whole day, after which he claimed he had received word from the Almighty that he should postpone his ascension. After this, enthusiasm for his programme dwindled and he was eventually declared insane and committed to the Bellevue Mental Asylum where he died in 1930.

Although Bedward's fantastic scheme was to be consummate, it was to instigate a reversal of present circumstances rather than totally to transform them. For Bedward, it was not so much the evil of the white race *per se* which needed to be extirpated, but the way in which that race administered the workings of society. In his vision the transformation would involve the return of black men in white skins. Martha Beckwith recounted how: 'He [Bedward] showed me his hands and told me how, in the new Heaven, and new Earth, they were to be as white as my own' (1923, p. 42). Bedward's slogan might well have been 'new skins for old'. In essence, he was unable to break the association of blackness and depravity and saw the alleviation of problems within existing frameworks. In his utopia, new incumbents would simply occupy old offices. His heresy was caught squarely in the jaws of orthodoxy.

Certainly the same could not be said of Marcus Garvey, a contemporary of Bedward but a man committed to fundamental social structural change to be organised and engineered by black peoples. Garvey was not interested in modifications of the present society but sought only one objective: the return of black peoples to Africa. And, although he subjected his basic philosophy to recantations later in his career, it was the notorious early Garvey of the 1920s which really ignited the sparks of the Rastafarian fire.

For Garvey, a native of Jamaica, the evil system of European colonialism had fragmented the Africans and dispersed them throughout the globe in places where they could not fully express themselves intellectually and culturally. Not only had blacks been physically suppressed but their consciousness had been stunted and they had lost the sense of pride and dignity in being black. The restoration of this lost pride was to be brought about by a complete rupture with the white world and the return of blacks to Africa. He summarised his own programme:

> We shall organize the four hundred million Negroes of the world into a vast organization to plant the banner of freedom on the great continent of Africa . . . If Europe is for the Europeans, then Africa is for the black peoples of the world. (*New York Times*, 3 August 1920)

The vehicle for this plan was the Universal Negroes Improvement Association (UNIA) which he established in Jamaica in 1914 but moved to Harlem, New York City two years on, after experiencing little response in his native land. Between the years 1920 and 1924, when he was deported back to Jamaica, Garvey captured the hearts and minds of American blacks and gave them not only dreams of a redeemed Africa unspoiled by Europeans but tangible proof of his intentions to realise this dream. He bought steamships and organised his Black Star Line for the specific purpose of transporting blacks to Africa, which he used synonymously with Ethiopia (for Garvey the whole continent was 'Ethiopia' before the Europeans sliced it up): 'The Black Star Line will sail to Africa if it sails in seas of blood' (Garvey quoted in James, 1938*b*, p. 69).

His spell in Jamaica was equally as spectacular and almost as trouble-torn. His reputation as a man of exceptional qualities with an extraordinary message had been conveyed to Jamaicans through the *Daily Gleaner* which carried reports on his exploits, and it came as little surprise when several thousand supporters thronged to greet his homecoming. The UNIA's flag of red, black and green (the Ethiopian national colours) was displayed prominently and Garvey embarked on his second major venture which ended in 1938 when, after several brushes with the law and a decline in popularity, he left for England and eventually died in 1940 – his dreams unfulfilled

Though he failed in terms of stated aims and returned no blacks to Africa, Garvey had seized the imaginations of blacks in the USA and more pertinently in Jamaica in such a way as to change their self-conceptions. Those accepting Garvey's doctrine would have taken fresh cognisance of themselves, their places in the world and their ultimate ambitions. He provided a blueprint for what he called the 'New Negro', a product of 'a second emancipation – an emancipation of the minds and thoughts of four hundred million Negroes of the world' (*Daily Gleaner*, 2 August 1929).

As his wife, Amy Jacques Garvey, was later to express it: 'Garvey instilled in them NEW CONCEPTS of their rightful place on earth as God's creation' (1968, p. 38). This I take as vitally important to both Garvey's project and the Rastafarian movement which was to take up the leader's cause. For here, for the first time in Jamaica's history, was an enterprise depicting evil as not only the white race which continued to subordinate blacks, but blacks themselves who had accepted definitions of the negro as inferior. For Garvey, the evil lay inside as well as out. It was the blacks themselves who had failed to recognise their own potential. It was a state of consciousness which Garvey analogised to Rip Van Winkle's long sleep; but the awakening was imminent: 'Like Rip Van Winkle we are rising from our slumber of the ages and shortly we shall bless mankind with the wonder and greatness of life as revealed to us through God from the sleep of countless centuries' (1967, Vol 2, p. 350).

Throughout his active phases Garvey remained unshakable in his conviction that this 'awakening' was to occur in the near future and that one consequence of this was a social transformation in which all blacks would gravitate towards their rightful homeland, Africa, where they would rebuild their once great nation. And it was this conviction in the inevitability of the transformation that was inspirational to the early Rastafarian leaders who saw in Garvey a man inspired, a precursory prophet foretelling the coming of a new age for black peoples.

By 1930 Garvey's movement had passed its phase of notoriety and paled as the fine dreams of a mass migration to Africa died away. Despite Garvey's failure to successfully implement his plan, he set in motion less obvious programmes which were to be taken up by groups of black Jamaicans in the early 1930s and given fresh interpretations. Some years after Garvey's death, his second wife Amy Jacques in a moment of prolepsis remarked: 'After Marcus Garvey had returned millions to Africa *spiritually* he had done his work' (in Essien-Udom 1962, p. 61). Such a view was not shared by many Jamaicans, for them Garvey had only just started; the important work was still to be done.

1934–54. BEHOLD THE LION: ENTER THE RASTAMAN

The myth surrounding Marcus Garvey was to grow immeasurably bigger than the man himself, and the disparity between the two was bridged by the attribution of a single, undocumented phrase: 'Look to Africa when a black king shall be crowned, for the day of deliverance is near.' Around this an entire belief system, indeed a new conception of reality, was created.

In November 1930 the Prince Regent, Ras Tafari, was crowned Emperor of Ethiopia and invested with his official title Haile Selassie I, King of Kings, Lord of Lords, the all-conquering Lion of the Tribe of Judah. Now, during his Jamaican period, Garvey produced a publication for his followers and, according to Theodore Vincent, 'articles in Garvey's *Black Man* on the nobleman Ras Naribu had helped generate interest in Ethiopian royalty' (1976, p. 227). Certainly, the coronation in Ethiopia struck responsive chords among some sections in Jamaica, for the link was made between Garvey's black king, and the Emperor. His crowning was to portend a worldly transformation in which the white colonial structure was to be dissolved and all black peoples returned to Ethiopia, like Garvey used interchangeably with Africa. Further, Ras Tafari himself was to instigate the transformation and it was he who would arrange for the blacks to be collected and returned to Africa. His ability to do this was based not merely on the belief that he was the king spoken of by Garvey, but he was, indeed the Living God, the messiah who would lead black peoples to their fatherland, Ethiopia.

The endowment of divinity to Ras Tafari was taken up by three Jamaicans quite independently. Vincent (1976, p. 277) cites Leopold Howell and a certain Ferdinand Ricketts, who came from a family of active Garveyites, as the first leaders, whereas Michael Smith and his colleagues (1967, pt 1, pp. 6–7) reckon Leonard Percival Howell, Joseph Nathanial Hibbert and H. Archibald Dunkley were the first to develop the idea. The exact personnel, however, is less important than the impacts the thinkers had on the minds of other blacks; for some forty years after their original formulation and even years after the death of Haile Selassie, the commitment to his divinity and his intention to execute a transformation was set hard and fast in the minds of blacks not only in Jamaica, but in Canada, the USA, France and England.

How the early believers arrived at the conclusion that Haile Selassie was their redeemer is rather unclear, for at no time did Garvey acknowledge the legitimacy of their beliefs and, far from foretelling the coming of Haile Selassie as the redeemer of black peoples, he denounced him as 'a great coward' and 'the ruler of a country where black men are chained and flogged' (in Cronon, 1974, p. 162). Smith *et al.* (1967, pt 1, pp. 5–6) point to the Bible's book of Revelation as the clue to linking up Garvey's prophecy of Ras Tafari.

And I saw a strong Angel proclaiming with a great voice. Who is worthy to open the book, and to loose the seal thereof? And no one in heaven, or on earth, or under the earth, was able to open the book, or to look thereon. And I wept much because no one was found worthy to open the book thereon: and one of the elders saith to me, Weep not: behold, the Lion that is of the tribe of Judah, the Root of David, hath overcome, to open the book and the seven seals thereof. (Revelation 5: 2–6)

Certainly there are strands in Garvey which are highly suggestive of the apocalyptic struggle in Revelation; for example in his collected *Philosophy and Opinions* (1967, Vol. 1, pp. 73–4) he claimed: 'I see the Angel of God taking up the standard of the Red, the Black and the Green and saying "Men of the Negro race, men of Ethiopia, follow me."' 'I see' indicated that Garvey's privileged position had enabled him to perceive the process before it had even started. Whether Garvey himself ever felt he was personally endowed with inspiration from God is of less importance than the fact that his Rastafarian supporters believed him to be. It seems his *amour propre* prevented him from ever explicitly denying this and there are passages in his speeches and writings which give credence to this belief. He was himself a Roman Catholic and constantly sought Biblical sanction for his programmes, at one stage augmenting the UNIA with the African Orthodox Church. The church's leader, George Alexander McGuire, instructed his followers to tear up pictures of white Christs and Madonnas and replace them with black versions (*New York Times* 6 August 1924):

Our God has no colour, yet it is human to see everything through one's own spectacles, and since white people have seen their God through white spectacles we have only now started to see our own God through our own spectacles . . . We Negroes believe in the God of Ethiopia, the everlasting God. (Garvey, 1967, Vol. 1, pp. 33–5)

The conception of a black God, although by no means original was immensely influential in stimulating blacks to search for proof of that God; events in Ethiopia seemed to gel perfectly. Garvey's 'God of Ethiopia' and his 'black king' were to be one and the same person and so it was presumed the African redemption could not be far away. As Garvey himself proclaimed: 'No one knows when the hour of Africa's redemption cometh. It is in the wind. It is coming. One day, like a storm it will be here' (1967, Vol. 1, p. 9). And here the millenarian threads in Garvey's philosophy become apparent. For although he desisted passivity and urged his followers to work pragmatically for their redemption, there were occasionally lapses when he looked to God for deliverance: 'Oh God help the Black man and rescue him from the outrage!' (1967, Vol. 2, p. 412). And again: 'We have gradually won our way back into the confidence of the God of Africa, and He shall speak with the voice of thunder, that shall shake the pillars of a corrupt and unjust world and once more restore Ethiopia to her ancient glory (1967, Vol. 2, p. 324).

My point is that whilst it is conventionally thought that Garvey dissociated himself from the early cult, there are seams of concepts and categories which suggest a strong continuity in enterprises. Every element in the Rastafarian belief system could be found in Garvey's philosophy, the new followers merely gave them a different interpretation. After all, it was Garvey himself who bade his followers: 'If I die, look for me in the whirlwind or the storm, look for me all around you. For with God's grace I shall come and bring with me the countless millions of black slaves' (in Cronon, 1973, p. 122).

Those making what Michael Barkun (1974, p. 37) calls the 'quantum leap' from Garvey's plans of a pragmatically achieved redemption to a vision of the world miraculously transformed by Haile Selassie (referred to as *Jah*, the form of 'Jehova' used in Bibles before King James's version), began preaching their doctrine in and around Kingston during the early 1930s. (See Figure 1, where I have attempted a pictorial representation of what I believe Barkun intended.)

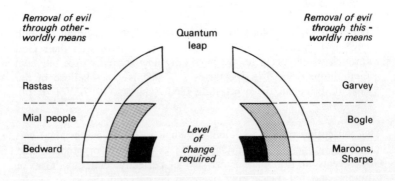

Figure 1. *The Quantum Leap in Thought*

Garvey's importance was in the provision of at least blueprints for new 'conceptual maps', a metaphor employed by Ian Jarvie who explains:

People living in a society have to find their way around it, both to accomplish what they want and to avoid what they do not want. We might say that to do this they construct in their minds a conceptual map of society and its features, of their own location among them, of their possible paths which will lead them to their goals and of the hazards along each path. (1972, p. 161)

In positing fresh targets for black peoples, to original ways of reaching them and changed roles for the 'New Negro' in this process, Garvey offered his followers a conceptual map of society; in other words, a new way of making sense of the world. But it was the exotic manner in which the Rastafarian leaders manipulated Garvey's blueprint that led to the rise of a set of beliefs somewhat at variance with Garvey's own.

Howell seems to have been the most influential in the dissemination of Rastafarian beliefs, due in part to his scrapes with the law. In 1933 he was arrested for using seditious language and so used his trial as a platform. Here it was revealed that blacks were to be regarded as the true descendants of the ancient Israelites who had been enslaved by whites, the agents of Babylon. Soon, however, Ras Tafari would arrange for the dissolution of white domination and send ships to return his children to Ethiopia.

Perceiving the possible inflammatory effects of such beliefs, the court dealt Howell a two-year gaol sentence and his accomplice, Robert Hinds, twelve months' imprisonment. Similarly, Dunkley, who had by this time given his movement the title King of Kings Mission, was fined for disorderly conduct in the same year and later detained at Bellevue Asylum.

1935 saw the appearance of Nyabinghi, a vehemently anti-white wing of the cult which had drawn inspiration from a misinformed article in the *Jamaica Journal* which told of a 'secret society to destroy whites' whose members afforded Haile Selassie messianic status (Philos, 1935). These may have been the first to cultivate the long, unkempt coils of hair which became known as dreadlocks and remained the central overt symbol of the Rastafarian movement (though Smith *et al*, 1967, pt 1, p. 9, believe the locks first appeared in the 1940s). On his release, Howell organised what he called the Ethiopian Salvation Society and in 1940 took his 1,600 followers to an abandoned estate at Pinnacle, St Catherine where they set up their own self-sufficient commune (Smith *et al.*, 1967, pt 1, p. 8). In the interim, Ricketts joined forces with one Paul Earlington, to form a more secular branch of the cult; Earlington turned this into the Jamaican 'local' (as they were called) of the Ethiopian World Federation in 1938. Hibbert, who had presided over his organisation the Ethiopian Coptic Faith, was committed to the Bellevue Asylum in the same year.

Howell's commune was subjected to periodic raids from the police and after one notable incident in 1941, in which Howell's followers had attacked neighbouring dwellers, it was revealed that Howell had insisted that he was Haile Selassie, an interesting acknowledgement of the inherence of God in man; this idea was to be elaborated into the principle of 'I and I', the unity of all people. After two years' imprisonment Howell decided to rigidify the Pinnacle commune, installing guards with watchdogs and exercising his leadership almost tyrannically. The parallels with the Family cult which emerged in California in the 1960s are irresistible. Its despotic leader, Charles Manson, was said to wield a strange mesmeric control over his followers, luring them with his apocalyptic vision of Helter Skelter, the ultimate confrontation between blacks and whites, and commanding them to murder figures representing 'straight society' (see Sanders, 1971). Manson's cult used the hallucinogenic drug LSD, Howell's used ganja, a marihuana cultivated on the estate, to which many Rastas were to attach religious significance. Both leaders gained inspiration from reluctant sources: in Howell's case, Garvey, and in Manson's, the Beatles whom he claimed had sent him messages through their recordings.

When the first phase closed the movement exhibited no cohesive organisational form and few points of ideological agreement outside the central acceptance of Haile Selassie as the divine redeemer and his intention to organise and execute the African redemption. Howell's was probably the most infamous of a surfeit of small groupings, with individual leaderships, but no single figure emerged with enough power to introduce organisational strength and ideological discipline.

There is a temptation to analyse the cult in terms of two distinct strains in Jamaican movements: the Rastafarian and Bedwardite movements and mial people constituting the millenarian responses; with the Maroons, Sharpe, Bogle and Garvey comprising the secular responses. But, in the context of Jamaica, distinctions between the religious and secular spheres were not rigidly maintained, and, as Barkun detects: 'Where a society does not distinguish between secular and religious realms, millenarian movements quite naturally articulate political problems in what we regard as religious terms' (1974, p. 23).

What I have hoped to show is that the Rastafarian movement slotted into a tradition making no differentiation between the two. In particular, Sharpe used Biblical sanction for his revolt, Bedward was blatantly political in his critique of white dominance, and, of course, Garvey hinted at the divine sanction that backed his endeavours. More fruitful distinctions lie in the perceptions of evil and the type of vision these prompted. Prior to the mial people and Garvey, movements did not envisage total transformations of social structures, but only rearrangements of existing ones. Even Bedward sought only to reverse positions. Garvey and later the Rastas looked to wholesale changes; it was merely the manner in which they could be achieved which brought disagreement. The asymmetrical relationship between Garvey and the Rastas was strong and, as I will show, an enduring one which lasted well into the 1970s.

1955–9. EXODUS: PROPHETS AND PROFITS

Both Garvey and the early Rastas wanted change, complete and utter change. They differed only in the way they approached the change. Garvey perservered with steamships, sedulously promoting a sense of nationalism amongst his followers and imploring them to break their links with the Americas. Howell and the others, however, were less concerned with the complexities of cultivating support and organising a mass migration to Africa. For them, the secrets of how the transformation would come about lay with their God and redeemer, Haile Selassie, who would surely implement his programme in the near future. Like Garvey, they were implacable and nothing short of a total transformation would satisfy their demands.

Since the movement had first emerged in the 1930s, its members had inflexibly retained a commitment to the inevitability of the transformation which would climax with the destruction of Babylon and the return of blacks to their fatherland. By 1954, political changes had resulted in the creation of the Jamaica Labour Party and, later, the People's National Party which were formed after civil unrest in 1938. Emigration to the USA and Great Britain had also got under way, indicating that at least some progress was being made to alleviate the miseries of the predominantly black working class.

A year after the eventual closure of the Pinnacle commune in 1954 and in the same year as the general election, Jamaica received a visitor from New York City. Maime Richardson was an official of the Ethiopian World Federation which had been established in 1937 by Melaku Bayen under the direction of Haile Selassie, who had probably envisioned the venture as a way of enlisting support for his country, by then occupied by the Italians. Though a secular organisation, the EWF's Jamaican 'local' was opened by the Rasta Paul Earlington in 1938 and was used very much as a vehicle for Rastafarian principles. At a public meeting Richardson touched upon a number of issues which seemed pertinent in the Rastafarian cause. For example, Leonard Barrett quotes her: 'The Emperor Haile Selassie is now engaged in building up a Merchant Navy . . . and the time is not too far distant when ships from Addis Ababa would sail to American ports. There was a possibility too that ships would one day call here . . . in Jamaica' (1968, p. 78). Read through the eyes of an uninterested observer the comment expresses little more than optimism

in the future expansion of Ethiopian trade links. Read through Rastafarian eyes, however, it was to mean something rather different.

In 1955, a certain Mr Branford of Kingston was reported to have
approached city merchants with a view to buying Ethiopian garments.
During a dream, Haile Selassie had visited him and told him to
prepare for the transportation to Africa (Smith *et al.*, 1967, pt 1, p.
12).

Later that year and throughout 1956 various groups of cultists
gathered at Kingston piers to await the ships of Ras Tafari. This was
to be the advent of the millennium.

The first part of a two-pronged climax of the new fervour occurred
in 1958 when a self-styled Prince, Edwards C. Edwards, circulated
handbills to announce that his Coptic Theocratic Temple at Kingston
Pier was to be the point of departure for the return to Africa.
Edwards claimed to have received a message from Haile Selassie in
1943, instructing him to prepare; he also insisted that he was in
spiritual contact with Howell (recurring 'I and I' principle?). Preceding the expected transportation were several days of celebration,
with nightly dancing, fires, rituals and incessant drumming. It was
even rumoured that the head of a policeman was to be collected as a
sacrificial offering to Ras Tafari the Emperor.

The Rastas' enthusiasm spilled over into an attempted armed
insurrection and 300 cultists moved to a nearby market place, proclaiming their intention to capture the city of Kingston. Attempts by
the police to disperse them produced a violent confrontation.

Needless to say, there were no transportations but within a few
months more pragmatic attempts at a solution were under way when
nine Rastas invaded the Jamaican Governor's official residence and had
to be forcibly evicted after a week of occupation. Clearly, the cultists
who had for long after the cessation of the Howell's affairs, been
regarded as harmless participants in a large-scale folly, were re-emerg-
ing as what I might warrantably call 'folk devils'.

One year after Edwards's abortive enterprise saw the coming into
prominence of the most significant leader in the Rastafarian movement since Leonard Howell. The Jamaican Claudius Henry had lived
in the USA for several years before returning in 1959 when he founded
the Seventh Emmanuel Brethren which was later changed to the
African Reform Church. He announced himself as 'God's Annointed
Prophet and Repairer of the Breach' and sold 15,000 tickets which
entitled the holders to travel to Africa: 'Please reserve this ticket for
removal. No passport will be necessary for removal.' Thousands sold
their property and possessions and flocked to Kingston in expectation
of travelling to Africa. Once more their expectations evaporated and
Henry's profitable exercise had brought him tangible rewards but left
his followers homeless and stranded. He was subsequently charged with

fraud and disturbing the peace, for which he was bound over to be of good behaviour for twelve months; it was barely six months before he was at the centre of another controversy.

The incidents of the late 1950s climaxed almost thirty years of waiting since Garvey's prophetic utterance was translated into an apocalyptic foretelling of the salvation of blacks and the fate of the white world. During those years nothing constructive had been done to facilitate the passage to Africa or the downfall of white society. The extent to which expectations of the cataclysm were sustained is measurable by the 15,000 followers of Henry who bought tickets. Presumably the personnel of the movement had changed over the span, but the vision of a redeemed Africa had certainly not dimmed in the imaginations of new recruits. To them, the African redemption was as attainable and inevitable as it had been to the first believers.

Events of the second phase in Rastafarian history indicate the enormous credulity and suggestibility of blacks in Jamaica looking for prophetic figures on to which they could project their hopes and ambitions. Receptivity to the idea of a transformed social cosmos was a common feature of the followers of figures ranging from Bedward to Edwards, from Garvey to Henry. Such a receptivity was fired by the realisation that the evil that needed to be eliminated in order to gain release from present miseries was so strong and ubiquitous that supernatural aid was required to destroy it and replace it with a more acceptable existence.

The two upsurges in enthusiasm came after a protracted period of anticipation during which the movement had generated vast reservoirs of millenarian energy. It needed only the detonating influences of Edwards and Henry to fire the explosions. But, when the expected transformation failed to materialise and expectant Rastas were thrown back on their haunches, the nature of the millennium had to be reconceptualised. Perhaps some human assistance was needed, after all. Events after 1959 suggest that at least some factions of the movement saw themselves taking up an active role in encouraging the transformation. The vision of a redeemed Africa did not recede but the actions it inspired were of a totally different order than those of previous phases.

1960–3. ASSISTING THE MILLENNIUM

Disappointed and dejected at the non-arrival of the ships bound for Africa, the movement was left in what James Beckford in his discussion of the Jehovah's witnesses calls an 'ideological vacuum': 'the apparent failure of the prophecy to materialize in the anticipated form led to neither the disintegration nor to the strengthening of the Russellite group . . . but it left the group in an ideological vacuum'

(1975, pp. 19–20). Such a vacuum resulted in a change of complexion for the Rastafarian movement during its fourth stage of development, with hard-headed figures emerging to rescue the cult from a contemplative phenomenon and inject into it an activist dimension. The supernaturally wrought transformation would surely arrive in the near future, but there was no harm in using human power to hasten it.

The first murmurs of the changes in orientation came with the occupation of the Governor's residence in 1959 mentioned above. Public attention had been alerted to the violent potential of the movement and the militancy it could provoke. Claudius Henry was still bound over following his ticket-selling venture, when his Kingston residence was raided by the police in April 1960. Discovered were home-made bombs, dynamite, detonators, guns, machetes, swords, batons, clubs and conch shells filled with cement. Henry was arrested along with twenty-four of his followers and accused of conspiring to overthrow the government. He was charged with breaches of the Firearms Law, and Gunpowder and Explosives Law and the Treason and Felony Law. It was something of an epoch-making arrest as this last law had not been invoked since the Morant Bay rebellion (see *The Times*, 12 April and *Daily Gleaner*, 17 April 1960).

Subsequent raids at the Clarendon branch of Henry's African Reform Church produced further evidence which was stacked against the offender at his strictly guarded trial. The charge read:

Before or after December 5th, 1959 with other persons unknown [the accused] did feloniously intend to incite insurrection against the Government of the island in order to intimidate and overthrow the Governor, Legislative Council, House of Representatives.

The raids had also thrown up correspondence between Henry and the Cuban President, Fidel Castro. Commenting on the charge the Chief of Police was quoted as saying investigations turned about 'an intention to overthrow the government by violence' and 'a plot to attack the police' (*The Times*, 12 April 1960). Henry was found guilty and sentenced to six years' imprisonment.

Henry's arrest was a prelude to a more interesting sequence of events beginning in June 1960 when a party of police and military discovered an arms cache at a Rastafarian hideout in the Red Hills district. For some time previously there had been rumours of a mock military exercise being carried out by Rastas. During the raid, two members of the British Royal Hampshire Regiment were killed and their assailants fled to Sligoville in a hijacked vehicle.

Days after the raid three members of Henry's African Reform Church were found shot through the head and buried in a shallow grave, presumably executed by other militant Rastas who were distrustful of them. And, so started one of the biggest manhunts in Jamaican's history: over 1,000 members of the police and military combed the island. After just over a month of island-wide panic four men were captured as they lay sleeping on the floor of a shop in Sligoville and another six rounded up in the days that followed. All were charged with felony, and eight with murder. One of those eight was Claudius Henry's son, Ronald.

The case opened up a number of questions regarding the island's security. First, because seven of the men arrested were Americans known to be members of a New York-based black terrorist group, the First African Corps; secondly, because all the men were armed with automatic firearms and ammunition which were traced to a Brooklyn dealer and it was speculated that they had been smuggled into Jamaica in refrigerators (see *New York Herald Tribune*, 4 April 1961). A rumour arose that the American group had forged links with Cubans who were backing their enterprise to team up with Rastas and to instigate a revolution in Jamaica. The mounting panic was reflected in a *Sunday Guardian* article (1 May 1960) headlined, 'Jamaicans Live in Fear of Rasta Men' in which the movement's membership was estimated at 6,000. To neutralise some of the panic, the government commissioned a University College of West Indies team to collect information on the doctrines, history, organisation and possible future of the movement. The team, comprising of Michael Smith, Roy Augier and Rex Nettleford produced a short report (1967) and some possible proposals, one of which was a mission to Africa with a view to implementing a migratory programme. This was accepted and a mission, which included a Rastafarian contingent, travelled to various African countries and returned with a report. The migration, however, remained purely in theoretical realms and was never put into practical operation.

Ronald Henry was hanged for murder in March 1961, but any hopes that this would be an end to the Rastafarian violence disappeared twelve months later when a group of Rastas attacked a petrol station at Coral Gardens, ten miles from the Jamaican tourist centre of Montego Bay. They had surprised the black attendant with guns, spears and machetes and knives and told him: 'Since you are one of us you can fly away from this place' (*The Times*, 13 April 1963). Having robbed the station of £35 they burned it down and moved on to a nearby hotel where they killed one of its guests, an estate salesman. The Jamaican Premier Alexander Bustamante hurriedly organised troops and police in a frantic effort to round up the group. Repercussions would have had a detrimental effect on the tourist industry, second only to bauxite in its contribution to the island's gross national product. But, shortly after this, a mobile police unit was attacked and an inspector chopped to death with a machete. The gang invaded a private house, around which the police threw a cordon. A siege ensued with three Rastas and two policemen being killed. Three cultists were held for murder and within twenty-four hours 170 more were arrested following a series of raids.

Officials of Montego Bay were reported to be unperturbed by the trouble and 'were not alarmed by the incident', which was caused, they reckoned, by a small gang with robbery as its motive (*The Times*, 13 April, 1963). Their confidence was obviously not shared by the government which urgently sought to defuse what was seen as an explosive situation. In the immediate aftermath of the incident Bustamante launched a full-scale campaign to eliminate the ganja plant on the island. Now, the use of ganja was not unanimously accepted by all Rastas; as Smith and his colleagues observed: 'Some brethren will have nothing to do with ganja, while others accord it religious significance' (1967, pt 1, p. 26). But generally the 'herb' (as it was known) was associated with the cult in much the same way as other drugs were linked with religious movements, such as the Yakan or Allah water cults and Kamajo or Peyotists and the cactus plant *Lophophora Williamsii* Lamaire.

It was convenient to view the problem not as some social structural inadequacy, but rather the ganja, tracing a causal path from drug consumption to violent behaviour. A debate on the effects of ganja followed but it proved inconclusive. Whatever the outcome of such a debate, the single important consequence was that the movement had been imbued with a new dimension: that of being a fully fledged threat. Writing in this period, the novelist Ian Fleming (1971, p. 84) illustrated this view of the movement by having his hero, James Bond, mixed up with Rastas who were portrayed as ruthless mercenaries available for hire to representatives of various Caribbean political interests, including Cuba, or United States crime syndicates. Asked whether he carried a gun when dealing with them, one of Fleming's characters answers: 'Of course. You don't go after Rastas without one.' (Bond later kills a Rastafarian assailant.)

During this period, the movement and the rest of society had entered into what Barkun calls a 'mirroring relationship': 'Each sees each other as a threat and a source of evil, in a mirroring relationship. Each confirms the worst suspicions of the other' (1974, p. 51). To the Rastaman, the wider society was Babylon, the agents of which were conspiring to suppress him with whatever means available. Not only had they foiled Henry's plans, they had hanged his son, jailed several other brothers, destroyed the ganja crops, dismissed plans for a migration and generally discredited his whole enterprise. To the wider society, the view of the Rasta was probably best summarised by Clinton Parchment who wrote in the *Daily Gleaner* (30 April 1960):

There may be a few sincere and decent Rastafarians in this odd semi-religious, semi-political sect, but it is self-evident that the majority are lazy, dirty, violent and lawless scoundrels mouthing religious phrases to cover up their aversion to work and their ill habits.

The Rastas and the wider society held a mirror to each other and both saw evil.

1963–78: THE POLITICAL PROMISE: REDEMPTION OR REVOLUTION?

Ironically, the incidents of the early 1960s despite producing the popular image of the Rastaman as a folk devil, succeeded in generating enormous interest in the movement. The university report and the mission to Africa had given the cult some semblance of legitimacy and, although migration negotiations collapsed, the possibility of a physical break with Jamaica was supported by the growing numbers of emigrants, many of whom travelled to England. Added to these, was the emergent popularity of American black power replete with its 'black is beautiful' slogan, clenched fist insignia and Afro hairstyles, imploring black people to recognise their African heritage. Together, they blended to 'produce a fresh nucleus of interest in the Rastafarian movement' and it was of this nucleus that the electrons and protons of the latest phase were born. Barrett (1977, p. 172) in his discussion of the contemporary movement in Jamaica reckons that the important change in orientation evidenced in the 1960s was stimulated by a myth said to have originated during the visit of Haile Selassie to Jamaica in 1966. The Emperor is thought to have told the Rastas to liberate themselves in Jamaica before turning their sights to Africa. Accordingly, many of the newer accepters of the faith, who included university students and, most importantly, musicians, were less interested in a physical removal to Africa, and summarised their objective with the phrase 'liberation before repatriation'. In other words, it was sufficient that they realise the fundamental Africanness without recourse to returning to their fatherland. I, for one, would not dispute Barrett's contention but would only suggest that the notion of African redemption within the movement is rather more complex and deserved a deeper analysis (to this I return in Chapter 11).

Barrett (1977, p. 219) further contended that the new affiliates had the effect of bringing the movement out of its religious shell and transposing it into overtly political phenomena. Here he finds agreement with Rex Nettleford who writes of 'functional Rastafarians': 'A group of such young people are found among the University undergraduates and may be termed *functional Rastafarians* who have served

to secularize the movement away from its strongly religious orientation' (1970a, p. 94).

The argument runs that the contagious growth of Rastafarian belief
symbols, motifs and emblems wrenched the movement from its preoccupations with a return to Africa and imbued it with a political
reflex, however incoherent. Such a view certainly draws support from
contemporary neo-Marxist commentators on the movement, who read
into Rastafarian beliefs a disguised analysis of society. Dick Hebdige
says of the Rastaman:

> he could undertake a highly critical analysis of the society to
> which he owed a nominal allegiance. For the rest, the Biblical terms,
> the fire, the locks and Haile Selassie et al. served to resurrect
> politics, providing the mythical wrappings in which the bones of the
> economic structure could be clothed so that exploitation could be
> revealed. (1975, p. 152)

Stuart Hall (1976a) has argued along similar lines and Linton Johnson
even goes so far as to argue that the contemporary movement 'repre-
sents a particular stage in the development of the consciousness of the
oppressed Jamaican' and 'is laying the spiritual and cultural foundations from which to launch a struggle for freedom' (1976a, p. 407).
Even the university report included the ominous reminder that:
'Revolution becomes Redemption with Repatriation as the issue provoking bloodshed. The Marxist vanguard wears a Nyabingi cloak'
(Smith et al., 1967, pt 2, p. 28). Under the searchlight, the fourth
phase of Rastafarian history is characterised by a 'politicisation' in
which preoccupation with a supernaturally inspired return to Africa
cedes place to a more political orientation. Presumably, then, the
fifth phase would be one of violent, revolutionary change.

All contemporary commentators, with one exception (A. Kuper,
1976), have theorised along similar lines and some of the arguments
are persuasive indeed. However, they are not sound on examination.
To be sure, phase four witnessed the almost contagious spread of the
movement's popularity. Rastafarian beliefs, objectives and ideals were
subjects of university debates and political discussions. Musicians
specialising in the sphere of reggae began weaving into their songs
tales of the destruction of Babylon, the return to Africa and the roots
of the Rastaman. Even Jamaican Premier Michael Manley phrased his
successful 1972 election campaign in an apocalyptic idiom, berating
white capitalism and its attendant evils, and exhibiting his rapport with
the movement by proclaiming himself the new Joshua poised to lead
his suffering children to the promised land. To enhance the image he
utilised a staff given to him by Haile Selassie, and promised 'Power
for the People'. In fact, the incorporation of Rastafarian themes into

the already established People's National Party proved to be an inspired political strategy, for Manley assumed power in 1972 and consolidated his position with a landslide election victory in 1976 when his policies were endorsed by the Rastafarian musician Bob Marley who played concerts on his behalf (though Marley refused to pledge his support publicly for Manley). The premier skilfully manipulated Rastafarian ideas to his own end by serving the infectious spread of enthusiasm amongst the majority of blacks (constituting 78 per cent of Jamaica's total population), whose support he needed, and harnessing this to his own party.

But this, I argue, is the movement's major political impact for, while Rastafarian representatives have made independent endeavours to instigate political change, they have been unsuccessful. Dismissing for the time being the attempts of the Henrys to implement change, the first serious political challenge from Rastafarian ranks came with the excursion of Samuel Elisha Brown who in 1961 campaigned as a candidate for Millard Johnson's revival of Garvey's People's Political Party (PPP) – more popularly known as 'The Black Man's Party'. Johnson had been to Africa and championed its values, preaching black solidarity and pride without ever trespassing on the issue of a mass migration; as Katrin Norris puts it: 'He confined himself to those who were interested in bringing the mountain to Mahomet' (1962, p. 58). His appeal to blacks fell upon stoney ground; all sixteen of his candidates were crushed, each losing their deposit.

Although, throughout the later 1960s the spread of enthusiasm for the movement suggested a broadening 'black consciousness' among the negro majority, the consummate failure of the PPP and the successful incorporation of Rastafarian themes into party politics, gives rise to the view that the enthusiasm had been accommodated by existing political interests rather than feeding an open challenge to them. Further, the 1961 election turnout was a record high – (78 per cent) and this was improved upon in subsequent elections, suggesting a strengthening support for the institutional facilities available.

Although there have been the occasional efforts of Rastafarian groups to organise themselves into political alignments, their attempts have made little impression on what would appear to be a strong political structure. The influence of the movement on social change has been largely in the sphere of party politics where some of its themes, though not the central one of African redemption, have been taken up and utilised as a means of maintaining the social order rather than destroying it.

As the 1970s drew towards a close the Rastafarian movement housed such a diversity of levels of political sophistication, orientations to Africa, willingness to co-operate with the rest of society and preoccupation with the destruction of Babylon that it is impossible to draw out any single statement on its overall condition and therefore its future as a political force (but see Barrett, 1977, pp. 210–85 for an attempt). But because I have rejected the theory of the movement's metamorphosis into a revolutionary force, this does not imply that I dismiss its overall contribution. Errol Bowen (1971), Nettleford (1970a) and Barrett (1977) himself have all stressed the importance of the Jamaican movement in artistic achievements, and even then I believe they underestimate the importance of Rastafarians in creating a culture. In the 1970s, manifestations of the movement appeared in such places as New York City, Hartford Connecticut, Toronto, Paris and, of course, the urban centres of England. It came to be one of the most vital and exhilarating forces in the lives of young blacks, who believed themselves to be denied a culture which was truly their own. They set out to revive what they believed to be the lost culture of pre-colonial Africa, coined by English Rastas as 'The Way of the Ancients'. They rode out the seemingly iconoclastic death of their deity in 1975 and persisted in their efforts to realise their essential Africanness, whether in Jamaica, England or the USA. How one version of the movement was able to manage this and create for itself a distinctly Rastafarian reality in the apparently incongruous context of modern industrial England is the central question in forming the remainder of this book.

Figure 2 *Rastafarian Milestones: Jamaica*

1927–9	Garvey's Jamaican period
1929	Sixth International Convention of UNIA at Kingston
1930	Coronation of Haile Selassie I of Ethiopia

Phase 1:
  Behold, the Lion

1930–1	Howell begins teaching divinity of Ras Tafari
1932	Hibbert forms Ethiopian Coptic Faith
1933	Dunkley forms King of Kings Mission
1935	Garvey leaves for England
	Nyabinghi wing appears
1938	Earlington forms Jamaican local of EWF
1940	Howell forms Ethiopian Salvation Society at Pinnacle
1941	Pinnacle raided and Howell imprisoned
1941	Howell released and returns to Pinnacle
1954	Pinnacle commune closed by police

Phase 2:
  Exodus

1955	Visit of EWF's Maime Richardson to Jamaica
	Branford prepares to leave for Africa
1956	Congregations at Kingston ports

1958   Edward's convention
         Violent outbursts
1958   Henry's Seventh Emmanuel Brethren redemption scheme
         Edward's camp burned down by police

Phase 3:
Assisting the Millennium

1960   Howell detained at Bellevue Mental Asylum
         Henry's arms cache discovered
         Henry Jr and his group's violent activities
1961   University report released
         Mission to Africa
1963   Coral Gardens episode
         Campaign to eliminate ganja

Phase 4:
The Political Promise

1966   Haile Selassie I visits Jamaica
1968   Spread of 'functional' Rastas
1970   EOC officially established in Jamaica
1971   EOC's Abba Mandefro visits Jamaica
1975   Death of Haile Selassie

Numerical Estimates of Rastas in Jamaica

1955c	1,800	(Simpson)
1960	60,000	(Carter and Went, in *Sunday Guardian*, 1 May)
1964b	10,000–15,000	(H. O. Patterson)
1973	70,000	(Llewellyn Watson)

Chapter 3

From Evasion to Truculence

Legal emancipation from slavery did not bring about the psychological liberation of the Afro-Caribbean. Despite generations of 'free existence' he continues to suffer from self contempt. This affects his behaviour towards the white man. He tends either to evade the white man or be aggressive and truculent towards him.   *Dilip Hiro, 1973*

EVASION: THE PENTECOSTALIST RESPONSE

It was Garvey who first located the evil confronting black peoples as lying not only outside them in the shape of the white-dominated colonial system, but inside them; their images of themselves as inferior and subordinate to whites. For the black leader, the New Negro would have to emerge, invigorated by his changed self-conceptions and armed with a fresh knowledge of his capabilities to follow Garvey to 'a new world of black men, not peons, serfs, dogs and slaves, but a nation of sturdy men making their impression on civilization and causing a new light to dawn upon the human race' (M. Garvey, 1967, Vol. 2, p. 126). Such an ideal lay at the root of the Rastafarian enterprise – only the methods for its achievement were changed.

The English version of the movement which manifested itself in the late 1970s was fuelled by the Garveyite imperative to cleanse blacks of their self-conceptions and take fresh cognisance of themselves. Extirpating this particular evil was of central importance to them as their observation on their parents demonstrated: 'We believe that perhaps the majority of blacks in this country are still in a state of mind that can be described as not a conscious state of mind'; 'Fooling themselves; they're never going to be treated as equals in this society.' 'Misguided by European Christianity', 'blinded by Babylon' or just plain 'brainwashed' were phrases chosen by Rastas to describe the first-generation immigrants to England. For them, only the Rastaman had reached the plateau of enlightenment from where he could see 'the light of Africa' and therefore the true ambition of the black man.

The first-generation blacks on whom the Rastas were to pour so much scorn were much more accommodating in their postures towards whites. They came to England, as did most migrants, hopeful in their expectation of improved social conditions and a better chance for their children. Whether planning to settle permanently in the new country, or remain temporarily with a view to a future return, enriched after a profitable adventure, the migrant looked to the new environment as a source of hope. Few would have anticipated a hostile reception; indeed, if Daniel Lawrence is to be believed 'in an important sense the Jamaicans came here already feeling part of this country: Britain was not an alien society' (1974, p. 30). His view finds support from Sheila Patterson (1963, pp. 224–5) whose earlier study indicated that the blacks' first contacts with whites proved a grave disappointment. Even if their initial reasons for leaving Jamaica and other parts of the West Indies were negative, for example to escape deteriorating conditions, expectations of a reasonable reception in England were upheld.

The presence of blacks in Great Britain dates back to the sixteenth century, though the period following the end of the Second World War eclipsed anything which preceded it in terms of sheer numbers. Tens of thousands of blacks arriving in the 1950s and 1960s met with disquieting receptions typified most dramatically with the 1958 uprisings in London's Notting Hill and Nottingham's St Ann's Well Road area when blacks and whites clashed. The emergence of the Teddy Boys as intimidators in the late 1950s was a continual reminder to blacks that they were not valued, at least by some sectors of the white working class (see Downes, 1966, pp. 119–29). Worsening relations between blacks and whites hastened the passage of the 1962 Commonwealth Immigrants Act which sought to 'prohibit discrimination on racial grounds'. Its effectiveness was tested by a study carried out over 1960–7 in which it was concluded that 'substantial discrimination' still existed in those spheres not covered by the Act – employment, housing and services (Daniel, 1968).

The response of the first-generation blacks to the white racialism they experienced was what Dilip Hiro (1973, p. 17) would characterise as 'evasion'. They withdrew, not always voluntarily, into district enclaves, giving rise to a residential patterning called 'ghettoisation'. The growth of peculiarly black communities in such urban–industrial areas as London, Birmingham and Manchester had cultural consequences in terms of the emergence of all-black clubs, shopping facilities and, most importantly for present purposes, churches. Moves to establish and run churches to cater almost exclusively for blacks, seem to characterise the efforts of the first generation in response to the felt discrimination. Nowhere was there a hint of an articulation of anger at conditions. Instead, the West Indians turned inwards on their haunches making use of their limited material and cultural resources to built and maintain self-sufficient churches.

Of the more celebrated assemblies the Pentecostal churches best characterise this evasion. Basically, Pentecostalism extended the tradition of Native Baptist movements, which it will be remembered emerged out of Jamaica in the late eighteenth century. Strictly speaking, the Pentecostal Church was American in origin, but underwent so many mutations that it would be unwise to view the British churches as straightforward derivatives. Many of the British Pentecostal churches developed links with Jamaican and American counterparts, but were distinct assemblies in themselves.

Doctrinally, the churches revolved around the Day of the Pentecost spoken of in Acts 2:1–2.

And when the day of the Pentecost was now come, they were all together in one place. And suddenly there came from heaven a sound as if the rushing of a mighty wind, and it filled all the house where they were sitting.

The Pentecostal members, or 'saints' were to await this Day of Judgement when they would reach their salvation and in the meantime were to retire as far as possible from the contaminated outside world. But on occasions their actions betrayed this: buying property, recruiting new converts, sometimes building new churches. Malcolm Calley (1965), in his study of the movement took the view that the commitment to the Day of Judgement worked more as an ideological sanction for maintaining separation from the world than as a principle governing the day-to-day lives of members. Although they were to be the elect, the chosen ones who would be plucked from the earth on the Day of Pentecost, they could use this as a way of withdrawing from the world which had denied them a full range of rewards and accorded them only poverty and deprivation; as Calley puts it: 'In rejecting the world, members claim to be superior to it' (1965, p. 135). They opted out of the race for conventional rewards and found contentment in other, less visible spheres.

This opting out was evidenced in the Pentecostalist's strict observance of ethical rules: forbidden were the consumption of alcohol and tobacco, the wearing of jewellery or cosmetics, the using of bad language and the practice of sexual laxity. Avoidance of contact with the contaminated outside world was recommended. Observance of these rules and adherence to Pentecostalist practices ensured the believer a special relationship with God, expressed through ecstatic experience in which the individual became 'filled' with the spirit of God and threw convulsions, twitching and became able to speak in tongues: 'And they were all filled with the Holy Spirit, and began to speak with other tongues, as the spirit give them utterance' (Acts 2:4).

The success of Pentecostal churches in the 1960s illustrates the desire of black migrants to somehow break with what they perceived to be a hostile world by attempting to transcend it. Calley detects the start of the churches in 1954 when Wolverhampton-based blacks began Pentecostal services at private homes. By 1967, Clifford Hill (1970, p. 187) revealed that a single branch of the movement, the New Testament Church of God, alone commanded a following of 10,861 congregations, employed fifteen full-time ministers and owned its own buildings, including a theological college for training its ministry.

But while the growth of Pentecostalism indicated a general evasion, it did not signify the Pentecostal member's rejection of society, for as Hill reminds us: 'He still has his traditional strong regard for the "British way of life" and desire for acceptance into British society' (1970, p. 39).

Radical rejection of white society was not the driving force behind the Pentecostalist growth: the members still retained their respect for the society but used the church to lessen their profiles and in so doing lessen the bumps and jolts of the uneasy relations with whites. They lowered their profiles as a primarily defensive measure.

The Pentecostal movement may not be totally representative of first-generation postures during the 1960s, but it does point up the ways in which a great many black migrants responded to a hostile reception in England. By attempting to develop their own autonomous religions and find satisfaction within them rather than in the fierce outside world, the blacks de-emphasised their presence and passively withdrew into their racially distinct enclaves where they could find mutual support and encouragement from fellow blacks.

ASSERTION: THE RUDE BOYS

The middle years of the 1960s witnessed the emergence of possibly the most improbable youth cultures: the volatile combination between the indigenous skinheads and the migrant rude boys. Skinheads were working-class teenagers who cropped their hair, hoisted their trousers up to mid-calf and eased their feet into 'Dr Marten' brand toe-capped working boots. The latter were known as 'bovver boots', deriving from the bother the skins sought to cause. Skinheads specialised in aggravation, abbreviated to 'aggro' directed at anyone noticeably deviant, but most often Asians, overt homosexuals, motor-cycling Hells Angels and long-haired affiliates of the hippie persuasion. John Clarke (1975, p. 102) speculates that these almost ritualistic attacks on these groups were manifestations of the skinheads' endeavour to defend what they thought to be a deteriorating working-class tradition from new challenges; what he calls 'the magical recovery of community'. Their whole enterprise was reactionary: it eulogised machismo, racism and sexism – a sort of Alf Garnett with claws!

The rude boys, like the Rastas who came later, were an English offspring of a Jamaican phenomenon. Michael Thomas describes the Jamaican rudies as 'the hustlers and ratchetmen and small-time super-flies of West Kingston. They haven't been to school and they can't get a job and a lot of the time they can't is because they don't want work' (1973, unnumbered).

It is not clear whether the English rude boys were transplanted, unemployed youths of Kingston travelling with their parents to a new home and finding ready allies in the skinheads, or British-born blacks growing into a world they had little respect for and adopting the styles of Jamaican rudies. They were probably a mixture of both. Whatever the personnel, the young blacks fused with their white counterparts to produce a violent and reactionary movement which attracted some tens of thousands of adherents.

The *accouplement* was made possible, first by the similarity of posture of the two groups. Like the skinheads, the rude boys were aggressive, in that they seemed to derive gratification from non-instrumental violence, racist in that they hated Asians, and sexist in that the movement had a predominantly patrifocal orientation. Their 'uniforms' were also similar: shorn hair, hitched-up trousers, boots and braces, with preferably mohair suits for evening attire.

The musical form known as 'rock steady' was an outgrowth of early Jamaican attempts to imitate American rhythm and blues. It acquired a property of its own through peculiarly Jamaican production tech-niques and the habit of disc jockeys to 'dub over' their own voice on to sound tracks (see Kallynder *et al.*, n.d.). Ska music which later developed into rock steady championed the rude boys, extolling their virtues of 'roughness' and 'toughness' and encouraging them to resist authority at its every manifestation. And it was the skinheads' affinity for this music that brought forth the fusion.

Rock steady was as important to the skins as rock and roll was to the Teddy Boys of the 1950s and new wave was to the punks of the 1970s. Many of the Jamaican-produced songs such as the 'Return of Django' and 'Longshot Kick the Bucket' were elevated to the status of anthems and even obscure, lesser known numbers were enthused over. Another popular sound was the interestingly titled 'Israelites', the significance of which was to be realised some years later. It was because the young blacks were so knowledgeable of this musical form that they gained acceptance by a group committed to the destruction of most other 'outsiders'. Being born in Jamaica or having Jamaican parents placed the blacks in the advantageous position of being aware of new sounds, many of which were not available through conventional distri-butors and had to be imported. They were also expert at the dance which accompanied the music, a coupled affair in which both partners would lock their knees into each other's crotch and perform a continuous rubbing motion; it blended perfectly with the sexually explicit flavour of some rock steady records, one notable example of which was Max Romeo's 'Wet Dream' which was banned by BBC television and radio.

The interface between black and white youths between about 1968 and 1971 produced a terrifying alliance which was afforded grand media exposure. Unprovoked attacks on Asians, a practice which was called 'Paki-bashing', were commonplace and this became the subject of almost hysterical debate.

The 1950s had seen the first-generation West Indians as subjects of systematic assaults by the Teddy Boys, but by the beginning of the 1960s they had as George Melly put it 'Crawled back under their stones' (1970, p. 57). The skinhead–rude boy adnascence had revived the pattern – but with a twist. This time, blacks had joined whites and singled out the other major immigrant group, and as I shall later show, West Indian youth never really purged itself of this antagonism towards Asians.

In a way, the attacks on immigrants were understandable. Writing of the Teddy Boys, Paul Rock and Stanley Cohen offered the view that 'There was enough latent hostility to make the object of the Ted's aggression irrelevant; as it happened, the object – a coloured racial minority group – was visible and very relevant' (1970, p. 314). And, in a similar vein, Clarke theorised that Paki-bashing involved 'the ritual and aggressive defence of the social and cultural homogeneity of the community against its most obviously scapegoated outsiders' (1975, p. 102).

Young blacks were welcomed by skinheads not only because of their musical tastes but also because of their similarity of style, the are of being 'cool' their non-encroachment in commercial spheres unlike the Asians who were making inroads into property, shops) and their predilection to fight back if attacked which was something the more passive Asians would not do.

The Asians would not have such relevance for the rude boys but the violent pursuit may have held a different sort of gratification for them. Possibly the type of pleasure some derive from appreciating works of art, listening to music or, more vividly, participating in sport, if only vicariously. Paki-bashing may have been indulged in for its own sake: it possessed an expressive, non-instrumental value; hence, the ritualism in the activity. Further, the activity brought them the attention of the media: they were under the spotlight as aggressive thugs, but they were still in full public view. In other words, they were making themselves conspicuous. Whereas the postures of the first generation defined something of an evasive measure, the rude boys presented an assertive gesture; not so much of defiance but of presence: just to show people they were here and could not be pushed around. They could make things happen and thereby neutralise the sense of fatalism, rather than sitting back and accepting the positions offered them by society. By becoming involved with a group which was rapidly ascending to the realms of folk devils and integrating violence into their repertoire of social behaviour, the rudies could demand attention, however unfavourable, from the rest of society. The rudies and the skins constituted the first meaningful association between blacks and whites, but one which lapsed as the 1970s drew on, both groups wandering in their different directions. Commercial interests took grip of the skinheads, developing them into viable material for exploitation: records, films and books about the skins proliferated. The rude boys were less amenable, they retreated into the ghettos, maintaining much of their style but without the skinhead partners. Importantly however, the rude boy phenomenon left a legacy: an ongoing structure for the stable interaction of peers – the prototype black gang. (This characteristic of the second-generation West Indian community was to become vital in the later transmission of Rastafarian themes.)

Gang formation had begun prior to the liaison with the skins, but the *accouplement* probably stabilised it. At any rate, once the pandemonium had died away the second-generation blacks were organised in a series of gangs with flexible memberships ranging from, say, eight to twelve. What is more they remained permanent features of black youth and this proclivity to crystallise into such units was to have important consequences in the later development of the Rastafarian movement.

TRUCULENCE :   BRITISH BLACK POWER

Black power enjoyed a relatively brief but eventful period of notoriety in England, principally through two organisations, the Racial Adjustment Action Society (RAAS) and the Universal Coloured People's Association (UCPA). The leaders of both groups were heavily influenced by the then radical American movements of the 1960s, which developed as reactions to the more moderate Martin Luther King's Southern Christian Leadership Conference. In a way, the British equivalents were similar reactions to the inadequacy of existing organisations, the chief one of which was the Campaign Against Racial Discrimination (CARD), established shortly before the passing of the 1965 Race Relations Act with the intention of creating an 'umbrella organisation' under which all similar bodies could affiliate.

The motivating force behind black power was to generate self-serving resources, thus reducing the dependence on a white-dominated society which denied black people equality. Paternalistic influences in the shape of white leaders and administrators were regarded as super-

fluous and the real need was for blacks to help themselves, build their
own organisations and develop their own leaderships.

Evidence of the rising popularity of black power came in November
1967 at the 3rd Annual Convention of CARD. A motion that the
organisation's white officials should be replaced was carried but failed
to command the two-third majority necessary for a constitutional
amendment. The convention was highly controversial with the meeting
being adjourned after allegations that various radical groups had sent
bogus delegates to inflate the all-black vote. *The Times* (6 November
1967) carried the headline: 'Campaign to Oust Whites Fails: Black
Power Confusion.' This 'black power confusion' which effectively
signalled the demise of CARD was due to the incursions of two
distinct but similar organisations, both of which had grown to
prominence over the previous three years, and by 1967 carried formidable bodies of support from blacks in England. 1964 saw the visit
to England of Malcolm X, the militant black power leader and
member of the separatist Nation of Islam, better known as the Black
Muslims. During his stay, X met with a Trinidadian, Michael de
Freitas, whose other names included Michael Abdul Malik and
Michael X. Obviously impressed by the meeting, de Freitas moved
to organise what he intended to be a British version of the Black
Muslims. In RAAS, de Freitas envisioned a vehicle for the promotion of exclusively black interests; he implored his followers to stop
turning the other cheek when encountering white hostility: 'Stop
twisting and hit back . . . our last name is Black' (*Observer*, 4 July
1965).

Prior to the foundation of RAAS there were a handful of black
militant groups, many of which preached neo-Garveyite philosophies,
but as black leader Obi Egbuna has noted:

> At a time when it was considered the climax of absurdity to call
> a 'West Indian' African, they attracted little membership . . . the
> easiest way to get thrown out of the 'respectable' Black meetings
> was to walk in with a Black Power badge pinned on your jacket.
> (1971a, pp. 17–18)

Egbuna himself was responsible for creating a second national organisation based on similar lines to RAAS, though without the religious
dimension. His mentor was the infamous Stokely Carmichael who
addressed an audience at London's Round House in July 1967. By
this time black power had already aroused controversy through its
entanglement in the Courtauld dispute at **Preston**, Lancashire where
racial discrimination was rumoured to be at the root of an unofficial
strike by 300 Asian workers (Torode, 1965). De Freitas and his
movement pledged their support for the strikers and simultaneously
drew the attention of the national press.

On the international scene the total rage of American blacks in the Watts district of Los Angeles in August of the same year seemed to magnify the general disenchantment with the more liberal black movements.

So, by the time of Carmichael's visit, cells of black militancy were congealing; his appearance was, as Egbuna puts it, 'like manna from heaven' (1971*a*, p. 18). Almost overnight black power spawned another organisation. The UCPA invited Egbuna to lead them in translating their more moderate line into a fully fledged black power ideology.

It would be possible to see the UCPA as a pragmatic counterpart to RAAS's idealist wing of black power. Amongst its formal aims were 'the establishment of separate educational, political and economic institutions and the encouragement of pride in the separate ideology of the black man' (Hiro and Fay, 1967, p. 8). The organisation would have appealed to those who found RAAS's religious overtones discouraging.

Shortly before the 1967 CARD convention, Carmichael was deported and four members of the UCPA were indicted under Section 6 of the Race Relations Act for allegedly inciting racial hatred. The growing threat to social order posed by the two groups was brought to public visibility most dramatically at the unruly November Convention and in the same month de Freitas was accused of inciting racial hatred with a speech delivered at Reading, for which he was later imprisoned for one year. At his trial he insisted on taking the oath on a specially cleansed Koran. Within months of this, Egbuna and two others were arrested and charged with conspiring to murder white police officers, for which the black leader received a three-year suspended sentence. During his Old Bailey trial he spelt out the philosophy and plans of his newly created offspring of the UCPA, the British Black Panthers.

Despite the martyrising effect of these two incidents, they cut away both movements' leaderships and presented black power followers with an example of the sanctions to be drawn from the same type of behaviour. Deprived of their loci of authority and without local ideological direction the two movements splintered and eventually faded into insignificance.

At the beginning of this chapter I quoted Hiro who contended that the black man tends either to evade the white man or be aggressive and truculent towards him.' Black power was most assuredly an example of the latter. The response of de Freitas and Egbuna was based on the premise that only by vesting power into black hands could improvements be made. They followed the tenets of American leaders, many of whom wanted not only remedial measures, but social transformations. In particular, Malcolm X and Carmichael considered the sources of black and white conflict as firmly embedded in the social structure. X, when visiting Britain months before his death, had reformulated his original Black Islamic philosophy to embrace a catholic conception of universal struggle in which non-whites in the Western world would need to link with their third-world brothers and violently overthrow the whites' dominated order (X and Haley, 1966). Carmichael in the mid-1960s committed himself to the elimination and the necessity of rebuilding separate black communities (Carmichael and Hamilton, 1967; Lester, 1971).

The British movements strained to maintain continuity and, unless the messages of de Freitas and Egbuna are to be dismissed as tub-thumping rhetoric, harboured a similar commitment to total change. Anything less was cosmetic, as Egbuna explained: 'Integration is beautiful . . . but it's a mirage. You just can't achieve it' (in Hiro and Fay, 1967, p. 8).

In complete contrast to the early migrants, especially the Pente-costalists who saw the evil in their lives as alleviable through passive withdrawal, the black power followers saw the malevolence as rooted in social structures which perpetuated the subordination of blacks. They sought to mobilise and eliminate this evil through violent, pragmatic means. The two opposing orientations illustrate once more how the manner in which evil is depicted affects the ways in which it is responded to. Whereas the Pentecostalists sought their salvation in other worldly realms, black power adherents sought theirs in a violent confrontation – in this world.

Numerically, British black power may have achieved little, but it is my contention that it was important to the genesis and development of awareness necessary for the growth of the later Rastafarian movement. Despite its relatively short life-span the black power movement rose to infamy because it acknowledged the existence of certain sets of problems common to all blacks and pointed fingers at specific and recognisable sources of those problems; but most importantly con-ceived of ways of solving those problems, and therefore rejecting the idea of the obduracy of white control. Like the Jamaican movements of Bogle and Bedward which cited the white man as the cause of the black's distress, black power linked up the social and racial spheres and this was an effective node in the minds of blacks.

Prior to Bogle, general patterns of thought in Jamaica were localised and highly particularistic in their location of evil. Similarly, in England the early migrants sought personal gratification and social satisfaction through primarily spiritual means; addressing sources of power in other-worldly realms and not in the social environment. Pentecostalism demonstrated many of the elements associated with the obeah-myal complex, parts of which later metamorphosed into Native Baptism. The solutions sought were designed to generate feelings of well-being and even euphoria for the adherent; ecstacy, filling with the Holy Spirit and healing were typical to both traditions. Such solutions were not designed to make any significant impact at a more tangible level. Bogle broke with such traditions invoking collective violence to effect a solution. Though the programme involved change it was intended to leave the constitutional framework unaltered, as did, indeed, the Bedward scheme which identified evil differently and so chose different methods for eliminating it. Both were important in loosening the belief in the impossibility of change, and although they both failed in conventional terms, they made the connections between race and subordination which were to prove so important to the Garvey and Rastafarian movements.

Even the careers of the individual leaders exhibit a marked similarity, which was no doubt influenced by the somewhat heretical tasks they set themselves. Most obviously they were all involved with agencies of social control at some level. (Bogle being hanged for treason and Bedward being imprisoned and later committed to a lunatic asylum; de Freitas jailed for incitement to racial hatred and later hanged in Trinidad in 1975 for the murder of his cousin Joseph Skerrit, and Egbuna charged with conspiracy.) The entanglements reveal the extent to which their schemes were regarded as potential attractors of sentiment and therefore inherently dangerous and, although they could have contributed to the leaders' possible martyrdom, they more likely deterred any other would-be subversives.

Once a particular awareness of a situation has been raised it has a habit of enduring and becomes hard to erase by simply removing the personnel promoting that awareness. RAAS and UCPA were the first organisations to voice black opinions in a manner contrary to the ambitions of the government and voluntary bodies; they constituted a reversal of the desired pattern of race relations in that they staked out a polarity, and declared integration an unattainable 'mirage'. Black power's appeal in the 1960s was not sufficient for it to overcome the obstacles because of the preference of the first generation for stability.

But the complexion of the situation changed in the 1970s. Black power likewise functioned to produce a stunted but appreciable theoretical awareness of how a common social position amongst blacks was ultimately determined by racial stock. Because at least a minimal level of such theoretical awareness had been achieved it meant that the Rastafarian movement did not have to build upon a totally unscarred surface.

Black power, like the Rastafarian movement, was an adoption of sorts but could not escape the traumas of birth: it had to work on an unprepared and unresponsive surface. Sights on the future had not been adjusted sufficiently to focus on anything more ambitious than a progressive integration into society. It was an early, untimely response to the felt distress of blacks in Britain. It was without precedent and it lacked widespread support; its life-span was short and its success nugatory. But, in its own way, black power established an awareness of the intimate relationship between social position, blackness and, most crucially, the commonality of identity on the basis of this relationship. Such a relationship was to be fused with new life by the Rastafarian movement which followed in the wake of black power.

Chapter 4

Rasta Renaissance

I'm from Ethiopia, but I was born in the West Indies.
Ras Anthony, London, 1977

AFRICA IN ENGLAND : THE COMING OF JAH PEOPLE

While during the 1960s it might have seemed, as Egbuna would express it, 'the climax of absurdity to call a West Indian African' it became in the 1970s a vitally significant reminder to young blacks that they had a rich cultural heritage on which to draw for support and inspiration. The association between second-generation West Indians and Africa was perhaps the most socially consequential phenomenon in the history of the black presence in England.

Black power had attempted to articulate the grievances of the West Indians at an overtly political level; it was radical, to some revolutionary, seeking a comprehensive transformation of social structure in such a way as to accommodate the demands of blacks the world over. Its attempt to upgrade morally the black man by appealing to his skin colour, symbolised in such slogans as 'black is beautiful', constituted a total rupture with white society, a desire to rid the black man of any dependence on the white world and instil in him the self-confidence to advance along his own channels. But mere blackness was insufficient to bring together the fragmented groups of West Indians in England; what was needed was a superordinate reference point; some tangible focus for the underlying cultural unity of blacks.

Mindful of this, blacks began to organise along different lines. In the late 1960s a number of Jamaicans in London came together with the intention of forming a black consciousness movement. They had seen the demise of black power as proof of the inadequacy of trying to mobilise black sentiment on purely political levels. Clearly, the black power assumption that blacks knew well their own best interests and would align themselves with movements dedicated to the further-ance of those interests was a faulty one. The criteria used by blacks for determining their ultimate preferences were far more complex and multifaceted than the strictly rational procedures envisaged by de Freitas and Egbuna. People like Immanuel Fox and Gabriel Adams (later changed to Wold) were sensitive to such problems of organisation and mobilisation; they recognised the overwhelming majority of successful West Indian movements were founded on the leader's or imputed leader's validation of authority through resort to supernaturally endowed power. In the history of Jamaican movements leaders had needed special qualities to substantiate their claims: Bedward and Garvey, Native Baptist leaders and even the more contemporary Pentecostal leaders in England needed to perform healing miracles, exhibit ecstasy, claim divine revelations, and so on in order to clinch social recognition of their elevated status. The whole tradition, or culture of successful Jamaican movements was encrusted with the belief in someone's or some group's claim to supernatural power of a particular order. Ras Tafari was charged with such a spirituality. By the 1960s it had spread to embrace thousands in Jamaica and its followers claimed to have been 'passed over' by the divine spirit of Jah, Haile Selassie, who they had accepted as the divine creator and deliverer. They had divided the world into two portions, good and evil, or in their thinking Zion and Babylon, and, as the true children of Israel, they were to be saved on the final consummation of history when the path of salvation would open to those accepting the faith. The status of Rasta was in itself a claim to divine power; the experience of Rasta sanctified the individual's life: 'God is in I because it is his nature to be within man as well as above him,' I was informed by a Rastaman.

By the end of the 1960s, a nascent organisational form had emerged in London. The movement attempted to satisfy the conditions of a mass all-black enterprise, sanctioned by supernatural power but with inherent potential for collective action. Modelled basically on Garveyite lines, the Universal Black Improvement Organisation (UBIO) had as its main architects two Jamaican-born London residents, Immanuel Fox and Gabriel Adams, both of whom were familiar with the growing importance of Ras Tafari to blacks in Jamaica. Accordingly, they sought to incorporate Rastafarian themes into a basically black consciousness-raising vehicle as a way of creating interest and enthusiasm among blacks in Britain and possibly provoking them into collective action.

Not that their interests ended there: they developed an ancillary political wing to the UBIO which they called the People's Democratic Party (as opposed to Garvey's People's Political Party) and adopted as its colours the red, green and black of Ethiopia in much the same was as Garvey had done for his movement. At this stage the UBIO and its political branch had no clear programme; it was not strictly Rastafarian in doctrine, philosophy or ambition; nor was it a straightforward political interest group. It was literally a mixture of Rastafarian concepts and themes built on to a neo-Garveyite structure. As an ex-member told me: 'We hadn't the conception of the Lord God Jah Ras Tafari as our one and only guidance.' Numerically, its success was limited but the interest in Ras Tafari generated through its meetings in London stimulated its leadership to embark on another, more ambitious venture designed to elevate Rasta to ideological paramountcy.

To this end Fox, Adams (Wold) and two others (called, I was told, Wight and Christie) travelled to Jamaica where they obtained sanction from the Ethiopian World Federation to set up a local branch in London. Barrett summarised the EWF's task thus: 'We, the Black Peoples of the world to effect Unity, Solidarity, Liberty, Freedom and Self-Determination, to secure Justice and retain the integrity of Ethiopia, which is our divine heritage (1968, p. 78).

The Federation was started in Jamaica in 1938 by Paul Earlington, a Garveyite who recruited the support of the original Rastafarian prophets, Archibald Dunkley and Joseph Hibbert for a while before organisational and ideological tensions resulted in fissions and fragmentations into smaller groups bearing the title of 'Ethiopian' (for example, the United Ethiopian Body and the Ethiopian Coptic Church). By the time of the UBIO leaders' arrival in Jamaica the original EWF had almost dissolved into a surfeit of different Rastafarian groups utilising EWF principles to combat the organisational precariousness which had characterised the early cult; though there was no expropriation of authority from these fissure groups to the Ethiopian body for sanction of doctrinal innovation and interpretation.

The ideological conflict which beset the EWF's relationship with the Rastas had never been resolved. The orientation to Ethiopia as a strictly cultural locus as opposed to a physical or even spiritual centre of gravity, as in Ras Tafari, was an obvious source of disagreement and the position of Haile Selassie as the movement's patron, and in no sense its divine figure, prompted further unease. But by the time of the visit to Jamaica the EWF still maintained a thoroughly Rastafarian character and was without doubt the single most impressive African-centred organisation displaying the important features of centralised authority and, therefore, a degree of social control over its members.

Though organically separate from the EWF, the Ethiopian Orthodox Church (EOC) was the officially recognised religion of Federation members. As a representative of the major area of Eastern Christianity in Ethiopia it was introduced to Jamaica in 1969 (established officially in 1970) as a religious augmentation to the EWF and from that date continued to recruit support from EWF members and other Rastafarian groups seeking affiliation to what was considered a legitimately institutionalised religious body. Here is not the place to discuss the origins and doctrines of the EOC (but see Ullendorff, 1973; Barrett, 1977, pp. 201–9); suffice to say it was the recognised church of Ethiopia and was therefore designated the gnostic counterpart to the EWF.

On their return to London, the leaders transformed the existing UBIO into a new 'local' (as EWF branches are called) of the Federation and began to preach the doctrines of the EOC to all its members. By 1971, the first truly Rastafarian organisation had been established with the EWF at the centre, the People's Democratic Party as its political wing and an EOC-inspired set of Christian teachings as its religious mandate. Premises in the heart of London's market district of Portobello Road were used as headquarters (Local 38) and its members began a campaign of vigorous proselytising to recruit new members. Amid the subcultural backcloth of the late 1960s and early 1970s the emergence of young blacks growing dreadlocks and adorning themselves with Ethiopian-coloured garments did not appear incongruous. The American hippy phenomenon had seared its way through Britain's white youth provoking new stances of anti-authoritarianism and corresponding symbolic gestures: long hair – the longer the better – unconventional attire and beads were the somewhat exotic orders of the day; and tales of drug-taking abounded. Though unique in their own way, the new appearances of the Rastas would have prompted little surprise from a wider society confronted with its native youth extolling the virtues of being 'weird'.

Sometime in 1972, Claudius Haughton, a Jamaican living in Birmingham, came into possession of EWF literature. Haughton, for a while an associate of the militant black power Afro-Caribbean Organisation, was dissatisfied with existing forms of black organisation in England and saw in the EWF the opportunity for a totally fresh, original mass movement based not only on political directives but on a total and comprehensive appeal; the EWF offered just that. After discussions with the London leaders, Haughton returned north and set up the second British offspring of the Federation. Unsupported and without any premises or finances, he marshalled the assistance of a small band of other new affiliates and began recruiting in Birmingham.

By 1973, the English version of the Rastafarian movement had a rather loosely assembled organisational structure and a small but growing membership. But, while interest in the EWF and its Rastafarian themes was spiralling, the membership itself was a more or less temporary association of enthusiasts organised around the common interest, its belief system was a broadly based synthesis of ideas and practices gleaned from whatever sources were available (often supplemented by individualistic interpretations) and its leadership was dispersed, thus denying the movement any formal locus of final authority. As a consequence it had little or no resilience against schism, as was shown when one of the founders named Pepe branched off to form his own separate Rastafarian group, the Twelve Tribes of

Israel, again a branch of a Jamaican group. Further, it lacked the sophisticated level of organisational equipment required to absorb the growing popularity of Ras Tafari into its structure.

All of this is not to suggest that Ras Tafari in England was totally a product of the 1970s. Indeed, Sheila Patterson (1963, p. 360) documented an abortive attempt of new migrants to organise a Rastafarian-oriented United Afro-West Indian Brotherhood in 1955 which made only a nugatory impact on the black community. Later she was able to report that: 'Early in 1958 a group of bearded and rather conspicuously dressed young men were noted in the Brixton market area. Several local informants confirmed that these were Ras Tafarians but no further information could be obtained then or later' (1963, p. 354n).

It seems that many migrants brought their religious beliefs with them to England and had to transmute them to fit new circumstances (Pentecostalism, for example). As Ras Tafari was in the mid-fifties a rather obscure and disreputable cult in Jamaica (Simpson, 1955*a*, 1955*b*) it seems unlikely that any migrating affiliates would want to advertise their membership for fear of stigmatisation.

Whatever the dispositions and motivations of Rastas in the 1950s, it seems their numbers remained small and their social importance minimal. Indeed, it was not until after 1973 that the gestation period seemed to approach an end and the movement really experienced birth in the West Indian community. But when it did, it blossomed into what might warrantably be called a Rastafarian renaissance; great chunks of the young West Indian community were swallowed up in enthusiasm as Ras Tafari manifested itself in England.

In 1973, Colin McGlashen was able to report on a 'Grand Rasta-farian Ball' in London at which he described 'two men of dreadlocks, splendid and terrible with thick matted tassels of hair hanging past their shoulders'. As Hebdige reflected, 'the men of dreadlocks began to make an incongruous (*sic*) and sinister appearance . . . on the grey streets of the metropolis' (1975, p. 151).

Apart from the localised influences of the EWF, depleted by the return to Jamaica of Fox, regarded by many as the most formidable and energetic personality in the movement, and the Twelve Tribes, interest was perpetually stimulated by the growing volume of Jamaican reggae music which was being imported by migrant West Indians. As I will show in the next two chapters, the music, replete with Rasta-farian concepts and categories, fell upon receptive and suggestible ears.

The rising popularity of reggae music amongst blacks and whites in England ensured it a wide distribution after 1974 and, in particular, the phenomenal success of the Jamaican Twelve Tribes member, Bob Marley, facilitated the easy identification of black English youth with their Jamaican progenitors. Familiarity with Rastafarian beliefs and values, ideals and ambitions came principally through the music but also through continued social interaction with other, possibly more knowledgeable enthusiasts.

The EWF had by then received the Head Administrator of the EOC in the USA and Jamaica, Archimandrite Abba who instructed in baptisms and appointed deacons. It was publishing its own newsheet, *Rastafarian Cry*, as a way of disseminating information about the movement and the Twelve Tribes members were also busily recruiting and promoting through their very professional publications (for example, *Praise I* and *Love I*). But the vast majority of young blacks were not interested in affiliating to any institution; the magnet was Rasta; as an EOC member put it: 'Rasta is more exciting.' For here was a ready-made package which as black persons they could find socially significant and personally meaningful. It provided them with new conceptual maps; new modes of comprehending the workings of the world about them, for understanding not only their current position but their history and future, for explaining ways in which they might escape their present circumstances and aspire to higher goals and for identifying who they were. As a conceptual scheme for explaining the world and providing the nucleus of self-identity, Ras Tafari totally eclipsed anything which had preceded it. Its appeal was remarkable yet, on consideration, understandable; deprived of any acceptable method of answering such perennial questions as 'why does the logic of the world work to continually subordinate the black man?', 'who am I as a black person born in the West Indies but living in England?' or 'what should the ultimate ambition of a black man be?', the black youth accepted willingly the remedies to these problems offered by Ras Tafari.

To argue that the appeal of Ras Tafari was purely in its provision of a vehicle for raising black consciousness, or of an explanation of the world or of a new identity and that young blacks' affiliation to the movement was a product of a deliberate and self-conscious exercise would be a simplification. Certainly, these dimensions were implicit in the movement and, as I will argue in the next chapter, were responsible for drawing young blacks into the ranks. But immersion into Ras Tafari was a much less deliberate process of drift culminating in the acceptance of Haile Selassie: 'Ras Tafari passed over I'; 'Ras Tafari found I'; 'Selassie I was always in I'; 'It was in us from creation.' were illustrative Rastafarian comments. The motion was guided gently by underlying influences: the facilitating ones being the loss of commitment to parental modes of life and the social order which they seemed to symbolise; the promotional ones being the availability of Rastafarian concepts and the social apparatus for their transmission, like reasoning sessions and the distribution of Rastafarian music: 'Maybe music was the inspiration for the movement but through reasoning a better understanding was reached,' a Rasta explained.

During the 1960s, West Indians' attachments to the existing order had been loosened by the rude boy complex. The rudies' affinity with the skinheads was founded upon principles of anti-authoritarianism, violence, racialism and short-run hedonism. The young rude boys, like their Jamaican predecessors, effected a weakening of ties to parents and brought into being for the first time in the history of the English black presence a cleft between first-generation migrants and their children. Rude boys crystallised into gangs comprising of a core numbering about eight to twelve and an outer ring of many more.

The rough-hewn ideology of the black gang, whilst not submerging individualism, was centred around group loyalty and the paramount importance of the gang as a unit.

Now, although the rude boy complex as a stylised subculture dissolved as the 1970s approached, it left behind the legacy of a gang structure which remained a socially important feature of black youth in the years that followed. The style of the rudies passed away but the structure of the gang remained – and this was a significant factor in the growth of Rasta.

The enduring structure of the gang provided ready-made channels for the communication of Rastafarian concepts and categories; the smooth transmission was lubricated by regular and intense patterns of social interaction among young blacks. Homogeneity, similarity of orientation and social condition ensured a more or less uniform reception. Familiarity with Ras Tafari was self-generating once the initial awareness had been gained by one or more gang members. Full comprehension of the doctrines and normative prescriptions was not necessary for the incipient drift, for the act of becoming a Rastaman was always a process of becoming: as I was repeatedly told: 'The learning never stops.' Knowledge of the movement was always penumbral and to ever claim full insight was tantamount to a breach of the faith. But once the peripheral boundaries of Ras Tafari had been broached then the process of drift towards the nucleus of the beliefs and the new cognitive and normative directives it held could begin.

The dislocation from the parental culture became more attenuated as Rastafarian subscriptions intensified. Gangs became breeding grounds of Rastafarian themes and their interpretation through 'reasoning' dialogues. And, as Ras Tafari took grip, the gangs' dissociations deepened: though they were rarely total. This dislocation from conventional culture was always likely to occur with second-generation West Indians; perceptions of rejection and the patterns of social and residential segregation that they fostered were highly conducive to the development of the idiosyncratic mode of thought which substantially cut Rastas off from other groups. 'The ghetto or culturally distinct enclave can breed messianic dreams of its own' (Barkun, 1974, p. 175); and the dream of Africa was a powerful magnetiser of emotions and sentiments.

Increasingly, the gaps between the drifting Rastas and the wider society became more visible: dreadlocks grew longer, Ethiopian coloured garments more apparent and home-made makutarias, or prayer sticks, more evident. The 'exteriorisation' of Rasta made dissembly virtually impossible and confirmed the dislocation. Modes of conduct and expression became progressively eccentric: the Rastas developed their own stylised walk – a sort of loose-limbed bouncing motion – and cultivated a brand of Jamaican patios as their own way of communicating replete with its own special vocabulary (concepts such as 'suffering', 'pressure' and, of course, 'Africa' were charged with new meanings). What might have seemed relatively insignificant differentials were by the mid-1970s very revealing indeed; the new Rastas were staking out a social gulf between themselves and the rest of society.

Whilst drifting into Rasta ways, the young blacks acquired those symbols, ideologies and terminologies deriving ultimately from their Jamaican predecessors, but which could be used in the different environment to lace them together as a social unit and minimise their associations with the 'outside world'. Contacts with the discredited agents of Babylon were restricted and primary group or in-gang associations were promoted. The company of other drifters or those that had accepted the faith was valued and the noxious influences of the wider society were avoided. Processes of inclusion (of brethren) and exclusion (of outsiders) worked to seal members into a practically impermeable subworld, a closed sphere.

The drifting process entailed a concomitant closure of ranks to outsiders. Relationships with outsiders suffered as a result of increased involvement in the movement – 'They see that Rastafarian make it bad for your own group, you know, and in a way they don't believe in themselves as black people' – so the Rastas were almost forced to abandon outside relationships with other blacks (and relationships with whites would have been minimal anyway). Breakdowns in outside relations were of little consequence to the Rastas because they considered themselves to be the 'enlightened ones' and so had little to gain from those who had not 'seen the light'. As the movement grew and processes of mutual reassurance went into effect, relations with outsiders were valued less and less and primary relations were restricted to in-group members. It became clear that the incomprehending wider society would never accept the validity of Rastafarian beliefs, so trying to maintain good relations with its members was something

of a self-defeating exercise: 'Them never understand I and I; so I
don't need them. I know it is the truth I have and so I'm prepared to
struggle for it' commented a Rasta; and another: 'The faith is the
strength to overcome the oppression.'

By 1975, Rasta had developed from an interstitial phenomenon to
the stage where it engulfed vast sections of the young West Indian
community. The movement's magnetic attraction was undeniable; it
drew devotees from the black working class of London, Birmingham,
Leicester, Liverpool, Manchester and Bristol, by then becoming
increasingly familiar with the messages of Bob Marley, Big Youth and
Burning Spear, not to mention the less available and far obscurer
concepts of Ras Joseph and the Sons of Negus and Nyabinghi.

But the abundance of dreadlocks and prayer sticks had opened the
movement up to inspection and events after mid-1976 were to introduce tensions from both the outside and the inside. In June 1976,
the movement gained the attention of the *Reading Evening Post* which
wrote of a 'West Indian Mafia organisation called Rastafarians . . .
an International crime ring specialising in drugs, prostitution, subver-
sion and blackmail.' Its syndicated members were said to favour fast
cars, wear their hair in 'long rat's tails' and 'walk about with "prayer
sticks" – trimmed pick-axe handles'. The EOC responded with legal
action but nothing of consequence transpired (see *W.estindian World*,
15 July 1976). As much as eighteen months later, in December 1977,
the publication of the even more damaging *Shades of Grey* report
demonstrated what little understanding of the movement had been
achieved despite its prevalence and urgency. The report was based
on dubious knowledge and was totally destructive in its attack on the
Rastas, bringing into focus what was called a dangerous 'criminalised
subculture'. Clearly, the young West Indians lacked the effective
power to resist the attention of others and their attribution of the
status of folk devils – or 'red devils' as the *Reading Evening Post*
would have it!

In late 1975, the whole movement faced its most severe crisis since
the non-materialisation of the expected millennium in the late 1950s
and early 1960s. If the criterion for membership was the acceptance of
Haile Selassie as God, then his death might warrantably be understood as totally and irrevocably destructive to the whole system of
Rastafarian belief. At this stage in the movement's development it
exhibited few points of organisational or ideological unity, its membership was fluid, there was only limited normative consensus, vague
and disturbed leadership and no definition of roles. The characteristic
for evaluating Rastafarian status was the acceptance of Haile Selassie
as the divine power who would transform the world through the
destruction of Babylon. The drift to Ras Tafari was, in effect, accompanied by the acquisition of Rastafarian concepts and categories and

culminated in the realisation that Haile Selassie was, indeed, the true God. His departure was to place the entire Rastafarian belief system under stress.

THE 'DISAPPEARANCE' OF HAILE SELASSIE

The death of Haile Selassie on 27 August 1975 under circumstances so dubious that his son Asfa Wossen demanded an autopsy was probably the most taxing event for the movement since the repeated failures of the millennium to materialise in Jamaica during the late 1950s and early 1960s. Ethiopia had been troubled by civil discontent since before 1973 when a failure of the annual rains resulted in a disastrous famine in many areas, some of whose populations were already at the subsistence level. Matters were exacerbated by the world rises in food prices, a series of strikes and eventually a serious mutiny of armed forces. Malcontents pressed for the Emperor's resignation and radical constitutional changes, some of which were implemented. But throughout 1974 his authority waned drastically and unrest flourished until September when a Co-ordinating Committee of Armed Forces seized power and proclaimed his deposition. Accusations of corruption followed and Haile Selassie was confined to an army barracks for three months, after which he was returned to the Grand Palace at Addis Ababa where he underwent an operation for a prostate gland complaint, an illness which was given as the official cause of his death but which his son contested. (See also *The Times*, 28 August 1975; *Guardian*, 28 August 1975.)

To digress slightly, when the ships did not arrive in Jamaica in the 1950s and 1960s and the expected signal of the coming holocaust did not appear thousands of members retreated to their disbanded communes or Kingston 'dungle' (slum) dwellings to cultivate fresh visions, enliven old ones or even anticipate more earthly attempts to encourage and assist the transformation. After the cult's inception in the 1930s it generated communities of followers geographically dispersed but all utterly convinced of the divinity of Haile Selassie and his ability to organise and execute their return to Africa. The very presence of people sharing such a belief afforded some kind of insulation from the discrediting forces at work when the ships did not appear. As Michael Barkun argues: 'The existence of a community of believers is insurance against the traumatic effects of disconfirmed predictions, for within that community there are mutual sources of reassurance and rationalisation' (1974, p. 115).

In a similar fashion, the seemingly iconoclastic death of Haile Selassie was buffered by the growing collection of Jamaican followers convinced of his divinity and who were prepared to employ strategies designed to preserve the validity of their belief. So that, writing just after Haile Selassie's death, Leonard Barrett was able to report:

The central tenets of the Rastafarians have not changed to any great extent. Haile Selassie of Ethiopia (even though he was dethroned during my research, and died within a few days of my return from the field), is still god. The returned messiah in the flesh, he is now even more powerful in the spirit – a belief central to the movement. (1977, p. 171)

The death stimulated a series of ingenious responses from members of the English brotherhood; these can be summarised in three categories:

(1) Haile Selassie was still alive; his death was a fabrication of the Western world and its allies.
(2) He simply assumed another form.
(3) His death was inconsequential because Haile Selassie was merely a 'personification' of God.

It becomes immediately apparent that (2) and (3) closely resemble Barrett's inferences. I split them into two because for some Rastas Haile Selassie was indeed God when still alive as a person and God as a spirit after his death, the assumption of a spirit form reducing neither his power nor his status. In the (3) formulation, however, Ras Tafari was never to be conceived of as God even during his life; he was merely an exteriorisation of God, or a vehicle for the transition of God into this world; it was expressed more succintly by a Rasta: 'When I looks at a photograph of Selassie I, I am not looking at God; nor if I look at Eyesus Christus; these are merely representations for God is I and I and always has been.'

The belief that Haile Selassie was not dead at all, but simply in hiding where he bided his time waiting for a return to power was a claim made by the most politically aware members. Those who were to some extent involved with the movement by 1975 and were familiar with events in Ethiopia could find some support for their belief in the suspicious and sinister circumstances surrounding the dethroned Emperor's departure. So strong was their conviction that Haile Selassie was their God that it was not to be shaken by events so shrouded in mystery and confusion that even the incredulous son of Haile Selassie insisted on an autopsy which was subsequently refused by the succeeding military government.

Those holding to this particular version were amongst the most sophisticated early thinkers in the movement; those taking a keen interest not only in the movement but in the movements relationship with the outside world. They were acquainted with the conspiracy theory which accounted for the entire history of the black man in terms of the white's propensity to suppress him by whatever methods he had available, physical or mental (discussed more fully in Chapter 7). The uncertain disappearance of Jah fitted in almost too perfectly with the malevolent forces of Babylon's efforts to perpetuate the black man's enslavement. Haile Selassie's death doubtless remained a powerful validating support of the Babylonian conspiracy theory and actually worked to reinforce the belief system by providing evidence of the white world's determination to continue its dominance.

Often the events of 1975 were cited as supportive of the conspiracy theory: 'Babylon took Jah 'cause it knew its days were up. It knows Selassie I was ready to "throw" the world; him come to cause the deliverance, man. But Babylon on the run, him scared, man – do *anything* like make believe Selassie I dead. But him no dead, man; Jah lives; always will.' And another Rasta 'Colonialism will always try to suppress any attempt of the black man to gain his independence; just look at what happened in 1975. They [the whites] want I to believe His Imperial Majesty is dead.' A small number of Rastas believed the conspiracy had taken on a new dimension with the disappearance of Haile Selassie, holding to the view that Selassie had consented to the coup after realising that his position was so vulnerable that the takeover was inevitable: 'The press never said anything, but His Majesty probably knew the takeover was going to happen and so negotiated it himself.'

The sources for this conspiracy belief to account for Haile Selassie's death or 'disappearance' are unsure. Adrian Boot and Michael Thomas in contrast to Barrett, contend that: '*Most* Rastas don't altogether accept the apparent fact of his death, and those that do await his imminent resurrection' (1976, p. 80). (My italics). It is certainly possible that those members subscribing to this belief in the immediate aftermath of the death, gleaned their ideas from the Jamaican movement with whom the institutionalised branches were in communication. Adherents to the view that Haile Selassie was forcibly taken into captivity and not allowed contact with the outside world came predominantly from the Twelve Tribes and the EWF (which experienced an ideological upheaval as a result of this some months after the death). Some went as far as positing the view that the disappearance was arranged in consort with Haile Selassie himself and that, mindful of his inability to check the civil unrest, he willingly became a party to his own disappearance; the reluctance of the military régime deposing him to reveal details was seen as supportive of this. My study suggests that the ideas dismissing the death were very immediate reactions by those who were members of Rastafarian organisations in 1975; but the phenomenal growth of the movement took place after this date.

Although I would not go so far as to contend that only members of one of the two institutions were in a position to formulate the first response due to their greater familiarity with world events and their closer contact with their respective Jamaican branches, the vast majority of non-institutional affiliates tended to house a more spiritual interpretation. This might well have been due to the fact that most of them drifted deeper into the movement at some time after the death, by which time it strained credibility to believe that he was still alive. By 1977–8 most Rastas had adopted either (2) or (3) as a way of confirming their belief in the divinity of Haile Selassie and thus solidifying their status as Rastafarian. The pattern of belief between (2) and (3) was fairly randomly distributed and equally split: about 40 per cent suggested that Haile Selassie had simply metamorphosed; another 40 per cent contending that to think of Haile Selassie as God was a misconception, for his body was more of a vehicular unit for the carriage of God and his death was of no consequence (the other 20 per cent subscribing to the 'disappearance' view). It is a fine distinction but an important one. The second of these interpretations, (3), grew in prominence among the ranks of the EWF after a series of events which threatened to undermine the whole enterprise.

The difficulties arose when the EWF, eager to strengthen its links with the original EOC, one of the most ancient branches of the Christian Church, made efforts towards this end by inviting a high-ranking official of the Church to grant his approval. Realising that the Rastafarian impulse was encompassing vast sections of the black community and that some youths were, through their exuberances, bringing the name of Ras Ṭafari into some disrepute, the Church members sought to consolidate their own positions as serious and devoutly religious people who had not on any occasion transgressed the boundaries of orthodox Christian faith or practice in the process of becoming Rastafarian. The Church's Abba in London consented to conduct baptismal duties in 1976 but at the same time took the opportunity to declare two correctives which struck at the core of the Rastafarian belief system. First, that if they were to be righteous EOC members, they should cut off their dreadlocks. His second directive was more serious: that members should erase from their minds the 'erroneous belief' in the divinity of Haile Selassie (given the political situation in Ethiopia, this request was understandable). The first instruction was dutifully carried out by many Church members but the second was disturbing and totally unacceptable. After the initial shock, however, a resolution was discovered. Ostensibly, the members adhered to the official doctrine of the EOC, performing services, ceremonies and rites according to Eastern Christian teachings. For the overwhelming majority the conviction in Haile Selassie's divinity would not fade and they retained their fidelity to the Rastafarian movement by making this a personal commitment and never articulating it at Church services etc. In such a way, they were able to remain an EOC member without impairing their Rastafarian status. Those who had modified their physical appearance through shedding their locks dismissed their action as unimportant, stressing the implicitness of God in all men irrespective of their hair; to quote two members: 'I am a baptised member of the church, but still a Rastaman. This is not contradiction as you say. Because we do not recognise this in ceremony does not mean God is not within I; nor that Ras Tafari is present in the church'; 'Locksing up was a way of showing the world that Ras Tafari was alive. Now they know and so the locks are no longer important to the movement.' Others were more insistent on the need to keep the locks: 'There is certain vows that Moses himself set aside for the Nazarite . . . so we are just fulfilling what was spoke unto our fathers . . . and we are in the faith and spirit of the Nazarene. This is the cause of the locks.'

Superficially, then, the EWF had brought its members into line with the official Church doctrine, worshipping Haile Selassie as the Supreme Patriarch of the Church without publicly attributing to him any greater status. The prevalent view in the Church at the time of my research (1977–8) was that Haile Selassie was *the* central figure in the whole Rastafarian movement, but that in many ways his divinity was open to misconception. He was a 'personification' of God but his death bore no lasting effect on the future of the movement for God was implicitly residing in all men. Haile Selassie had personified God for a while: 'How can Ras Tafari be dead when he is in all men? The body of Haile Selassie I may have been terminated but the spirit of God lives in all mankind.' (An interesting after-effect of this ideological movement in the Church was that some members eventually felt compelled to concede that they had been hopelessly mistaken in their previous thinking that Haile Selassie was God and that, in view of their new conception, they should renounce their Rastafarian status, admitting, as one ex-Rasta did, that: 'My King is not my God' and 'I am no longer Rasta, my work is for God not for a king.')

The steadfastness of any religious movement can never be taken for granted, especially when the central tenets of its belief system hang on threads slender enough to be snapped by invalidating events. Ultimate ambitions of, for example, redemption can be fomented in isolation and made invulnerable to disconfirming realities; other items are more vulnerable. Haile Selassie's death might well have been viewed as the final falsification of Rastafarian beliefs: Haile Selassie was a king overthrown by a military coup, and, in all probability, killed by his adversaries; therefore he was not God after all; existing Rastas would have been proved wrong and future aspirants deterred from joining the movement. But, of course, this did not happen: Rastas employed a range of strategies to defuse the traumatic events in Ethiopia and membership swelled astonishingly after 1975.

Those accepting the faith after August 1975 would not have faced the same kinds of potential dissonance as older members, for they entered the movement with the recognition that Jah was no longer a living king as well as the messiah. The responsibility was on the existing brethren to reassure the new accepters (a term I prefer to 'converts') that the conceptual transformation was genuine and unshakable. One beauty of this process was that in assuring others that their beliefs were true ones the older members were able to reciprocally gain assurance in their own correctness: 'The individual who assures someone else that his act was right also assures himself. And when he sees the effect of his reassurance on the other, he is again confirmed in the rightness of his own position' (Barkun, 1974, p. 114–15).

In Rastafarian terms, this reciprocal reassurance process was known as 'reasoning'; members came together in informal social interactions to discuss spontaneously practically any issue concerning them personally and how this related to the movement. Throughout the course of the dialogue some members might disappear, others might join in the activity and the contours of the discussion might undulate continuously in a rather flighty fashion. Topics were sometimes unremarkable; at other times profound and exceptional. I point to this procedure of reasoning as one of the vital techniques through which the potentially injurious events in Ethiopia were assuaged. Once in command of a rationalised interpretation of the death, the individual Rasta could, through reasoning, persuade others of its validity and reaffirm their ability to discover the truth when all about them were struggling in ignorance. Those not entirely convinced of the correctness of the beliefs were discouraged from 'fence-sitting' by having their doubts allayed and their convictions reinforced. It became a self-perpetuating cycle as the movement grew numerically and more and more young blacks became acquainted with the beliefs and passed them on to others; Ras Tafari developed an internal dynamic.

The assimilation of Haile Selassie's death into the Rastafarian belief system rested on the ability of its most sophisticated and influential members to endow outside sources of information with a negative status and simultaneously validate their own interpretations, a process Berger and Luckmann (1972, pp. 132–4) call 'nihilation', 'to liquidate conceptually everything *outside*' (in this case outside the Rastafarian subworld). Rastas neutralised the challenge of events in Ethiopia by creating their own interpretations of them in terms of Rastafarian concepts and disallowing other versions any credibility except as evidence of the general Babylonian conspiracy: 'nihilation *denies* the reality of whatever phenomena or interpretations of phenomena do not fit into that [socially constructed] universe' (Berger and Luckmann, 1972, p. 132).

The death of Haile Selassie could therefore be discounted as having ontologically inferior status and therefore not meriting attention except as a product of Babylon's anxieties; or accepted by being reinterpreted in concepts derived from a Rastafarian belief system; or simply dismissed as a misconception and irrelevant to the movement. In all cases, the external events in Ethiopia were incorporated into a Rastafarian frame of reference and used as resources for the validation of the belief system. Effectively, the liquidation of other interpretations served to affirm the status of the Rastafarian interpretation and thus reinforce existing conceptions. The numerical growth of the movement and the reciprocal reassurances through procedures of reasoning strengthened the plausibility structure of Ras Tafari; each new addition to the movement gave supportive evidence for those already accepting the beliefs, and growth fed its own dynamism.

THE CONTOURS OF THE MODERN MOVEMENT

The conditions under which the movement emerged and blossomed in the 1970s were, as I see them, six-fold. First, and quite obviously, the concentration of an homogeneous black population in urban areas, sections of which housed sets of aspirations which were to remain systematically unfulfilled. As I will argue in the following chapter, the discrepancy opened up by the difference between expectation and experience was a vital motivating factor in the apprehension of racialism and the process of becoming a Rastaman. This, in turn, led to a condition of suggestibility among that section of the populace; dismayed and disillusioned by their being denied what was understood as full participation in society they became receptive to new ideas and ambitions. Thirdly, and very importantly, was the availability of Rastafarian concepts and themes made possible through music and the social apparatus for their transmission. Ease of communication of these concepts was facilitated by the existence of a pre-formed gang structure; patterns of stable and regular social interaction had been established during the rude boy era and lingered on as the principal unit of second-generation West Indian associations. Out of this initial set of conditions developed a growing intimacy of knowledge with Rastafarian ideas and messages and a concomitant rise of self-awareness, not simply of being black but of having an underlying cultural unity and one which united all Rastas in the face of adverse conditions, or 'pressure'. This dawn of realisation was summarised by one Rasta as 'the revival of our true self and the discovery of our history'. During this acquisition of knowledge came the familiarity with the important theoretical elaboration I call the Babylonian conspiracy. The final condition to be satisfied was the perceived loss of legitimacy in the dominant moral order, including the educational and social control systems, and a corresponding adherence to the legitimacy of the Rastafarian order, or 'God's law'. Such a perception stimulated an active rejection of old allegiances, the ties to which had been loosened in earlier periods and, following from this, two complementary procedures: the shut-out of parental influence and elimination of their significance; and the enhancement of the peer group's socialising importance – in-group reasoning became perhaps the most valued unit of social intercourse.

The breach with the parental culture was articulated through calling parents 'brainwashed', 'misguided' or even 'blind': 'They [older blacks] are not in a conscious state of mind. They still believe they are perhaps inferior'; 'They are bound to fall'. Acceptance of Ras Tafari for the overwhelming majority symbolised their complete dislocation from their parents and the moral order they represented. Mutual accommodation occurred for some, but only at stages where both parents and children became more tolerant of each other's beliefs.

With all of these conditions fulfilled the Rastafarian movement was able to take firm root in the black-populated areas of England's industrial centres. During 1976 and 1977 it grew virtually day by day, attracting the majority of Britain's young black working class and impelling them to new postures and social behaviours. The 'spell of Africa' exerted an unparalleled influence on black youth; the acceptance that Haile Selassie was the divine king alluded to in Garvey's prophecy brought with it a totally fresh and enlightened conception of the world. Garvey had provided his original Jamaican followers with new conceptual maps with which to make sense of the world but his impact was equally as dramatic in England. For the neoteric Rastas, Garvey, 'the black prophet of the sky', was still talking to them: 'He was the one who told us that we must look to Africa when a king shall come . . . and he told us that we must ask for deliverance through the rise of Ethiopia and worship God through our own spectacles,' observed a Rastaman. He was just as alive and subjectively real in 1978 as he was in 1923; as it was expressed to me in the February of that year: 'Marcus Garvey *is* a servant of God . . . God gave him the inspiration and vision to see certain things about the world which come about.'

Furnished with their new vision, the Rastas were able to take fresh cognisance of the world and their place in that world. Answers to such questions as 'Why does the logic of the world work to subordinate the black man?'; 'How can he rid himself of this condition?' and even the very basic 'Who am I?' were revealed in the unfolding Rastafarian dialogue of reasoning.

The superbly enriching understanding of 'I and I' became arguably the most important theoretical tool apart from the Babylonian conspiracy in the Rastafarian repertoire. I can elaborate no better than

Rastas themselves: 'I and I is an expression to totalise the concept of oneness. It is derived from the expression that God always addressed himself by when he speaks of himself as "I". You know, so when Ras Tafari speak of himself as "I" he means it in a sense of total uplifting of one's self, total dignity of one's self and expresses that so his fellow brethren is the same as himself. When he's addressing a brethren as himself, he says "I am I" – as being the oneness of two persons. So God is within all of us and we're one people in fact.' 'I and I means that God is in *all* men. The bond of Ras Tafari is the bond of God, of man. But man itself needs a head and the head of man is His Imperial Majesty Haile Selassie of Ethiopia. This is a man that binds all the hearts of man.'

As I will argue later, this perception of a unifying bond of brother-hood, or brethren expressed in I and I was to prove vital in the move-ment's maintenance of a distinctly Rastafarian conception of reality. It bound the members together in a single unit so that even without formal organisation it constituted a coherent and definable movement as contrasted to a loosely structured aggregation. And within that movement, Rastas were able to cultivate and develop a new and exhilarating view of the world, one which divided the universe into good and bad, right and wrong, or Zion and Babylon.

By 1978 the contours of the modern movement were well estab-lished; apart from its internal developments it had reached the lofty levels of public visibility with the publication of the controversial *Shades of Grey* report and the plethora of publicity surrounding it. As well as the scathing attacks it underwent from Brown's report (1977) and its publicisers, the movement encountered opposition from the police, Asians and certain sections of the West Indian community. But such difficulties served to reinforce the conviction that Rastas were one people and their passage to Zion would be fraught with pressures from Babylon; but Ras Tafari afforded the devotee some resilience; as I was once told: 'The faith is the strength to overcome the oppression.'

The sense of awakening, or, given the Jamaican origins, cultural rebirth, swept the entire West Indian community, gripping the hearts and minds of the under 25-year-old population. Even those barely old enough to comprehend the importance of the movement, let alone its belief system, did not escape the spread of enthusiasm. Twelve and 13-year-olds adopted the colours of Ethiopia and sang jubilantly of 'Jah' and 'Rastaman Vibrations' (see Troyna, 1977*b*). By the late 1970s it was not necessary to be a Rasta to recognise that Africa was the true home of the black man.

Africa had left the black community spellbound; the recognition of that continent (used synonomously with Ethiopia – colonialism was responsible for 'artificial divisions' of the continent) motivated new loyalties and authenticated the new movement. Young West Indians saw themselves not as fractionated and culturally diverse but as one people, sharing similarities of backgrounds, of present circumstance and, more importantly, of future. Bob Marley spoke to his followers thus: 'We know where we're going, we know where from; we're leaving Babylon into our father's land' (from 'Exodus').

But while the concept of Africa was the most efficacious and emotive symbol of the movement it was also its most ambiguous and perplexing aspect. As with the later Jamaican movement it was never quite clear whether Africa was to be utilised as a spiritual or intellectual focus for black people, or as a geographical entity to which all blacks would eventually return. Rastas insisted it was both: 'Repatriation is spiritual and physical'; 'Africa is where all black men are descended from and so it's back to Africa we must go'; 'The only ambition of the Rastafarian movement is to see that all the black people of the western hemisphere return to their homeland.' But, despite the avowed intention to travel and settle in Africa at some future stage to be specified by Haile Selassie, there was a general agreement that recognition of that African heritage was a precondition for that enterprise to succeed. For the new Rastas it was not only possible to be African in England but an inescapable part of the preparation for the physical return. This is, by necessity, a simplification of the central ambition of the English movement, as the concept of Africa was replete with all the contradictions and ambiguities of its Jamaican original of which Barrett estimated 'that close to 50 percent of the movement's membership still holds to the doctrine of repatriation; that is, the miraculous return to Ethiopia by the supernatural power of the king' (1977, p. 172); the other 50 percent house the slogan 'liberation before repatriation.' I am slightly sceptical about the simplicity of the division, but if Barrett is correct then his finding bears little relevance to the English situation where the Rastas' orientation to Africa was a much more complex affair. To this I will return in the concluding chapter.

To summarise: the movement had developed an identifiable shape by the late 1970s; its adherents organised their lives around the divinity of Haile Selassie and his ability and intention to engineer and execute a redemption programme, the mechanics behind which were never systematically revealed. The gang structure evolving out of the rude boy complex remained and this facilitated communication of Rastafarian concepts and categories through procedures known as reasoning. Such groups were the principal unit of social interaction amongst Rastas and as the breach with parental culture was finalised they assumed over-riding importance as socialising vehicles: an EOC member captured it: 'Man learns through reasoning; this is how the brethren reaches enlightenment and comes to understand his true

self'. Informal group interaction was vitally important to the aquisi-
tion of Rastafarian concepts, values and norms and was a learning
process in itself.

The tendency of the English Rastas was to maximise their divergence from the wider society and at the same time solidify their own
commitment to exclusivity and distinctness as well as reinforcing a
particular conception of reality. The looks, the language and the predilection to minimise contacts with outsiders and restrict relations as
far as possible were all symbolic strategies in the establishment of an
exclusive, and in many ways élite group composed of people in search
of their 'true selves'. What might have been misunderstood as 'pre-
cocious independence' or 'sheer arrogance' was, in fact, part of the
endeavour to authenticate the reality of Ras Tafari as the chosen
people.

Before moving on to delineate some of the ways in which these
strategies were implemented and to what effect, I should perhaps
specify more accurately who were the Rastafarian members, what
changes they underwent in the process of becoming Rastas, and what
were the external influences so indispensable to the recreation of the
movement in the changed environment. The second two questions will
occupy the following chapters; the first will be dealt with in the
remainder of this.

SOCIAL ORIGINS

I will suggest in the next chapter that the drift to the Ras Tafari was
a creative response to confusion within the second-generation West
Indian community. After experiencing difficulty and anxiety in trying
to make satisfactory sense of what were considered to be important
matters of existence, they turned to the comprehensive world view of
Rasta where they found fulfilments of their need for an understanding
of the world and their place in that world, as well as a vehicle for
mobilising sentiments and reinforcing black solidarity. I will examine
the sorts of dispositions which spurred them into their particular
courses of action in due course, but for the moment need to establish
a balanced view by considering some 'objective' characteristics of the
brethren's background. Not that I am suggesting that such indicators
as social class, status, educational level or parental influence are
reliable determinants of forms of behaviour; merely that there are
discernible and patterned features of Rastas' backgrounds which can
be profitably used to elicit a social profile of the movement's membership.

One danger of sociological theorising is to posit relationships
between such variables as class, education or religion and draw out
conclusions. It is a central contention of my book that any understanding of social phenomena must take account of the actor's perspective,

his cognitions, perceptions and dispositions motivating him to act in certain ways. By considering both objective and subjective facets of the movement I hope to achieve a balanced appreciation.

If, for the sake of simplicity, occupation is accepted as a criterion of social class, it could be safely concluded that the Rastafarian movement of the 1970s was composed totally of young (modal age = 18) working-class blacks (about 70 per cent male), mostly of Jamaican descent but a few from other parts of the West Indies. There was a statistical predominance of unemployed (about 50 per cent) and manual occupations (45 per cent) including painters, carpenters, factory workers, packers and warehousemen.

Some were involved in higher-level labour jobs which would have required the actor to have had some training. A small number were enrolled at the colleges of further education on full-time or part-time bases. An even smaller number were self-employed, running small commercial ventures such as speciality food shops or one-man services. The range of occupational grades was rather narrow, suggesting that the movement attracted those at the lower reaches of the occupational hierarchy. Similarly, the Jamaican movement had always been composed of those anchored at the foot of the hierarchy, those members of the working class eking out a living by scuffling in the 'dungle' or performing menial jobs; though the spread of the 1970s tended to draw into the ranks some elements of the middle class, or what Leonard Barrett calls 'functional Rastafarians' (1977, p. 220). By and large, the English and Jamaican movements were, as Vittorio Lanternari puts it, 'religions of the oppressed' (1963). Members had very limited access to luxuries and, in Jamaica, even necessities – as their living on the wretched outskirts of Kingston illustrates. Wealth, status and power were not rewards accruing to Rastas: only a tiny number were in possession of their own property (mostly motor cars and bicycles); those boasting status based this contention on membership to musical bands.

The temptation here is to introduce theories of the relative deprivation kidney to explain the emergence of such a movement amongst groups subjected to oppression of some order, pinpointing the group's depressed social condition as the causal factor. Such theories have been influential in studies of millenarian movements, most notably through the work of David Aberle (1966) and Anthony Wallace (1956a). Stated *in puris naturalibus* the broad theory holds that when an actor or group of actors sees some other actor or group (which may or may not include himself) as being in possession of a certain material or quality (irrespective of whether they actually are) and also requires that material or quality himself he experiences relative deprivation (see Runciman, 1966). As his capacity for acquiring this material or quality remains unchanged, he becomes progressively more discontented and gives outward expression to his feelings by resorting to religious forms of behaviour, perhaps of the millenarian order. The theory relies heavily on the subjective orientation of the actor(s), for it is his gauging of his own position through the utilisation of others' as a measuring rod – a subjective individual judgement of conditions – which stimulates the propensity to act in the particular way. This gauging bears no necessary relationship to objective conditions for the deprivation is felt relative to another; but, of course, accepting the hypotheses deriving from the theory, the researcher would expect patterns of relative deprivation to be found among disprivileged groups, especially where they coexist with more privileged groups. The availability of qualitatively and quantitatively better-off groups as guidelines enhances the chances of felt deprivation.

Approaches stemming from this are riddled with problems, the most serious of which is that its concepts are so vague and flexible that it can be applied to practically all social situations. But its generalisability is so limitless that it is capable of explaining everything and nothing at the same time! To ask of it why millenarian responses are elicited among those feeling relative deprivation at some times yet not at others would be to overtax the theory; it simply cannot account for the breakpoint between millenarian and other forms of social dissidence: the difference between issues of challenge and protest against the existing order and the utter and unshakable conviction in the imminent transformation of that order to be instigated by some supernatural agency, 'the quantum leap.'

The actor's frame of reference is essential to any enterprise seeking to arm itself with relative deprivation as a tool of analysis and every effort must be made to ensure that the deprivation is felt by the group exhibiting the particular behaviour; objective conditions of deprivation provide only clues as to where to look for relative deprivation. My research indicates that the Rastas of the mid-1970s were not only deprived in the sense that their lowly occupational position denied them access to the spheres of wealth, power and status, but they genuinely regarded themselves as severely oppressed. 'Suffering', was always the critical unit of experience for the Rastas. Through believing themselves to be continually suffering at the hands of Babylon the whole history of the blacks' contact with whites could be conjured up in a moment: 'It's all about suffering.' It was a concept as relevant and immediate to the contemporary Rastas as they thought it to be to their enslaved ancestors.

But this is not to imply a propensity to value all the attributes of white society, for the Rastas were committed to a comprehensive transformation, not merely a readjustment of material circumstances.

But clearly there were social rewards available to whites which Rastas were conscious of and did value: dignity ('We *were* a people of pride and dignity'); social prestige ('The black skin has always been frowned upon'); culture ('The colonial system has stripped us of everything that has identified us as a people over the centuries'); history and identity ('It's for us to revive our true self and really know our ability by discovering our history'); education ('The education system worked to prevent the Rastaman realising his true self'); jobs ('You go for a job – you can't get a job. Certain places reject you. Why? Because you are black'). But importantly, they recognised these as having been denied them because they were black. Although they were valued attributes of some sectors of white society, in no way were the Rastas content to have them passed over to blacks; they wanted the total structure of their distribution transformed so that a new age would bring these qualities to the black man. It was the perception of racialism underlying the deprivation which provoked the Rastafarian response; the objective condition of disprivilege and the feeling of relative deprivation were necessary but not sufficient conditions. In other words, the young blacks who drifted into the Rastafarian movement were undeniably a deprived group chained to the bottom of the occupational hierarchy; they expected to be accepted on an equal footing with their white contemporaries but came to feel that this was never possible because they were black ('The black man can never be accepted here'). So although they felt relatively deprived by being denied full participation in society it was not just this feeling that impelled them to Ras Tafari but the understanding of why they were deprived. Without this, their response would have had no focus and, therefore, no effective critical impulse.

The perception of racialism as an explanatory variable must be added to the condition of disadvantage and the feeling of relative deprivation for a more complete account of the movement's emergence (I will develop this in the next chapter).

It will have become apparent by now that the rupture with the parental culture facilitated the drift to Rasta, so an examination of the family backgrounds of Rastas is desirable at this stage. No English Rasta had parents who affiliated with the movement (though young Rastas brought their children up in the faith once they themselves had accepted it); in every case, the Rastas came from conventional Christian backgrounds with Roman Catholicism and Methodism slightly over-represented – but not significantly. Parents' adherence to a more accommodating Christian mode of thought – but to Rastas, 'a distortion' – no doubt exacerbated tensions between the two generations. The process of becoming a Rastaman was accompanied by a decrease in the subjective credibility of parental religions and a concomitant disjuncture with the culture they seemed to augment. Not surprisingly, the awareness that their parents were 'brainwashed', 'misguided' or just 'blind' compounded that rupture.

Associations were made between the parents' religious affiliation and their social position. Occupationally, Rastas' parents were down the scale; including plumbers, machinists, carpenters, transport workers and car workers.

They lived in rented accommodation or small owner-occupied property and showed a very similar profile to their children in terms of wealth, status and power, none of which were evident. The Rastas saw the West Indian Christian churches as preventing their parents realising their 'true self' and thus rendering them malleable puppets of colonialism; they were 'in a state of mind that can be described as not a conscious state of mind; they still believe that they are perhaps inferior'.

The links between their parents' deprivation and their membership to a Christian church was a powerful one in the mind of the Rastas. The belief was that their parents and their Jamaican ancestors had been duped into accepting churches 'derived from the European' from the early days of slavery and this had proved an inhibitory mechanism stultifying their collective consciousness and therefore persuading them to accept their definitions of blacks as inferior. At times the church was seen as the handmaiden of the more privileged classes – not necessarily to manipulate blacks but to exploit the working class generally, for example, through the practice of confession which provided the upper classes with revealing insights into working-class life and so afforded them a means of control.

Consider the following statement of a Rastafarian sister who contended that to belong to established religions was 'to submit oneself to exploitation and control': 'This is what the Church of England and so forth used to do because it was also common history with the peasants of England that confessions within churches was only in practice a way of finding out what the villagers in certain communities were doing – their social lives in the community. When they used to confess to the priest and so forth this would give the priest and the ministry a certain understanding into the village and peasant life or to really manipulate it. And this is the kind of thing that Ras Tafari pursue and so you can understand why they are so resentful towards certain established religions today.'

Coming from Christian families and therefore being encouraged in church-going during their childhood conveniently prepared the ground for critical interpretation of the Bible, discussions of which characterised a great deal of reasoning procedures. All Rastas were to some degree conversant with the Scriptures and quoted liberally and accurately from the Bible, particularly the Book of Revelation which was thought to hold a special significance for Rastas: 'Revelations is the most important book in the Bible for Ras Tafari . . . this is the last days', predicted a Rastaman.

Rastas accepted the Bible as their central text with the proviso that much of its original material had been deliberately distorted during its translation into English, as a way of defusing some of its potential as a sanction for rebellion or even revolution (this was cited as evidence of the Babylonian conspiracy theory). It was necessary, therefore, to interpret the Bible as critically as possible and recognise the aspects of it which might have been flashed out, included or altered in meaning. The first generation had unwittingly accepted the document at face value without pausing for exegesis, but through involvement in the movement the Rasta was able to realise that he should view the Bible as more cryptographic, searching the text for hidden meanings and directives. Accompanying this was a process of 'mental erasure' in which the Rasta systematically wiped out the interpretations of the Bible learned in childhood and developed a more analytic approach. A Rasta expanded: 'The teaching of the Bible given to us by our parents was to be subjected to our master. These concepts we had really to erase from our mentality . . . we had to erase all these concepts and find something that was a gift to I and I; and His Imperial Majesty came and set that alight.'

This mental erasure meant that, although Rastas and their Christian parents both regarded the Bible as their central text, their interpretations were so different that they found little ground for an affinity, still less for discourse. This was seen by some as an extension of the Garveyite imperative: 'He [Garvey] told us that we must ask for deliverance through the rise of Ethiopia and worship God through our own spectacles. So now we know that it is written in Revelation.'

For a variety of reasons the Rastas lost their attachments to the religions of their parents, yet did not replace the former centrality of Christianity in their outlooks with a radical alternative. What they did was to approach Christianity differently, applying an interpretation based on Garvey's contention that

> Our God has no colour, yet it is human to see everything through one's own spectacles, and since the white people have seen their God through white spectacles, we have only now started out (late though it be) to see our God through our own spectacles . . . We negroes believe in the God of Ethiopia, the everlasting God – God the Father, God the Son and God the Holy Ghost, the one God of all ages. That is the God in whom we believe, but we shall worship him through the spectacles of Ethiopia. (M. Garvey, 1967, Vol. 1, p. 34)

The loss of faith with their parents' religions was part of the more total dislocation from parental culture and increased identification with the peer group. As well as the more general criticisms of the first generation, Rastas complained that the traditional churches contained no element of African identity and showed resentment against the reluctance of church leaders to glorify their blackness; comments such as 'white man's puppets' and 'sell-outs' abounded.

Accusations from older church-going blacks of the Rastas' 'godlessness' or 'heresy' were totally unjustified. What happened was that the plausibility structure of formal Christian beliefs became less firm for Rastas after they reached the awareness that their parents' position of disprivilege was in some way connected to their religious propensities. As the structure crumbled there was an acute need for a new 'world-maintaining legitimation' (to borrow Berger's 1969 term) and the drift towards Ras Tafari was in satisfaction of this need. Once released from parental ties and in the limbo-like state of drift, the young West Indians became more suggestible to the messages filtering across from Jamaica which were beginning to be reasoned through with more and more frequency.

The Rastas' detachment from the wider society was seen by them to be a quite total and irrevocable break. Centrally, the disjuncture with the parental culture was a precipitating condition for the drifting process which I characterise as a gentle dynamic interplay between the proclivities of young blacks and the magnetism of Rasta. Such a process was stimulated and encouraged by their loss of commitment in the English educational system. Blacks found their parents' religions losing credibility prior to the drift into Ras Tafari and more and more incredible as they moved towards complete acceptance of Haile Selassie. The vast majority felt no compulsion to affiliate with an institution and saw the acceptance of the faith of Ras Tafari as sufficient (some justified this by saying 'My church is my home; Ras Tafari travels with I everywhere I go'); others turned to the more institutionalised forms of worship, the Ethiopian Orthodox Church and the Twelve Tribes of Israel.

The educational system was the subject of bitter abuse from Rastas but it was never made quite clear whether this could be used as evidence of dispositions before the drift or a reflective critique using the analytic knives of the Rastafarian cutlery. Perhaps a breakdown of educational background would be revealing. Most Rastas (about 80 per cent) had some level of schooling in England: those that were born in England had their entire schooling in the English system and those that travelled over from the West Indies before the age of 11 went through primary and secondary school stages (about 40 per cent). Those that had migrated with their parents after they were 11 (about 40 per cent) went through secondary school stages and a tiny minority had no schooling at all in England (about 5 per cent). The majority of those schooled in England went to comprehensive and secondary modern schools with a few others going to grammar schools; some went on to institutions of further education on part-time or full-time courses usually for purposes of vocational training. They left school at 16, though some, though technically still at school, disaffiliated themselves as early as 14 and practised truancy as a full-time operation. For the most part their educational qualifications were negligible: more than two General Certificates of Education were uncommon and Certificates of Secondary Education were only slightly more prevalent. Those that had continued into further education were obviously the best qualified, an Ordinary National Certificate being the highest achievement.

Whether the sense of alienation at school was the cause of the general pattern of under-achievement or a rationalised *post factum* in the light of their failures is a matter of some doubt. Since no Rastas were still at school (though there were schoolboy sympathisers) it was impossible to draw anything like a conclusive statement. I would suggest that the failure to reach any significant level of educational attainment was a result of loss of interest and meaning in school work and, in a self-fulfilling way, the eventual failure provided validation that the educational system was structured in such a way as to disadvantage the black youth. During the process of becoming a Rastaman the youth came to acquire the theoretical equipment enabling more comprehensive analyses of the system in a way compatible with the general conspiracy theory. Rastas would constantly invoke what I call the 'all that glitters' theme because it was introduced to me by a Rasta quoting Bob Marley and Peter Tosh thus:

> It's not all that glitters is gold,
> Half the story has never been told.
> So now you see the light
> Stand up for your rights.
> ('Get Up, Stand Up')

The other half of the story was the history and culture of Africa, its achievements, heroes, the atrocities its people had to withstand and the reasons why they should ultimately find release from their Diaspora and reunite in the black man's Zion. It was called by some the 'missing dimension': 'I and I didn't really find ourself could fit in within the schooling because there are certain numbers, dimensions missing. Now, we were always confronted by wonders, you know, and curiosities about this missing dimension and it wasn't until I realised the true self in the concept of Ras Tafari, by looking within and seeing our potentials, right? And you could say that our scope opened towards the value of education; and then to venture in and pursue the certain missed dimensions about the facts that we have been denied by the western hemisphere.' In this sense, the whole

Rastafarian enterprise was a learning process ('a learning which never stops for I and I') of erasing some concepts and acquiring others. The Rastas saw themselves as enlightened; quite literally they had 'seen the light' and were able to articulate a vehement critique of the educational system which they saw as inhibiting black potential.

Almost without exception, Rastas found the education they received in England totally unsatisfactory; even those engaged in further education at the time of my research tended to devalue the benefits of conventional education. Involvement with Ras Tafari was regarded as a much more meaningful way of learning about the world. As well as the basic involvement and the sharpening of analytic knives through reasoning, a great many took to reading about African history and culture and Ethiopia, in particular, was a topic for study; the appearance of Edward Ullendorff's book, *The Ethiopians* (1973) on many Rastas' bookshelves was illustrative of this.

Being a Rasta *was* learning: the very state of consciousness informing the drift to Ras Tafari was an 'insight'; a new way of looking at and comprehending the world, or as I have expressed it before, a new way of mapping the world conceptually. To repeat Marley and Tosh, Rastas had 'seen the light' and were aspiring to new levels of knowledge denied them by conventional education. Their under-achievement was attributed to lack of interest compounded by 'racist biases' in school curricula (meaning that black history was virtually ignored).

Perhaps my involvement detracts from 'objectivity', but I find the cycle of lack of interest → under-achievement → acquisition of theory to explain the under-achievement a credible one and see no reason to be sceptical in intuiting the property of rationalisation. I do not believe the Rastas' criticisms were simple justifications for their failure but articulate and persuasive comments on a system utilising curricula ill-designed to accommodate the interests of black youth. But here is no place for policy issues; what is needed is some specification of at what point the disinterest translated into a conscious rejection of the educational system using Rastafarian concepts.

No Rastas affiliated when at school, though it is very difficult to pinpoint when they accepted Ras Tafari due to the hesitancy in revealing such information; instead remarks such as 'Jah was always in I' and 'passed over I' were more common. I stress that there is no legitimate concept of conversion in Ras Tafari but an unsteady process of becoming aware of the divinity of Haile Selassie and the eventual acceptance of this. To specify the precise moment of acceptance would be a rather arbitrary exercise, imposing a static notion on a process. With caution, however, I can estimate that most Rastas reached acceptance about two years ater leaving school with many others accepting over the following two years. The general pattern suggests that after doing rather badly at school the West

Indian youths spent between, say, one and four years in states of drift during which time they became aware (through music and peers) of Rastafarian concepts and categories and later accepted the central tenet that Haile Selassie was their redeemer. Once familiar with the critical Rastafarian theory of a Babylonian conspiracy, the reasons for their failure at school were more apparent; they 'saw the light' and were, therefore, able to formulate their critique of the educational system.

Before moving on to an examination of the cognitive changes involved in the drift to Ras Tafari, I should make some mention of the role of women in the movement. Just over one-quarter of the membership was comprised of women and their role in Ras Tafari was very much a subordinate one. It was a role graciously accepted by the sisters themselves; new feminism, or women's liberation was regarded as 'foolishness, because a woman should do what a man tells her to do'. The movement was seen as men's property: 'The Bible shows us that man was created in His image, the likeness of God and the woman was created for the company of man. God gave the man the movement.'

The general subject of sexual relations for Rastas stems from the lack of family structure in the days of slavery. The matrifocal emphasis led to children never having fathers on a permanent basis and they came to be reliant on females, a reliance which continued after slavery (see E. Clarke, 1974). For the Rastas in both Jamaica and England the reliance on women was seen as a vestige of colonial domination and its ramifications, including the emasculation of blacks. Part of the Rastafarian imperative was to restore manhood and a sense of dignity, to upgrade morally black men; sexual attitudes have to be set against this background. This observation helps link the modern Rastas with their Jamaican predecessors.

Kitzinger, writing of the Jamaican movement, noted that: 'Incorporated in Rasta faith is a model of a social universe in which the accepted norms of social relations current in Jamaican society are negated, in which the mother is usurped, and in which a new male identity is established and finds expression' (1969, pp. 260–1). The stability and strength of the black man was regarded as threatened by a continuance of the age-old reliance on females which led to 'man's loss of initiative and manhood'. Rastas created for themselves a father-image and God in Haile Selassie and his presence in all men gave them virtual omnipotence; women had no such recourse: 'Jah is I's father and the earth I's mother.'

In contrast to conventional Jamaican forms, Rastafarian sex ethics had a pronounced paternalistic orientation which accorded the dominant position to men generally and heads of families in particular. Concubinage was seen as a viable type of union (though many Rastas were married legally) and sexual activity within such arrangements was agreeable. Homosexuality, on the other hand, was stringently decried as 'unnatural' and 'ungodly' as was birth control, a clever device of the Babylonian conspiracy to prevent the multiplication of black men and therefore check their numerical strength.

The antipathy towards feminism, homosexuality and birth control were to be seen as vilifications of the 'moral decline of the West', a slide into decadence which heralded the imminent collapse of Babylon in much the same way as it did the Roman Empire: 'A moral decline in the West has caused women to embark on a road of women's lib.' mused a Rastaman. The Rastaman's preservation of his male superiority was a way of insulating himself against the infectious forces of Babylon; he remained untouched by the decadence as the *fin de siècle* approached. Women, though in a numerical minority and lacking the status of the male, saw themselves as fulfilling an important role in the insulation by supporting their men: 'The women should be subjected to the man because the man should be king in his own house.' Though most sisters approved of their men regarding them as 'Queens.'

My purpose in this section has been to answer the basic question: who were the Rastas? I have looked at the composition, constituency and the members' social origins in an unsatisfactory but necessary manner. But, having established who they were, it is now important to look at the ways in which they came to affiliate to the movement and accept the divinity of Haile Selassie. This process involved a number of sometimes complex cognitive changes along a route which I characterise as the 'journey to Jah'.

Chapter 5

The Journey to Jah

In Jamaica children are taught all about Britain, its
history, its heroes etc. So coming over here we knew what
to expect, or at least thought we did.

Tony E., 1977

THE THREE RS:
RESTORATION, RETROCESSION AND RETALIATION

The process of immersion into the Rastafarian movement can be
analytically divided into two segments: first, the existence of states of
suggestibility and predispositions to become involved in the movement; and, secondly, the availability of Rastafarian concepts and
categories and the social mechanisms for their transmission. In
Chapter 6 I will describe and analyse the vehicles of transmission and
their impact on black youth, but for the moment wish to concentrate
on the facilitating cognitive conditions for affiliating with the movement. In short, the changes underlying the process of becoming a
Rastaman.

Affiliation should be considered as a complex and not always
unhindered transference of allegiance. It involved the transgression of
certain rules and principles peculiar to West Indian life in England
and the crossing of new psychological bridges leading to the new faith.
As such, the passage encountered resistance in the form of familial
pressures, obstacles in the form of public stigmatisation and restrictions
in the form of denials of validity and legitimacy to the religion. Yet,
despite these roadblocks, the Rastaman possessed the equipment to
overcome deflecting influences and carry through his journey to Jah.
In general terms, the Rastas sufficiently adjusted conceptual maps
to be able to confront such forces, recognise them and transcend them.
In order to be able to do this, the potential adherent had to undergo
a series of cognitive rearrangements which were triggered off by
experiences and apprehensions of what I consider to be a specific
nature.

The Rastafarian response of the 1970s was preceded and stimulated
by a pattern of critical events, the experience and apprehension of

which predisposed West Indian youths to states of suggestibility. Throughout the 1960s and early 1970s black children had stored up sets of expectations of what they were likely to contribute to and receive from British society. Coming from a conventionally Christian background they entertained a basic set of religious and, indeed, moral assumptions transmitted by their parents whose socialising influences defined a basic series of views about the world. Most Rastas had migrated to England with their parents between the ages of 6 and 13 (though some were born in England). They carried with them clusters of partially formed expectations of the new life ahead of them. Such expectations were the result not only of the contagious optimism of their parents but also of their schooling in Jamaica where curricula had for long been closely geared to English models. England was seen by migrating blacks as the starting point for a new life and such conceptions filtered down through the family. As a Twelve Tribes member told me: 'In Jamaica children are taught all about Britain, its history, its heroes, etc. So coming over here we knew what to expect, or least thought we did.'

Additional information derived from formal education about England, its history, achievements, and so on provided a solid basis for something like the following expectations: the English are typically characterised by moral rectitude; they are honest and fair; scrupulously impartial in their distribution of opportunity; though giving the appearance of being reticent and unobtrusive they are hospitable and accommodating; as a consequence they would welcome the arrival of their fellow commonwealth member and offer no resistance to full integration into British society. A Rastaman reflected: 'I remember how my mother was always telling me about how good and nice English would be once we arrived. I was 10 years old then and foolish enough to believe her.'

Such was the 'typical Englishman' and attitudes towards him understandably ranged from positive to (at the worst) neutral. It was reinforced by the migrants' contacts with whites in Jamaica who, though in a numerical minority, were nearly all in positions of prestige and authority; the association between wealth, education and power with whiteness was carried over into the new situation. The possibility of being accepted by and integrated into an order of such eminent individuals (if only for a period) no doubt spurred the migrants' ambitions and positive identification with 'the British way of life' (S. Patterson, 1963, pp. 224–5; Lawrence, 1974, pp. 39–45). Children's attitudes were correspondingly positive and, because of their insulation in family units, less susceptible to alteration than their parents.

Two patterns of events in England shattered, for many, what Nancy Foner calls 'the mystique of whiteness' (1977, p. 134). First, the subjection to rejection in various spheres such as housing, employment

and general social activities on the grounds of being black gave rise
to the dual awareness that they were not only inescapably black, but
also regarded negatively by the typical Englishman because of that
fact.

Secondly, the whites encountered in England were not typically
holders of prestigious offices, or wielders of power, but nearly all
members of the working class and, in material terms, only marginally
better off than themselves. The interaction with whites had the effect
of stripping away the salient features typically associated with whites.

> Indeed, judging by the migrant's former criteria English working-
> class whites do not merit deference: like poor light-skinned
> Jamaican villagers, they have, besides their skin colour none of the
> characteristics (wealth, good jobs, education, or cultural traits) which
> deserve respect. (Foner, 1977, p. 134)

Comparisons with conditions in Jamaica gave support to the belief
that present circumstances, though not as desirable as expected, were
nevertheless preferable to those left behind. Unequal treatment on the
basis of skin colour and the image-breaking encounter with whites
forced a modification of attitudes, but not of a radical variety; conditions
mitigating against this included the necessity of accepting prevalent
self-definitions of inferiority which received validation in everyday
life: the effect that 'we are in this materially and socially inferior
position because there is something inferior about us'. A Rasta later
described the legacy of this: 'The majority of blacks in this country
are still in a state of mind that can be described as not a conscious
state of mind; they still believe that they are perhaps inferior.' And
another: '. . . some West Indians are so trapped in society.'

Though parents would have been prone to feelings of despair, even
bitterness, after the failure of experience to live up to the high expectations, their children would not have been so exposed to the iconoclastic forces. The protective shield denying them the experience of
racialism in occupation-seeking, house-hunting, service-searching and
so on would be subject to removal only at later stages. In the sphere
of education, the destructive effects of discrimination stemming from
language would have provided a blockage along avenues of educational
advancement, and curricula changes after the move would have posed
problems of adjustment. But when the youth could take cognisance of
his parents' conditions relative to whites and the lack of privileges
resulting from the state of being black in a predominantly white
society he would be able to conceive of his own position as closely
linked to that of his parents by virtue of the common characteristic
of blackness. Such an awareness dawned at the later stages of formal
education and it was here that he was able to transcend the 'here and

now' of everyday occurrences and relate current situations with general conditions. As a most perspicacious Rasta observed: 'It is inevitable that we, as black people, were never and can never be part of this country where we do not belong; like a heart transplant, it rejects us.'

After the Education Act of 1944 which brought equal opportunities in schooling for the island's population, education in Jamaica had been conceived of as the major route to occupational advancement. Secondary schools, in particular, had been seen as important vehicles for the acquisition of qualifications and skills necessary for prestigious and remunerative jobs. After the 1950s, increasing numbers of Jamaican working-class children entered the secondary education from which they had been previously excluded. It seems reasonable to assume, then, that parents, knowledgeable of the even greater educational opportunities available in England, would project high aspirations on to their children and be reasonably enthusiastic about their chances in the new environment. This emphasis on the value of education would probably have gradually disintegrated as the migrants learnt that material improvements in England could be attained through channels other than education. Long hours on awkward shifts in manual jobs was one such channel and incomes afforded them items of 'luxury' and standards of living barely dreamt about in the West Indies.

Coupled with the overwhelming presence of racialism and the awareness that blackness in many respects presented an obstacle to advancement regardless of educational qualification, the decreasing importance attached to education by parents would have been transmitted to the children whose chances of educational improvement were impaired anyway. A Rasta explained: 'Education? What good is this to a black man? Qualifications; them mean nothing so long as you're black.' The retrenched emphasis on education in parents and children would not, however, have necessarily translated into a reduction in optimism about life chances. Whereas first-generation West Indians to a large extent straddled two worlds and were able to harken back to their old life as a comparative baseline for current experiences, their children would have only dim recollections and hazy memories of life as it was before the migration. Consequently, they cognised the new situation in absolute terms rather than relative to past circumstances: this was *the* world not an alternative to a past one. Thoughts of the future turned about raising aspirations and the probability of enjoying the full range of benefits available in the new society. Unlike their parents, they possessed no dreams of a return home – for this was their home. Asked if he could compare his present conditions with those in Jamaica, a Rasta answered: 'I couldn't rightly tell you anything at all about Jamaica; only the stories my mother used to tell me.' In effect, the two buffering factors of comparison with previous circumstances and the possibility of only a temporary stay were not available to second-generation West Indians and as a consequence ambitions floated upwards with each successive experience at school and at home.

When the awareness that their parents had been systematically excluded from positions of authority and prestige, choice accommodation and certain services and activities on what were considered to be racial criteria, that their inferiority was popularly regarded as rooted in their racial origin and that the opportunities open to them would be subject to limitations because of their colour, they had few resources to minimise the disappointment, and anxieties ensued. The awareness that their progress would be retarded by their blackness gave that blackness a fresh symbolic meaning and social arrangements came to be organised around those new meanings: 'When did I realise racialism existed? Just before I left school I guess, when it seemed people treated me different because I was black and for no other reason. Before that I didn't give the matter too much thought,' a Rasta recollected. Blackness became the basis for the orientation of activities in later school years: the crystallisation of early teenage blacks into distinct groups resembling the Jamaican rude boys. Less stylised variations on the black gang theme followed. A case study into this very phenomenon found 'that this withdrawal into racially exclusive peer groups results from the pupils' realisation of a common identity and shared destiny' (Troyna, 1978, p. 64).

But, whereas first-generation West Indians' social arrangements contained not even an implicit challenge to their inferior status, the younger members' organisational patterns revealed at least a muffled questioning of such definitions.

There were, of course, alternatives available: they could restore expectations and ambitions by trying harder academically and culturally, preparing to compromise and assimilate strenuously; they could retract their expectations and resign themselves to a limited and restricted participation in society, a retrocession; or they could retaliate by vigorously ·replying to their experience, seeking to make their presence felt urgently and consequentially. Of the three avenues, *restoration* was the hardest and possibly the most daunting, *retrocession* was defeatist and damaging to self-esteem and *retaliation* the most accessible and attractive – and overwhelmingly the most popular. It also had a resuscitation effect on the depressed morale of West Indian youth.

The formation of gangs was further facilitated by the exacerbating impact of familial fragmentation after migration to England. With one and sometimes both parents having to work long shifts and inconvenient hours the influence of the family unit on the young West

Indian became depressed. Less parent–child contact released the child from the socialising grasp and left him freer to find other agencies. Following this, the peer group assumed principal importance as the main secondary socialising force in generating and transmitting norms, values and expectations. Conventionally, it is thought that children derive their status and sense of social importance from the parents' location and achievements in society. But, for young blacks in England, their parents provided only models of degradation and deprivation which were hardly likely to engender any sense of value or selfhood. As one Rasta sister reflected: 'Our parents, you know, they have all been so brainwashed – well some of them anyway. They're shocked to see how we are going about as Rastafarian. You know, to see how we free ourself. They would not treat themself like we treat ourself in Ras Tafari, because we just natural.' And a Rastaman: 'How could our parents give I and I anything to live up to? They've been misguided by European Christianity, which is not acceptable to Rasta, and so are still suffering the consequences in their bodies and their minds.' The role of the family, then, was permissive of the shift in focus to the gang as the source of views about the world.

These changes in orientation and social arrangement were facilitated by a number of corresponding cognitive changes in so far as expectations on the basis of held typifications of whites were not met and the apprehension that they were not going to be met opened up a discrepancy which needed to be reduced by whatever measures necessary. Reformulation of the original conceptions of whites had no doubt been at work throughout the whole interactive period after migration, but the need to reformulate dramatically and abstractly arose when it was realised that the quality of blackness was the single most important factor militating against the parents and, therefore, the second generation's progress in the new environment: 'Fooling themselves; they're never going to be treated as equals in this society'; 'Racialism is too deep. I see this in my work, in each day I face racialism; too much to wipe away,' were illustrative Rasta remarks.

The possibilities for discrepancy reduction were three and all entailed attitudinal adjustment on the changed typification. Restoration necessitated an attitude of ambivalence towards white society, on the one hand accepting the legitimacy of its routes to success while on the other recognising the obstacles to blacks strewn along these routes. Retrocession needed little modification of a neutral stance to whites and acceptance of their definitions and their legitimate right to define. Retaliation implied a more radical stance, throwing back at whites the abuse they had meted out to their parents; but still a posture of assertion rather than hostility.

The conditions under which second-generation West Indians' attitudes were rendered fluid and amenable to change in respect to whites and, therefore, permissive of new social activities and arrangements were where the expectation to achieve a full and rewarding participation in the community and be accepted as an integrated member by white society was shattered by the realisation that blackness constituted an irremovable obstacle to progress. The imperative to reduce the discrepancy fed a number of alternatives, one of which was the reformulation of conceptions of whites, adjustment of attitudes towards them and the adoption of new stances or postures of assertion. Relaxed parent–child contact due to familial fragmentation after migration had led to the possibility of attitudes being reshaped by other agencies; in a great many instances the peer group took on a significant role in this process. And it was out of this nucleus of a secondary socialisation agency that the energies of the Rastafarian response evolved. Overwhelmingly, Rastas emerged from the involuted West Indian groups, the basic prototype of which had been established during the rude boy era : the black gang. The formation of a rudimentary social structure among young blacks was essential to the later generation and dissemination of Rastafarian concepts and messages.

DRIFTING TO THE CORE

The impact of acute rejection and, sometimes, hostility had lowered the morale of first-generation West Indians (cf. C. Hill, 1971); nevertheless, many of their children were to accept the challenge offered by the discrepancy between expectations and experience and strike up new attitudes and postures. Movements into nuclear gangs had the initial impact of closing the discrepancy partially and imbuing members with a greater sense of success and acceptance by peers; they belonged to groups where they felt needed and where their needs were also fed back to them from the group. The sense of belongingness which was so integral to the black gang phenomenon depended on the feeling of the individual that the group both needed him and sustained him; that the group was important to him and he to the group. As a Rasta said of his fellow group members: 'These are my brethren; I am to them as they are to I.' Morale, which I consider to be an ability to retain a high degree of expectation and purposeful activity in the face of adverse conditions, was extremely important to the cohesion of the gangs. It provoked feelings of affirmation as being a member of a group which was (to some extent) exclusive and improved the potential for collective action (one early manifestation of which was Paki-bashing).

Through membership in the gangs, a secondary socialisation process took place in which it was learnt that effective organisation and action could be best achieved through the group itself rather than the action of individuals. But, though in structure the Rastafarian movement built on the platform of such relationships established in earlier phases, it used them to communicate and convey goals; messages of a prescriptive and evaluative kind. By influencing the group to pull together and further the common purpose, Ras Tafari was able to subordinate individual interests to the interests of the group. The formation of gangs was, amongst other things, a morale-creating endeavour; yet its membership permitted the gratification of existing individual needs. Membership in Ras Tafari, as well as satisfying individual needs, introduced new individual needs on a higher level; new higher objectives. The gang was a culture for the breeding of more mature and ambitious goals, the achievement of which would entail some ethical imperative and promote feelings of prejudice to extant moral standards: 'Society and all that reject Rasta; so him come about and reject it,' asserted a Rastaman.

The development of the rude boy complex was a somewhat spontaneous reaction to a contradictory situation in which expectations were not met, thereby causing a discrepancy. The drift into Ras Tafari (as I have characterised the process) involved more of the element of conscious endeavour. Expressed differently:

> When you arouse anxiety, a very normal and very necessary process is first to scan the periphery and approximate the center rather slowly, for after all, when you have gained the security in relation to the periphery you may be courageous enough to strike out for the center. (Galdstone and Zetterberg, 1958, p. 104)

I see the retaliation route as involving a sort of cognitive scanning, moving aimlessly without clear sight of the source of discontent but reaching violently to phenomena which seemed to obscure clear vision. Rudie was more a visceral phenomenon, less an intellectual one. Once the stability of group structure had been established, however, and the mists began to clear, thanks in part to the stimulating influence of black power, the core of the problem could be approached. It became apparent that some social analysis would reveal the causes of current discontent as rooted in structure rather than individuals. And this awareness produced more conscious scanning for fresh ways to approach and tackle the problems. Ras Tafari was perfect: it gave new foci for shared interest and created issues on which to project concerns and pose fresh solutions for the resolutions of problems peculiar to the black man. As such it became a source of axis in morale-building among the young West Indian community by uniting them in a common struggle and providing a charter which, however ambiguous, exerted integrative forces on the members: 'It came to I that my brethren's struggle was also mine.'

Gang members of the earlier phases were neither imbued with

driving ambition nor a sense of ultimate objective. Their response lacked the benefit of an informing philosophy; it was a 'gut reaction'. Their behaviour violated certain norms about showing respect for authority, especially in the school, not threatening or aggressively interfering with other groups, not damaging property and generally being orderly and disciplined, but they were for the most part disobedient and rebellious young 'rascals' characterised by nuisance value rather than informed criticism; a Rasta made the contrast by using his personal experience: 'Since accepting Ras Tafari I am a "reformed man". I used to be in trouble with the police and all that rascally foolishness; but now I have insight enough to know I was foolish.' (Another admitted to having Jah pass over him shortly after his release from prison – where he had been detained on a burglary offence. There are many similar instances.) The course travelled from the former to the latter must, therefore, have entailed accompanying cognitive shifts: changing conceptions, perspectives, assumptions, beliefs and attitudes which predisposed them favourably to drift to Ras Tafari.

I suggest that the movement to Ras Tafari is best described as a process of drift in which the youth transiently existed in limbo, responding to different demands made upon him from different sectors of society without committing himself to any definitive posture of antagonism, positive identification, or anything in between. His ties with the 'conventional' values of his parents were loosened during later school years and his attempts to form an autonomous youth subculture were reactions to such relaxations. The rude boy venture was, to a great extent, self-defeating because of its members' impossibility of total escape from adult and authority surveillance; adolescent dependence militated against an enduring movement of unharnessed rebellion. However, once the links with the parent culture had been weakened sufficiently without any concrete alternative allegiances to turn to, the youth drifted into a chequered existence, flitting between the white squares of his parental background and the black of his gang enterprise.

According to my account, therefore, the process of becoming a Rastaman can be divided into four broad phases: first, the apprehension of racial disadvantage and the fresh symbolic meaning this brought to blackness; next, the loss of plausibility of the parents' beliefs and the structure they seemed to support; thirdly, the drift to Ras Tafari; and lastly, the acceptance of Haile Selassie as the divine redeemer of black peoples. (See Figure 3 for a representation of the way in which these phases link up.) The acceptance phase entailed all manner of new awarenesses and ways of making sense of the world and these will be considered in more detail in the chapters to follow. What is required now, however, is a more careful delineation of the routes followed during the important state of drift. For purposes of analysis I have sliced these into three channels of motivation: the need for identity; the need for explanation; and the need for mobilisation. Now, to examine these individually.

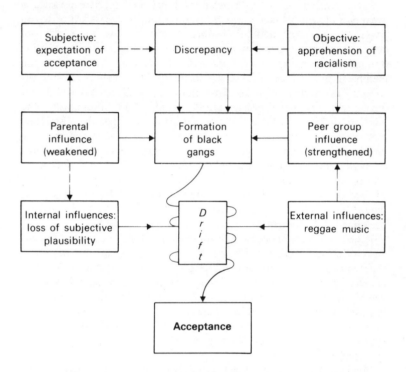

Figure 3 *The Process of Becoming a Rasta*

(1) *The need for identity*
The inescapable reality of blackness shaded and shadowed the West Indian child's emerging sense of self as he progressed through the later years of school into his early teens, making the development of racial identification an integral part of maturation. Blackness became inherent in his concept of self. This concept arose within a social context which assigned values to the perception of colour: positive and superior to white; negative and inferior to black. These two observations constituted a dualistic process in the cognitive movement to Ras Tafari: first, the growing realisation of the self as black and, secondly, the steadily accumulating awareness of the social evaluation placed upon that quality: '. . . certain pressures began to bear

on a man; especially in this society. You go for a job; you can't get a job. Why? Because you are black'; 'Each and every day pressure bears down on the black man; racism, unemployment and I would say injustice in the courts,' were two representative Rasta views.

In the earlier phase, a knowledge of his own blackness issued a definition of who the actor was by relating him to others, all of whom possessed the same defining features. Such an awareness was not achieved merely by self-examination, but through others' labelling him and identifying him in those terms, making his racial group membership the locus of his self-identity. This realisation and the concomitant ability to make distinctions on racial criteria was learnt during primary socialisation (see Morland, 1958; Proshansky and Newton, 1973, p. 181); but it was not until later that the distinction took on social importance; when it became an urgent and pressing social reality impinging on his subjective experience and informing his behaviour: 'As His Imperial Majesty says, the colour of a man's skin is no more important than the colour of his eyes; but ras, everyday we confront those with white skins oppressing I and making the black man suffer, like they have for 400 years; this is reality,' declaimed a Rastaman.

It was when typified characterisations of whites and blacks became etched in more detail with relevant evaluations, when they were charged with emotionally stocked judgements, that a clearer conception of what it meant to be black clicked into operation. And it was the seeping through into consciousness of this evaluative dimension which impelled West Indian children between the ages of, say, 11 to 15 to forge social relationships along racial group lines (see Troyna, 1978). Hence, the formation of black gangs solidified the existence of an exclusive racial group.

But it did not rid the black typification of the evaluative criteria attached to it; nor did the effects of under-achievement at school, low-quality accommodation, limited opportunities for advancement and the general treatment from the wider society. Clues about these were picked up from school and from the family and they confirmed the characteristic inferiority of the black man. This combined with the ambivalence of being black, but not being truly British nor truly West Indian and served to depress the self-esteem of many black adolescents and raise doubts about their own ability to compete in white society – within conventional frameworks at least: 'It became obvious to me that there was no place for the black man in white society; we so oppressed by the way we look.'

The formation of an English version of the Jamaican rude boy phenomenon was an acknowledgement of and resignation to the fact that West Indians were black and would be treated as black by other West Indians and, more significantly, by members of white society.

But it was also an acceptance that the nature of such treatment would inevitably lead to inferior status being conferred on all blacks. It was not in any way an enterprise designed to eliminate the negative connotations associated with blackness, nor even to reverse the tide. This is why Rasta was so appealing: it offered a very relevant alternative, which had been employed before, and eradicated any remaining self-doubts connected with black identity. Here was a comprehensive and exhaustive definition of who the black man really was ('the true self', not who the whites thought him to be), his history and, most pertinently, his future. It had consequences psychologically and behaviourally in terms of beliefs and dispositions and their effect on propensities to act in certain ways.

The conception of the white man implicit in Rastafarian beliefs was that of a treacherous and scheming agent of Babylon conspiring to repress the black man's potentialities as he had done for 400 years: 'One of the systems of breaking a slave was to strip him completely of his African culture'; 'Every day the white man denies the black his true culture.' Alternatively, the black man was reconceived as an intellectually and physically creative being who had not yet shrugged off the after-effects of his bondage. A Rasta speculated that: 'In many ways the majority of black peoples have not yet realised their true worth – their real potential – in arts, culture and such like.' Accordingly, attitudes towards whites were adjusted in consistency with the different conceptions; doubts and ambivalence about the black man's place in the world were removed.

Implications for self-identity were manifold: the underlying sense of inferiority was devastated; a sense of pride and dignity was created; conflicts concerning identity were wiped out; and a fresh nexus of identity was established: 'It's for I and I to revive our true self and really know our ability by discovering our history and by discovering our history we know what we were capable of in the past,' reasoned an EOC member. Ras Tafari disclosed to the black man a conception of his true self. Not the artificial convenience behind which he had masqueraded in his service existence, but an undistorted image of a creative being poised to revive his former culture, known to some as 'the way of the ancients'.

But this is not to suggest that the drift to Ras Tafari was an inexorable movement as, say, ballbearings to a magnet. Of course, the philosophy presented a set of packaged prescriptions and implications for the individual identity, but one should not lose sight of the motivations of young West Indians to shape for themselves the nucleus of a new understanding of the world and their place in that world.

In providing a kernel of new identity, Rasta brought with it a whole new array of expectations which owed little to white society and, indeed, tended in a direction contrary to conventional ones. The drift to Ras Tafari, then, was an expression of a quest for new landmarks for conceptual maps; old maps were simply not working. 'There were certain missing dimensions,' as one Rasta told me. In particular, the identity of the black actor was ambiguous, subject to internal contradictions and affected by the mutations inherent in a white racist society: 'This society still isn't sure what it wants the black man to be: some say equal and others say he is inferior.' The drift into the movement was activated by the effort to create a new and original identity, admittedly based on existing definitions (in Jamaica) but totally innovative in the English environment.

The route propelling the drift was characterised by the need to restore an identity, one which eventually linked the Rastaman to a version of the past and a vision of the future as well as to the rest of the world's black population; one which brought with it new expectations and aspirations – the return to Africa.

The critically important variable in the process was the cognitive need for a coherent and persuasive account of the self to solve the range of problems of identity and purpose in life (Argyle and Beit-Hallahmi, 1975, pp. 180–9). Such a need was incompletely fulfilled due to the social conditions outlined earlier and the influence they had on the cognitive development of West Indian youth. The availability of an image or model for shaping his own identity was a seductively appealing one and had the added advantage of providing positive evaluations to the quality of blackness. Drift towards the new identity was sustained by the gentle dynamic of ability and availability: the ability of young blacks to find and construct new conceptions of themselves and the availability of models for this construction.

(2) *The need for explanation*

The second route from the 'periphery' to the 'core' was characterised by the search for an answer to intellectual problems. There was an absence of satisfactory explanations to puzzling situations such as: 'Why were blacks systematically discriminated against?'. 'Why did they overwhelmingly occupy statuses and occupations of a lower order than whites?', 'Why were obstacles strewn in their way of progress?' and 'Why were young West Indians, schooled or even born in Britain, not accepted as British?' (Questions thematised from conversations with Rastas.) Solutions were sought and found in the Rastafarian belief system. Hence, the conception of Rasta as a problem-solving complex.

Different beliefs purport to explain ranges of phenomena. Those adopted by primitive actors might explain storms or earthquakes in terms of the will of the gods; those adopted by modern actors, armed with science and technology, might give insights into problems of morality and conscience. Acceptance of beliefs is a resolution of certain orders of problems, for the act of believing simultaneously cuts off ranges of alternative explanation which might otherwise be entertained and thus introduced problematics. Committed belief precludes the possibility of alternatives.

The spread of answers available to young West Indians came principally from parents' world views. I have noted how the Pentecostal-type churches offered explanations of present evils with reference to other-worldly states and the method they offered for alleviating them was through supernatural means. More conventional Christian churches offered gratification of a similar kind. Beliefs arising out of these traditions were accommodating and conservative in nature, issuing no challenge to existing states of disprivilege, impoverishment and inferiority. As such, they contained no imperative to make constructive efforts to resolve social and economic difficulties. In effect, existing belief systems, by offering explanations to current problems, acted as legitimations for their continued existence.

First-generation migrants, ever mindful of their conditions in Jamaica and other islands, found such beliefs compatible with their dispositions and outlooks. Second-generation blacks saw things differently and considered the solutions offered by their parents' beliefs less convincing; 'Just fooling themselves,' commented a Rasta sister.

Once the ties to parents' religions had been relaxed and thus an important source of social control weakened, the drifting black youth transiently responded to the demands of the gang as well as those of 'conventional' society, but without commitment. Solutions to the problems of existence peculiar to second-generation West Indians did not seem to represent an adequate explanation of their predicaments. Yet no alternative existed – until the advent of Ras Tafari. Then, as one Rasta put it, they 'had to do something black': 'After seeing the true self, other religions were without meaning. Pentecostal and Methodist and various other churches; you know, we didn't accept that because they derived from the European. We know that in ourself we had to do something black because we are black.'

Rastafarian solutions to the existential puzzles confronting blacks were penetrative and consistent; what is more, they presented a set of loosely defined directives for their amelioration. Ras Tafari offered a specific interpretation of evil and a course of action designed to deal with it. The black man's plight was explained in terms of his entrapment by the agents of the white man's Babylon, the essence of evil. The Babylonian conspiracy theory contained a comprehensive scheme for understanding and interpreting a whole range of phenomena including the black man's history, his future and his current circumstances. Here was the problem-solving complex *par excellence*: states of dis-ease and distress were rendered meaningful and therefore demystified; as a Rastaman captured it: 'I and I now understand how the Imperial Machine of the West and the religions that served it were designed to oppress all black peoples in the world.' In this respect, the compulsive attraction was the fresh understanding of problems; once this could be achieved, methods of eliminating them could follow.

(3) *The need for mobilisation*

Individuals in the social world apprehend, interpret and sometimes attempt to eradicate evil in a variety of ways. I have repeated Wilson's point often and illustrated its applicability to the Jamaican experience: as the manifestation of one omnipotent supernatural agency (Native Baptism and – in Britain – Pentecostalism), as the doings of human agents with supernatural powers (obeah-myal), as the product of the evil nature of certain factions of the human population (Bedwardism), or as the machinations of an exploitative system of human enterprise (Garveyism and black power). The reaction to the evil will depend on the conceptualisation of its source. So, whereas the black power response was informed by a set of principles for a totally transformed system of social relationships in which black men would re-make and re-shape their own destiny, the Pentecostalists were content to withdraw from what was understood as an intrinsically evil world and place their hopes for salvation in supernatural interventions. In both cases, the confrontation with evil was to take place beyond the horizons of the facilities provided by white society. Similarly, the Rastafarian movement was not characterised by an acceptance of institutional provisions for the satisfaction of goals; in its philosophy lay a critique of society. Its members were quite often self-consciously oppositional. This suggests that, although Rastas adopted critical stances towards society, the agents of which were regarded as irredeemably evil, they were not disposed to activism in attacking the causes of their problems because God would ultimately overturn the world and restore the black man to his rightful place, Zion. 'Must come' was the axiomatic statement endorsing the destruction of Babylon.

Quite obviously, there were variations in the interpretation of Ras Tafari and these had implications for behaviour: some regarded it as a mandate for attacks on any manifestation of Babylon, whether the police, store owners or property; some understood their role as more passive, comforting themselves in the belief that Jah would reconstruct society and elevate them from their lowly positions. In between these two there lay a plethora of variegated responses organised around Rastafarian principles.

The first two motivational routes were underpinned by a gradual process of drift in which the black youth moved steadily to a perception of the source of his problems; in other words, an identification of the core of evil, Babylon. Intensified awareness of causal processes contributing to perpetuating the plight led to criticisms of the central institutions of society rather than peripheral ones. They entailed movements from loosely held but largely unconnected sets of complaints and resentments to a clear and coherent vision. The third path was of a qualitatively different order. Here, the source of evil had already been identified and the shift to Ras Tafari was a much more instrumental endeavour designed to utilise Rastafarian concepts and categories to suit more political purposes: 'I've never really changed my views that much; I still see the cause of the black man's problems as the same. When I speak of Babylon it is, if you like, a more enlightened conception', contended a Rastaman.

Drifters travelling along this route (about 15 per cent of the membership) were selfconsciously motivated and aware of the possibilities inherent in the Rastafarian movement. Their interest in Rasta was in its potential for arousing young blacks and stimulating them into more militant postures.

The majority travelling along this path had been involved in some capacity with black power – though not necessarily with the organisations mentioned in Chapter 3. During this phase they had formed attitudes and struck up postures of a radical nature, borowing theories and stances from their American counterparts who were active during the 1960s. They all in some measure rejected the mode of social organisation in the Western world which ensured the domination of the white man over the black, but set about changing it through strictly secular means, often through formal political channels.

The demise of black power in Britain left them with the tasks of theorising the reasons for its failure and producing a formula which would regenerate such a movement. The furores caused by de Freitas, Egbuna and their colleagues had barely subsided before the Rastafarian manifestation became visible and many black power followers began to see the answers to their questions unfold before their eyes. These (I am told) were the conclusions: black power had failed because blacks in Britain, being mostly West Indian, were familiar with and enthusiastic for religious forms of expression and, therefore, movements involving secular imperatives would be most successful if they were shrouded in religious imagery. Garvey had vividly demonstrated the attention-arresting puissance of allying political directives with Biblical prophecy, and those seeking to mobilise the British blacks were mindful of this chemistry when they recognised the potential of Ras Tafari. Like many Garvey supporters who had grown disenchanted in the 1930s and turned to the Rastafarian movement as an alternative mode of expressing protest (Vincent, 1976, p. 227), many British black power followers looked to the newer form of Ras Tafari as a source of hope for raising consciousness among West Indians. An

EOC member said: 'I used to be in the Afro-Caribbean [a militant black neo-Marxist movement] but I realise that something more was needed for blacks in Britain. The history of the British-ruled West Indies shows that black people unite with religion, not just with politics.'

Unlike the other two routes which were characterised by a sometimes glacial and unselfconscious drift from the periphery to the core, the need for mobilisation route displayed a much more hard-headed and resolute deliberation in which the actors were motivated by a singularity of purpose and effulgence of vision. Their apprehension of evil had been shaped by black power edicts and they saw in Ras Tafari a disguised critique of the social structure they sought to transform. Humiliated by what they considered to be the obsequious role blacks were forced to play in the British drama and despairing at the failure of black power to stir imaginations with any lasting effect, they saw the possibility of an agglutinated package deal of prescribed beliefs and activities, the cutting edge of which was considered a black power orientation. As a consequence, they conceived of the movement as a consciousness-raising vehicle, the religious dimension of which would act as an integument or cell membrane inside which blacks could band together in the face of outsiders. I commented to a Rasta that the two posters of Malcolm X and Haile Selassie, which were side by side on his wall, might be construed as contradictory: 'Contradictory, ras! Just different ways of expressing same thing, man. Ask yourself one thing: what they both fighting against?'

They envisaged the Rastafarian movement as restoring some of black power's former orientation as a source of morale strengthening and awareness-building among the black community. It would provide a focus for shared interests elicited so that blacks could be aware that they participated in a common experience, caused ultimately by the existence of evil; what black power had identified as evil, white supremacy, the Rastas called Babylon. In short, the creation of a reference point for a shared focus of concern would enable blacks to interact within a framework, thus crystallising groups through the realisation of commonality.

The mobilisation group's drift to the movement was of a fundamentally different order than the others – though, of course, group members shared the benefits of identity and explanation offered by Rastafarian involvement. They held a prestructured conception of the white man which made for an almost wholly negative set of attitudes towards him. As a function of their antagonisms they associated only infrequently with whites and restricted primary contacts.

They were drawn not from the black gang structure, but largely from more organised groups with political, or at least activist orientations. Goals were fairly well defined and regarded as congruent with

Rastafarian objectives (the means employed to achieve them were obviously at variance). In Ras Tafari they saw the seeds of a new mood of militancy in black youth; a manifestation of bitterness. Here was the opportunity to persuade blacks of the necessity of pulling together to further their common purpose: as Rastafarian Bob Marley's panegyric to militancy stated: 'Get up, stand up, don't give up the fight.' The Rasta response had the effect of metamorphosing private grievances into public issues, and this was perfectly suited to those pursuing tangible objectives such as those of black power.

Whether these factions used the movement, or vice versa, is largely a matter of perspective. They offered a stimulating political input and sought on occasion to mobilise Rastafarian sentiment – usually unsuccessfully. Many later disavowed their allegiance to Ras Tafari, complaining of excesses of 'turning the other cheek' and dwelling on the divinity of Haile Selassie instead of engaging in more forceful means of publicising their troubles. The Rastas' failure to contribute actively at any politically coherent level disappointed many of those initially attracted by the militant promise of the movement: 'Sure, the potential was there; the whole deal was a consciousness-raising exercise. But they can do no good the way they are. What good is it going to do sitting around contemplating Haile Selassie and peace and love for all men?' They were lured by the instrumental rather than the symbolic aspects and were interested in phrasing political issues as religious ones rather than appreciating the dynamic interplay between the two dimensions, which was so central to the maintenance of the movement in England.

I have constructed three routes to account for the acceptance of the Rastafarian faith. My findings indicate that most Rastas experienced one of the 'needs', sometimes more than one, and had either satisfied them or frustrated them by involvement in the movement. I see the Rastafarian drift as an extension of the retaliation elicited during earlier phases of the West Indian experience. Rastas were overwhelmingly drawn from the ranks of the gang, the structure of which evolved through the rude boy complex. The process was also noted for its intensification of awareness of the source of evil, both personally and generally, which underlay the drift into Ras Tafari. In two of the channels, (1) and (2), states of suggestibility and malleability of attitudes or dispositions to act were necessary conditions for the drift, and situations creating discrepancies between expectation and experience facilitating this were present at the critical periods. In the other case, prestructured and predetermined attitudes about the target of the Rastafarian response informed a more extrinsic motivation. The three routes converged at the point of a desire to discover more about the movement. Such a desire was satisfied because of the existence of a set of Rastafarian beliefs and the social mechanisms for the transmission of them – including music. The next chapter will deal with these.

To conclude, I should stress that the predisposing process was complex and often subject to variation. My attempt to impose order by intuiting patterns and constructing categories into which they fall offers only some insights and invites objection from Rastas themselves who would challenge the contention that the drift involves a movement from peripheral attachment inwards; for the Rastaman believed himself to have been born as such ('It was in us from creation') and the moment of acceptance to be evidence of God's will as opposed to any self-conscious endeavour: the concept of conversion as such was not recognised. Recognised was the acceptance of Haile Selassie as divine creator and would-be transformer of the world, the living God. If I had to isolate a critical moment at which the drifter reached the 'core' and became a Rastaman, it would be upon accepting Ras Tafari: 'One day I came to accept His Imperial Majesty'; 'Jah passed over I'; 'In Jamaica and England there are many I man, all different; but all accept the truth of Selassie I as the Lord God Supreme' were three Rastafarian comments.

Parallel processes were at work as the actor made his cognitive adjustments consonant with a Rastafarian outlook; steady increases in knowledge of the movement and its objectives, heightening the awareness of belonging to a brotherhood, adoption of postures of lifestyle compatible with Rastafarian ambitions, strengthening of morale, dignity, self-esteem and polarisation from white institutions. The drift was multifaceted and I have dealt with only a few aspects of this creation of new meanings in an already established web of social affiliations; the incorporation of Rastafarian themes into the black gang structure. Now I shall consider how these themes became available and what relevance they were given by young blacks.

Echoes of Suffering

We're sick and tired of your easing kissing game
to die and go to heaven in Jesus name
we know and understand
almighty God is a living man
Bob Marley and Peter Tosh

REGGAE

Music builds up and brings the message from our brethren in
Jamaica, which is showing their tribulation; it is showing their glory
and it keeps us in contact with them, both spiritually and mentally.
(Henley, 1978)

Arguably the most important and influential music to ever emerge
from Jamaica has been reggae, an outgrowth of ska and rock steady,
but popularly used as a generic concept to characterise the more
general musical output of black Jamaicans. Reggae was unquestionably
an extension of the ska musical movement started by the early attempts
to reproduce American sounds and refined by the sophisticated productions of rock steady. Not unnaturally, both were seized upon by
uprooted Jamaicans in England, who could salvage some semblance
of their lost community by maintaining links with this, the most
accessible and untainted cultural form from Jamaica.

The unification of the rude boys and their English equivalents, the
skinheads, was ephemeral and inconsequential to the general pattern
of race relations. Developments in both traditions and in the distinct
cultural hybrid militated against any permanent allegiances being
forged. The skinhead enterprise fractured under the successive onslaughts of consumerism and exploitation of style, leaving the rudies
to retreat into subterranean enclaves. Prior to the split, however,
certain progressions were made on the Jamaican musical front which
were to effectively throw a life-line to despondent blacks in England.
The growth of a musical tradition and, in particular, the emergence
of a single exponent of that tradition were to prove vital and indispensable to the cultivation of a new identity for the black man in

England. They worked like a transfusion of consciousness, enlivening and reawakening the Jamaican's interest in himself, his ancestry and his future; the music was reggae and the individual, Bob Marley.

While the rudies and the skins were busily forging links in England, in 1968 a somewhat obscure Jamaican called Fred 'Toots' Hibbert was writing and recording a rock steady-influenced song which he titled 'Do the Reggay' (Pyramid label) and released with his group, Toots and the Maytels. Although enjoying a modicum of commercial success the song was rather more important for the interest it aroused concerning its title; no one quite knew what 'reggay' was. It has been speculated (by McKnight and Tobler, 1977, p. 43) that Hibbert derived the name from the Ragga, a Bantu-speaking Tanzanian tribe and simply added the 'y' on a whim. Alternatively, there have been those who stress the similarity with other words such as Rafa (the Indian form) or Reco (sometimes Rico Rodriguez), an early ska musician (Hebdige, 1975, p. 141). Personally, I believe the word to be etymologically related to the Jamaican expressions 'ragga-ragga', 'reggity' and 'reggid' which, according to Frederic Cassidy, denote 'The ugliness that comes from being ill clothed, ragged, untidy, dirty with its associated ideas of poverty and illness' (1961, p. 169). Whatever the origins of the word, it became re-spelled and elevated into an indispensable addition to the Jamaicans' musical vocabulary all over the world.

Whereas the earlier rock steady music had slowed ska down to a more immediately acceptable pace for Western ears and honed the lyrics down to 'near the knuckle' in order to titillate the imagination of its new followers, reggae signified a concentrated attempt to provoke social consciousnesses. I mean by this, that less accentuation was placed on the more ponderous and sexually thematic dimensions of rock steady: reggae music was for rebelling to and not making love to. The Jamaicans Kallynder and Dalrymple see the transition to reggae as symbolising a critical rupture in the pattern of Caribbean art.

Reggae was not conceived in a vacuum or conceptual negative but from a sociological, political and cultural situation that forced a possible physical and revolutionary position into a cultural one of music. That from the Caribbean comes a new fresh and vibrant music from black people who inhabit its precincts, testifies to the rest of the world, that though divested of our culture and language, we are still prepared to and must break out of the narrow constraints and cocoons of artistic values that have been set for us, and evolve our own. (n.d., p. 13)

In other words, they see reggae music as incorporating the collective sentiments of the island's black population, encapsulating a 'revolutionary position' in a cultural form. Whilst it is debatable whether the 'possible physical and revolutionary position' existed as a tenable reality or was merely a fiction of the authors' imaginations, it is certain that reggae most surely represented the most articulate and invective form of protest music to ever emerge out of the Caribbean. To be sure, the rock steady phase reflected a violence and anger unparalleled in previous Jamaican traditions, but raggae made the critical transition from straightforward musical discharges of growing hostility to calls for comprehensive social transformation.

Quite clearly the shift in emphasis towards and at the end of the 1960s and in a more pronounced manner during the 1970s came as a result of a number of circumstances. The prolonged violence in Jamaica, which had characterised the middle years of the 1960s, had by then taken on a new complexion with accusations and counter-accusations by the main political parties that the civil unrest was deliberately being manufactured by political interests to discredit the opposing party. States of emergency, gun courts, compounds and long prison sentences, together with perpetual police oppression had become integrated features of everyday life. Jamaica had learnt to live with the 'pressure'.

It had become apparent that no easy solution to the ever-escalating and seemingly endless sequences of violence at the street level would be found in the immediate future. Police–working-class relations were in a continual state of deterioration and depressed material conditions were static; no improvement was likely.

The rude boys' rock steady was vitriolic and sought to challenge authority without demanding a change in existing institutional arrangements. It asked not so much for alleviation from present conditions as a recognition of those conditions and the bitterness and anger that had fertilised beneath them. In other words, it was expressive of incoherent rebellious impulses; challenging but without any supportive theoretical basis to inform a demand for transformation; defiance but no insistence.

The period had seen a radiation of Rastafarian concepts and themes, in which certain fundamental tenets were disseminated throughout the society. The spread saw the rise of 'functional' Rastas. Most notable among the spread were the growing number of sympathising students, whose adoption of Rastafarian symbols and motifs signified their disenchantment with the extant political and social arrangements of Jamaica and their desire for an end to the miseries of their fellow blacks the world over.

But, more importantly (for present purposes), there arose a group of popular musicians demonstrating a keen awareness of Rastafarian principles and theories. References to Jah, Haile Selassie, Babylon and Ethiopia began to seep into the framework established by ska and rock steady, as musicians displayed an acute sensitivity to Rastafarian concepts. One such musician was trombonist Rico Rodriguez, who reflected: 'The bringing of the message of Ras Tafari into reggae was very important because most of the records I used to listen to in Jamaica were American, you know. And calypso which we used to play was almost dying out. So Rasta music was a different music coming into light in Jamaica.'

Assertions of defiance had been a formative response to the sense of hopelessness which followed the expectations connected with independence. But out of the deepening pool of despair came a more penetrating set of challenges and demands. The blanket of awe and apprehension which had fallen across Jamaica in the early 1960s remained significantly unaltered and the rude boy's call for an end to his suffering had gone unattended. The black musicians and, indeed, the rest of the black working class were looking towards a new mythical folk hero now that rudie had been emasculated; they found him in the figure of 'Natty Dread.'

> Oh Natty Natty,
> Natty 21,000 miles away from home,
> Oh Natty Natty
> And that's a long way
> for Natty to be from home.
>   Bob Marley and the Wailers, 'Natty Dread', 1974

Natty (derived from 'nutty', meaning weird and unstable) refers to the black Jamaican, impoverished but hopeful, suffering but resolute and refusing to give up the fight for improvement. He became the object and symbol of the new wave of Jamaican popular music. Natty Dread expressed the condition of the black man as the 1960s drew to a close. With no real improvement since independence and few hopes of relief through conventional channels, the younger dispossessed blacks looked for other means – and Ras Tafari offered at least a vision to orient towards. This is not to suggest that hope through established political and institutional organisations was entirely abandoned, the support for political parties at elections does not bear out such a contention. Nevertheless, the mood of the youth of Jamaica became increasingly critical and looked to the Rastaman for inspiration. So, whilst not totally immersing themselves in the cult of the Ras Tafari, the emergent new Rastas probed into the deeper layers of the movement in order to excavate concepts and categories which they could meaningfully relate to present-day circumstances.

Musicians, in particular, reaped a rich harvest from the Rastafarian conceptual package, virtually organising a total musical *genre* from the cult, its premises, concepts, themes etc. Linton Johnson said of them: 'The musicians have responded to changes in Jamaican society, incorporating the new pressures and tensions into the music, giving spiritual expression to the historical experience of oppression and rebellion' (1976a, p. 405). Whilst agreeing that music is most definitely and inextricably connected to the social context from which it emerges, I would add to Johnson's statement that it would be naïve to see the music as something like a direct reflection in a 'one-to-one' relationship. The commercial sounds of Jamaica were filtered through screens of commercial interest and governmental contingencies (e.g. the Jamaican Labour Party Premier, Hugh Shearer, imposed a ban on the highly acclaimed but severely critical 'Beat Down Babylon'; Peter Tosh's 'Legalize It' was also banned for a while). Hence, it does not follow that increases in the output of Rasta-inspired records necessarily represented an automatic response to an upsurge in popularity for the cult and its members. Of course, there was a process at work with more critical minds searching the Rastafarian treasure chest for the occasional theoretical gem, but I do stress the selectivity of such a process.

A more plausible way of looking at the spread into the musical sphere would be to see the musicians as articulating a form of protest directed less at immediate circumstances, more at the social structural arrangements which effectively subordinated the majority of the black working class, but burying their messages so deeply beneath a Rastafarian assortment of symbols and ideas that much of their critical sharpness was blunted – except for the recipients who were more totally aware of the context from which the music arose. Johnson again: 'the popular music of Jamaica, the music of the people, is essentially experiential music, not merely in the sense that the people experience the music, but also in the sense that the music is true to the historical experience of the people, that the music reflects the historical experience.' (1976a, p. 405). Further, he contends (rather romantically) that 'the musicians themselves enter a common stream of consciousness, and what they create is an invitation to the listeners to be entered into the consciousness'. His view would certainly find sympathy from Kallynder and Dalrymple who subtitle their work on reggae 'a people's music'. There can be no doubt that reggae, with its sometimes acidic statements couched in apocalyptic idioms, started from the perspective of a black Jamaican looking at the society around him and reflecting on 'what is wrong?' and 'what can be done about it?' This is hardly surprising once it is realised that nearly all the performers were drawn from the ranks of the urban working class (and were generally destined to stay there, thanks to the structure of the recording industry which had for long been heavily weighted in favour of the behind-the-scenes personnel and not the performers).

It would seem, then, that the messages of the music became more stringently challenging and suffused with condemnations of Jamaican society as the black militancy intensified. This would be an extremely difficult point to assess, but, as I have hoped to show in Chapter 2, the neo-Marxist theory that Jamaican society was seething with ever-expanding banks of rivers of revolutionary potential rests on a problematic set of premises. Indeed, rather than reflecting growing militancy and revolutionary fervour, one might contend that the changing form of music acted to slough off any latent militancy in the black working class. By translating the hostility into a musical form, rather than converting it into pragmatic proposals, the impetus towards mobilisation of forces was defused, leaving reggae as the principal source of expressing discontent. An English Rasta expressed concern at this: 'Unless we have this [political] element, Rastas will continue to have the reputation of reggae singers and do nothing constructive.'

However, such questions are secondary to the task at hand which is to delineate the ways in which reggae came to be the dominant vehicle through which Rastafarian ideas and demands were transmitted and disseminated to the young Jamaican population of England; how the links with the Jamaican brethren were established.

Superficially, it would appear that reggae had less appeal to English whites than rock steady. It had no particularly innovatory dance to accompany it as did its predecessor and, of course, by the time it had percolated across from the West Indies the pandemonium of the skinheads had died away leaving a slightly depressed interest in Jamaican sounds. The rude boys references had fallen on a receptive audience whose familiarity with the home-grown product and whose similarity to a comparable English youth culture facilitated a very smooth and simple association of Jamaican and English elements. Everything about rock steady gelled perfectly with the English situation.

Reggae presented a different proposition: the incursions of Biblical concepts, warnings of fires, burnings and future destruction, hysterical appeals to Jah for salvation and pleas for a return to Ethiopia were unlikely to arouse too much interest in a young white population which was being bombarded with the lurex and tinsel of the glittery glam-rock movement, the eye-catching vanguard of which comprised Gary Glitter, David Bowie and Roxy Music. The previous close connection with West Indian culture which resulted from the skinheads' liaison had come undone as new idols swept on to the popular scene. The sounds of Kingston slums were hardly pertinent enough to have any impact.

Jamaican artists were still carving out some commercial successes but by and large they reflected none of the impulses which were feeding the new patterns of music in Jamaica. Politically empty love songs by Johnny Nash and Dandy Livingstone, both utilising full orchestrations and polished production techniques, were the ones making most impression in England as the 1970s drew on and no one was really interested in the meaning of a rather strange record by Desmond Dekker which happened to top the best selling record charts in June 1969 and went on to sell 5 million copies. Its title was 'The Israelites'.

The parting of the ways of the skinheads and the rude boys coincided in almost chronological perfection with the increases of Rastafarian influences in reggae music. Jamaicans had withdrawn their presences into the more racially homogeneous confines of their own districts and contented themselves with an exclusively West Indian cultural sub-universe. West Indian 'blues parties', or 'shebeens' were well attended; these were run by itinerant disc jockeys who brought their own sound system on which they could play the Jamaican records. These disc jockeys were responsible for importing and dealing in Jamaican music, which was unavailable through English distributors. In this way, a steady stream of Jamaican sounds was brought to England, though by 1972 they were for the benefit of a virtually all-black consumer pool. Sales of single releases were estimated at 2–3,000 per copy, with the occasional one reaching figures of 50,000 – an extraordinary total considering such records were not on general release (see McGlashen, 1973, p. 12).

Contents were becoming more and more saturated with Rastafarian-inspired critiques or at least critical comments cast in Rasta language; they became heavily suffused with the quality of 'dread'. Artists gaining a reputation for such productions were (amongst others) Dillinger, I. Roy, U. Roy and Big Youth, the disc jockeys and bands such as Burning Spear and the Wailers who were to become the most internationally famous Jamaican band of all.

Topically, less emphasis was placed on the open sexuality of earlier sounds and more on immediate social problems in Jamaica and ways of overcoming them. The virtual starvation of black Jamaicans became a popular theme (e.g. 'Every Mouth Must Be Fed' – I. Roy; 'Them Belly Full But We Hungry' – Bob Marley and the Wailers). The persecution of blacks by the police was made highly relevant, especially after the introduction of the gun courts: 'This morning I woke up in a curfew, I was a prisoner too, yeah, could not recognise the faces standing over me, they were dressed in the uniform of brutality' ('Burnin' and Lootin' ' – The Wailers). Even inflation was to become an issue in later years: 'Everything is outa sight, it is so hard everything is going higher and higher' ('Time Tough' – Toots and the Maytels). Assurances that the day of deliverance would come in accordance with the wishes of Haile Selassie were frequent, even after his death: 'God is sleeping, God ain't dead' ('Jim Squashey' – Big Youth). In the

meantime, the poor Jamaican was instructed to 'shine up your hammer
and sharpen up your sickle' ('African Message' – U. Roy) and, above
all 'don't cut your dreadlocks' which was a 'Message from the Top'
(I. Roy). But, more generally, the imperative was to 'Praise Jah the
Lord God Ras Tafari'. The interpretation given to such messages by
English-based Jamaicans was to have interesting results.

Undoubtedly, many migrating Jamaicans who had arrived in
England before the 1970s were familiar with Rastafarian values and
demands. To some groups, the messages contained in the incoming
songs were practically hymnal and meaningfully interpreted as
expressive of the cry for Ras Tafari. Isolated Ras Tafari groups were
reported around South London at this time (McGlashen, 1973) though
it seems they were primarily reclusive and relatively invisible compared to the majority of Jamaicans in high immigrant areas. The
EWF and Twelve Tribes were in the process of establishing themselves.

To less informed groups, however, the newer reggae would have
been slightly more confounding and likely to provoke greater interest
in the cult, possibly asking more aware Jamaicans or studiously listening to the lyrics for clues as to the exact nature of the apocalypse of
which so much was spoken. Though most Rastas showed caution when
acknowledging the role of music in prompting their interest in Ras
Tafari – understandably in view of the insistence on the implicitness
of Jah – they would mostly agree and occasionally express this
openly: 'I suppose music was my first contact with Ras Tafari and it
was this which told me to look inside myself to find the true Rastaman
within I.' Asked whether it was through music that he began to realise
his roots, a Rasta answered affirmatively: 'Well, I can say so, yeah,
yeah; you can say that. I used to listen to music and sometimes a
certain record might stick in my memory and I would meditate on that
record. The words of it got stronger and stronger, began to make
meaning for I.'

Stories of 'fire in a Babylon' and 'blood up town and blood down
town' were bound to have prompted confusion; calls for a return to
Ethiopia could not have failed to stimulate an awareness of African
ancestry; descriptions such as 'and down here is the ghetto and down
here we suffer' would have fed a vicarious sense of desolation and
suffering. Suffering, or 'sufferation' shone through the lyrics of reggae
with crystal clarity; comparisons by English Jamaicans with their own
social position were inevitable: 'Music builds up and brings the
message from our brethren in Jamaica, which is showing their tribulation; it is showing their glory and it keeps us in contact with them,
both spiritually and mentally.'

It is part of the contention of this book that the messages of reggae
as gleaned by Jamaican youth from imported records, were largely

responsible for evoking the vicarious sense of suffering leading to identification of English Jamaicans with their less mobile counterparts and the emergence of a peculiarly English cross-fertilisation of Rastafarian ideas and values. But, of course, the messages were delivered through the sound systems by disc jockeys spinning impersonal pieces of plastic. West Indian night clubs and dances energetically tried to book original Jamaican artists, but it was a costly affair and likely to entail prohibitive admission prices. Messages in themselves would have been insufficient to provoke the kind of massive interest in Ras Tafari which came during 1976 and 1977 in which the awareness of every black youth in England was aroused and, in many cases, shaken. The message energising changes in thought and behaviour needed a personal focus. The cult of Ras Tafari in England had as its focus a Jamaican whose influence on the minds of Jamaican youth can be described as nothing less than seismic. The balance of this chapter will be occupied with an analysis of the biography and influence of this figure.

THE RASTAMAN COMETH: BOB MARLEY

Prior to the advent of Bob Marley and his music there had been a virtual absence of readily available millenarian themes among the West Indian community of England. Conditions in the comparatively new environment had brought to fruition an anxiety which had been simmering inside Jamaican youth. The younger members of the community had engaged in a brief and violent flirtation with the English skinheads, but such an alliance had been devoid of any ideological content which would have enabled them to direct their efforts towards systematically opposing the unwanted, evil influences forcing them to their positions of marginality. They seem to have floundered about, desperate to articulate some kind of defiance yet unable to find any set of ideas around which to organise. There was no clear conception of goals outside the immediate periphery and, more importantly, no individuals with a doctrine comprehensive and far-reaching enough to facilitate a crystallisation of efforts into a serious collective posture.

In the overview of the historical development of the cult of Ras Tafari I episodically touched upon the crucial relationship between ideas and leadership. Concepts and themes connected with social movements, whether secular or religious or mixtures of both, do not simply and spontaneously emerge out of social and political vacuums; they must be interpreted, stylised and refined by individuals and, where these individuals are not present, the ideas will not fortuitously appear.

My consideration of the influence of Garvey on the incipient Rastafarian movement and the critical role played by the triangle of

Howell, Hibbert and Dunkley in shaping and fashioning the alleged prophecy of the black king into a coherent religious and, in many ways, political ideology has sensitised the analysis to the sociological problems of why the prophet figure with a doctrine of hope and imminent rescue seems to emerge or be thrown up in times of severe doubt and depression. These two examples, plus the instances of Bogle and Bedward pointed up the inadequacies of explaining the appearance of influential figures at important historical stages as random occurrences arising in between the interstices of socially perceived needs and idiosyncratic personality gifts. The emergence of Garvey at slightly more stable junctures in Jamaica's history failed to emit anything like an exhilarating response from the working-class blacks to whom the messages were addressed. Bogle, Bedward, Howell and Dunkley (and much later Henry and Edwards) were at various times regarded as threatening deviants rather than prophetic messengers of 'great tidings'. Leadership patterns in Jamaica, or anywhere else, cannot be legitimately explained in terms of coincidence or chance. Seeming historical accidents are, under the sociological microscope, rarely accidents at all.

Accordingly, the emergence and popularisation of Bob Marley and his installation as a Rastafarian folk hero will not be analysed in terms of a random collision of, on the one hand, social tastes and, on the other, peculiar talents and idiosyncratic, psychological traits. On the contrary, I will argue that the availability of Bob Marley at the particular juncture he was required was neither the product of chance nor unrelated to the socially perceived need of the time. In other words, the appearance and success of Bob Marley amongst the black community of England owes more to cultural than to purely musical or even psychological variables.

It would not be exaggerating to suggest that Bob Marley was to the seventies wave of English Rastas what Marcus Garvey was to the first Jamaican cultists of the 1930s. He attracted attention, mobilised immense interest and disseminated ideas which were, in all probability, unheard of by many young West Indians before his rise to fame. He, more than any other individual, was responsible for introducing Rastafarian themes, concepts and demands to a truly universal audience; he translated the messages and prophecies of early believers into socially meaningful doctrines just as applicable and relevant to the contemporary setting of England as to the Jamaica of post-war years. As a Rastaman later put it: 'Music is a bond or a tie between the English Rasta and the Jamaican Rasta . . . through peace, love and harmony.' 'Bob Marley was, I suppose, almost like a prophet; like John the Baptist, bringing messages from I's brethren in Jamaica' (a view not shared by every Rasta). Regarded by some as an eccentric wildman and by others as a venerated prophet (and by others as neither, or both) Marley made the kind of impression on the imaginations of English Jamaicans that Garvey made on the imaginations of blacks in the 1920s and 1930s; he gripped their hearts, their minds and their passions. In the 1930s existing conceptual maps were called into question and subsequently overthrown as the quest for new orders of explanation of present circumstances was begun. This may be precisely the search that was undertaken by many aspiring English Rastafarian affiliates in the 1970s, to look for the 'missing dimensions'. They resumed the initiative to the West Indian community and were critically scrutinising their own identity, the nature of the society in which they lived and, most significantly, their own location within that society. Marley's messages were crucially important in providing at least some of the answers to such questions: 'He has the insight to see many things which others don't and tell his people about them', a young Rasta assured me.

The Marley phenomenon, as opposed to the man Marley, was a social relationship, not an attribute of his personality or a unique musical talent, and as such the strain is to remain ever-mindful of the vital link between the figure and the followers. Willingness to follow and a desire to recognise and honour qualities are necessary conditions for the production of Bob Marley as the archetypal Rastaman. They are not, however, sufficient conditions, in that the Jamaican predilection to seek out a cultural figurehead may well have gone unsatisfied were it not for events in Jamaica which made the emergence of Marley possible. Marley's role might never have been filled. Let me, therefore, turn to an overview of the background and progress of Marley and his emergence as the latter-day 'leader' of the English Rastafarian movement.

By a strange irony, the man who made such a profound impression on the black youth of England was himself of mixed parentage, having a white Liverpool-born father who died when he was 2 and a black Jamaican mother who cared for him up to his teens. Marley, the eldest of five children, was born on 5 February 1945 in the Middlesex Parish of St Ann, where Garvey spent his early childhood. Though his mother was a devout member of the Apostolic Church, she could not interest her son in religious pursuits. He went to school in Kingston. (Sources of information on Marley's biography: Dalrymple, 1976; McKnight and Tobler, 1977.)

Marley, unlike other school-leavers, did not show a marked penchant to 'scuffle' and hustle his way through his first years on the labour force and went to work in a welder's yard where he was introduced to music by a certain Desmond Dekker (McKnight and Tobler, 1977, p. 61). Jamaica was at this time going through an imitative phase with American black music forming the focus for most performers.

Dekker introduced Marley to one of the freebooter disc jockeys who were carving out a role for themselves at that time. Marley recorded a song called 'Judge Not' under the auspices of Ken Khouri, which was released anonymously in 1961. Other recordings followed ('Terror' and 'One Cup of Coffee'), but none achieved any significant degree of success and he was compelled to continue welding for his survival.

His musical presence recrudesced in 1964 when a ska group called the Wailin' Wailers installed him as their vocalist and chief song writer. On the release of their first recording, 'Simmer Down', their personnel was all black, with the exception of Marley, comprising of Peter McIntosh (later to be changed to 'Tosh'), Neville 'Bunny' Livingstone (later 'Bunny Wailer'), Junior Braithwaite and Beverley Kelso, the only female member. Later, the band was to change its name to the Wailin' Rudeboys to give it extra identification with the street gangs which had appeared in the slums of Kingston. Titles such as 'Rule Them Rudie' and 'Rude' gained the band members reputations as symbols of the new sense of defiance and rebelliousness.

After a slight commercial success in 1966, the unit was plagued by personal disputes and Marley became disenchanted. At the end of the year he moved to Delaware, USA where his mother was domiciled. In his absence, day-to-day violence continued to make Jamaica a cauldron of fermenting hostility. Marley's migration to the USA was no doubt prompted by the worsening dangers of living in Trenchtown where he resided during the 1960s, plus the threat of poverty which constantly hung over the heads of Jamaican musicians ruthlessly exploited by a system designed to yield maximum benefit to management and recording interests. It has been speculated that Marley first encountered the cult of Ras Tafari whilst in Kingston. Dalrymple (1976, p. 16) confirms that the musician came into contact with Mortimo Planno (or Planner) who formed part of the delegation on the mission to Africa in 1961. Planno was at this stage a very active cult member, proselytising vigorously on behalf of the Rastafarian movement and organising educational services in the instruction of African history, the Amharic language of Ethiopia and the Bible.

It seems that Marley could not have been over-impressed by his meetings with Planno for it was not long after that he decided to sever his ties with the Kingston slums and wholeheartedly embrace the whore of Babylon by going to work in a US car factory owned by the giant Chrysler group. Material rewards for this type of work were no doubt in excess of what he reaped from his musical pursuits. Two events hastened his return to Jamaica: he unexpectedly lost his job and so applied for welfare, whereupon he was informed that he was eligible for the draft to the army. Preferring the possibility of 'scuffling' and suffering in Kingston to fighting in Vietnam, he retreated to Jamaica in 1967 where he again enjoined forces with MacIntosh and Livingstone to form a band known simply as The Wailers.

Some of the numbers produced by this combo reflected the general enthusiasm for openly sexual lyrics and songs such as 'Bend Down Low', 'Stir It Up' and 'Put It Down' seemed a long way from the previously emotive cry of the rude boy. Quite characteristically, the group arrived at the wrong end of the royalties and so in 1968 decided to embark on their most enterprising venture, splitting with their recording company and creating their own 'Wailing Soul' label. Although the reputation of the band was at this stage growing steadily in Jamaica and their records were regular incumbents of top selling chart positions, the organisational problems of running a record company as well as a musical outfit proved too burdensome and the label collapsed after releasing only six singles. Exacerbating the situation was the arrest and subsequent imprisonment of Livingstone who fell foul of the government's sweeping proposal to cut down on the production, possession and consumption of ganja due to its connection with violence.

A stagnant period followed with Marley befriending Johnny Nash who was at that time experiencing commercial success in Europe unparalleled by any Jamaican performer. Marley accompanied him on a European tour with the apparent intention of writing his material, but the enterprise seems to have been fruitless (though Nash did include three Marley compositions and one collaborative effort on his album 'I can See Clearly Now').

Marley's return to Jamaica started badly when he was imprisoned for ganja possession, though he was publicly repudiated this and claims it was for a driving offence. On release, however, the seed of success was planted by a liaison with producer Lee Perry, whose studio band, The Upsetters had released a single, 'The Return of Django', which became something of a classic with English skinheads in 1969. Perry was obviously a very accomplished and professional producer whose familiarity with the English record market stood him in healthy stead. He changed the band's musical direction and created for them a sound which was uniquely their own. The association yielded many successfully selling records in Jamaica, including 'Duppy Conqueror' and 'Soul Rebel' which were later to be re-released on the Wailers' first significant British album, 'African Herbsman' and 'Rasta Revolution' which was issued on the Trojan label but made only a slight impact on the British market. At this stage it would seem that the Wailers' recognition in England was only negligible and the more general enthusiasm for West Indian music lay with the skinhead-adopted rock steady sounds.

The early seventies period also saw the intrusions of Rastafarian

concepts and motifs into the Wailers' work. The break with rude boy
and rock steady had left something of a void which the Rastafarian
messages seemed to fill perfectly. Marley was quick to capitalise on
the growing sympathies for the Rastas within the black community
of Jamaica. His lyrical posture transmuted from that of the anti-
authority rude boy, sniping and challenging, to that of a Rastaman,
critical of the whole structure of Jamaican neo-colonialism and optimistic about his ultimate salvation at the hands of Haile Selassie –
Jah. On release from jail, he offered the following consolation to all
those in similar predicaments:

> The bars could not hold me
> force could not control me, now
> they try to keep me down
> but Jah put I around
>
> Yes I've been accused (many times)
> and wrongly abused now
> but through the powers of the most high
> They've got to turn me loose
>
> Don't try to hold me up on this bridge, now
> I've got to reach Mount Zion – the highest region
> The Wailers – 'Duppy Conqueror'

This phase also saw Marley produce a number of other politically
motivated statements which were to add momentum to his already
escalating reputation as a social commentator rather than a pure
musical artist. The lyrics became less flippant and more thoughtfully
blended with social and historical conditions. '400 Years' constituted
something of a starting point for his personal plea to black persons to
discover and celebrate their African ancestry. The emotive 'Trench
Town Rock' warned of the consequences of allowing the black people
(children) to continue their suffering.

> And never let the children cry
> (Trench Town Rock)
> Or you got to tell Jah Jah why
> Bob Marley and The Wailers – 'Trench Town Rock'

Marley, of course, was not alone in his excursions into Rastafarian
planes. Notable disc jockeys such as U. Roy, Dillinger and Manley
Buchanan were also using amalgams of Rastafarian Biblical terminology and politically straightforward invectives to add fire to their
lyrics. Immediate and pressing social issues were tossed into the musical
arena, with the folk-image hero, Natty Dread, usually bearing the
brunt of the suffering. But what is important is the process whereby

situational deprivations were linked to the more embracing problems of 'searching for roots'. Present difficulties were not being perceived so much in an immediate idiom as in the context of the historical phenomenon of colonialism and its attendant evils. The first step out of the quagmire of colonially imbued values was to recognise the hallmark of Africa as a basis of affiliation and to generate an understanding of the black man's true roots outside Jamaica. In other words, the message was: make others fearful of your presence – 'keep your dread!'

> We have been stripped of our nature, our culture
>   and our language,
> Deprived of our religion
> Till we wonder will we really ever learn again . . .
> Keep your dread, Natty, know your culture.
> Big Youth – 'Keep your Dread'

With the radiation of Rastafarian values at work in Jamaica, the time seemed right for a more international cultivation of the *reggae à la Rasta* and towards the end of 1971 a comfortably rich white Jamaican, Chris Blackwell, approached the Wailers to record an album for his 'Island Records' label with which he had been energetically promoting the sale of Jamaican records in England over the previous nine years. Blackwell, along with another Jamaican called Lee Gopthal, had established the record label and a series of retail outlets devoted to black Jamaican music. Since their success with Millie Small's 'My Boy Lollipop' and the subsequent enthusiasm for Jamaican sounds, the enterprise had expanded into a veritable empire and they signed up the Wailers with a view to introducing them to an English audience. A deal was made between Blackwell and the Wailers in which the band was to make an album at the Dynamic Studios, Kingston, the cost of which was to be underwritten by Island, which would distribute the end-product in England.

The result was a rare collection of Rastafarian-inspired reggae with most of its raw edges chipped off by the technical sophistications of quality recording facilities. Aptly named 'Catch A Fire', one track of the record issued a prophetic warning:

> Slave driver the table is turn
> Catch A Fire so you gonna get burn.

The album was released by Island Records in England in March 1973 and its sales were boosted by a month-long concert tour of the universities later in the year. Supplementing this first exposure were a number of television appearances and a four-day booking at London's prestigious Speakeasy Club. A tour of the USA followed with the Wailers providing support for the principal act, Sly and the Family Stone.

For many young Jamaicans in England this would have been their first glimpse of Bob Marley, not yet sporting fully fledged dreadlocks but most certainly a figure of mystery with his thick patois-laden lyrics telling of the 10,000 chariots which would come to deliver his people after the destruction of Babylon. Marley was about to provide an indispensible impetus to the nucleus of Rastafarian interest which existed in England.

By now, West Indian migrants had learnt that they were not going to be allowed to be 'British' (in a cultural sense) even if they wanted to be. As a Rasta later explained to me: 'As the Bible shows I, the leopard can never change his spots and the Ethiopian his colours; it is inevitable that we, as black people, were never and can never be part of this country where we do not belong; like a heart transplant it rejects us.' Institutionally, advancements had been made to legally stamp out discriminatory practices but in real terms racialism was as prohibitive to integration as it ever had been. So, then, the prospective devotees of Marley began for a negative basis of racial rejection and disadvantage. But their magnetic attraction to Marley was not simply a matter of a retreat under regrettable circumstances; self-defence prompted by rejection by the majority. Obviously, such factors partially explain the enthusiasm for Marley which was to follow, but the attachment to him was not only a clawing of people in despair. Rather, there was another component: the restoration of selfhood. West Indians were in a situation which necessitated them organising themselves and adapting their qualities and resources to cope with existing situations. They were in an identity vacuum. Starved of the opportunity to be English and stripped of the material and cultural supports to sustain a wholly Jamaican character, the more energetic Jamaicans saw in Marley a ray of hope for a future identity based on an acute recognition of and sensitivity to the blacks' African ancestry and its bearing on future world events. The first exposures to the music and the physical presence of Marley were the first steps to the creation of an incipient corporate existence. For the Rastas, Marley brought the 'seeds' of a 'new consciousness': 'Personally, I accepted Ras Tafari long before Marley became big, but for many he brought across the message, you know, seeds to be cultivated in the different land, to grow into new consciousness.'

No matter how gifted a figure is, his leadership in the final analysis rests solidly on the willingness of others to accept him. Marley's attributes are less important than the extraordinary qualities the enthusiastic Jamaican imputed to him. Here was a home-grown Jamaican who had crashed into a (predominantly white) English market, sold records to white people, been fêted on television shows and appeared in front of white audiences. All this without diluting the content of his messages. No other Jamaican artist had succeeded in

such proportions whilst at the same time condemning the very structure of the white society which had given him the opportunity in the
first place. Bob Marley was singing to white audiences and simultaneously telling them of their own future destruction. Clearly Marley
was no ordinary Jamaican entertainer. *Rara avis erat.* Asked whether
he revered Marley as somebody special, a Rasta answered: 'Well man,
he's one of the brethren and all brethren are important. But he's
different; gifted perhaps with much insight.'

The second Wailers' album for international release was again a
Jamaican production entitled 'Burnin' '', a metaphorical description of
the state of the white-dominated world. 'Catch A Fire' had aroused
enormous interest especially amongst the black community of England
and his 'live' performances had been well received in general. No
comparable enthusiasm was in evidence in the USA, however, and so
the total promotional venture was only a partial success. Better things
were hoped of the second shot.

A tour designed to abet the sales of 'Burnin' '' crumbled to a complete disaster when lead guitarist, Peter Tosh, developed a bronchial
condition and was instructed to return to Jamaica. With ten tour dates
remaining the rest of the band refused to perform in Tosh's absence
and left for Jamaica. Popular explanations hold that internal frictions
had hastened the decision to return, although McKnight and Tobler
come up with the interesting theory that, after Tosh's illness 'The
band interpreted this as a sign of Jah's displeasure with their current
activity and so, to placate Him, they all returned to Jamaica' (1977,
p. 80). Subsequently, Tosh and another founder member, Bunny
Livingstone (now changed to Bunny Wailer), parted company with
the group to pursue solo careers. (Tosh released an album based on
the theme of Jamaican drug laws, appropriately entitled 'Legalize It',
published by ATU Music. The record was at first banned in Jamaica
though gaining acceptance in England and the USA. Despite lack of
radio air play the record was available through retail outlets. Wailer's
solo exercise, 'Blackheart Man: the ten messages', published by
Solomonic Music was a much more vitriolic and savage indictment of
white society, using predominantly Rastafarian scriptural imagery to
fashion the statements. Both records received recognition in Jamaica
without really gaining any kind of attention on the scale of Marley
and the Wailers. Tosh's popularity in England grew, especially after
he made a record with Mick Jagger in 1978, the year in which he
performed two concerts in London and Manchester.)

The 'Burnin' '' album opened with one of the most controversial
songs ever produced by Marley. A collaborative effort with Tosh,
'Get Up, Stand Up', was interpreted by most members of the music
fraternity as a battle cry to blacks the world over, to abandon Christianity and its conception of salvation and engage in the Rastafarian-

inspired struggle for this-worldly salvation. Part of its content issued the following statement:

> We're sick and tired of your easing kissing game
> to die and go to heaven in Jesus name
> we know and understand
> almighty God is a living man

The suggestibility and value crisis produced by the systematic rejections of the white majority and the experience of despair at the lack of meaningful improvement in race relations helped also to produce the audience desirous of instruction and guidance. In this same 'Get Up, Stand Up' Marley had provided a very influential tool for the English West Indians: a chisel with which to carve out guidelines along which to formulate a posture *vis-à-vis* white society. (It was the most oft-quoted song during my research and considered by many to be the single most important piece of music for the movement – though this was not a unanimous opinion.) The call to dismiss conventional Christianity and investigate the possibilities of a salvation on this earth primarily through fighting for recognition was a powerful message indeed, and one which many Jamaicans would have listened to attentively. 'Get up, stand up, stand up for your rights. Get up, stand up, don't give up the fight' was an urgent reminder that all was not lost despite the gloomy appearance of present circumstances; the fight was still to be fought.

In 1974, the leader–follower nexus forged even more tightly, stimulated by the release of arguably the most musically accomplished album to that date, 'Natty Dread', which was credited to 'Bob Marley and the Wailers' rather than to just 'The Wailers' (as were the other albums). Reception of the record was boosted by a well-attended concert tour of the USA in 1975, followed by a two-night performance at London's Lyceum ballroom where Marley unveiled a mass of corkscrewed dreadlocks to capacity audiences. The remainder of the tour to England was a success with the exotic Marley shouting messages of impending doom and destruction at his audiences. Marley on this tour was exemplary with his dreadlocks and Ethiopian emblems in full view and his speech in rich, slurred patois virtually incomprehensible to white members of the audience.

By now, the commercial product creation process was in full swing and Bob Marley was beginning to emerge as a marketable commodity. Respectable record sales and concert sell-outs stimulated an overnight interest on behalf of the media as well as the black community. Music papers and radio stations vied for interviews as Marley took his steps towards 'superstardom'.

The attraction of Marley for whites lay primarily in the form and content of his music. Ambiguities surrounding his sometimes confusing lyrics and his apparent anti-white intellectual position could be brushed aside and attention concentrated at the level of his music. American black music had commanded a strong following in England since the early 1960s and indeed 'soul' and 'funk' carved out a veritable tradition in contemporary popular music. Marley more or less slotted into this category, appealing to black music enthusiasts rather than the former devotees of rude boy music with its sexual overtones (though he later drew acclaim from the punks).

But for most blacks the attraction would have been more total, embracing both the music and the attendant intellectual posture. The colours, the locks, the messages and the by now commonplace exaggerated claims to consume large quantities of ganja daily, served to elevate Marley into something much more than just another Jamaican rock performer; clearly he was special. (I should mention that Marley's relationship to the Rastas was of a different quality to the relationship of someone like Stevie Wonder to his followers. Articulate though Wonder was (especially in the early 1970s), his lyrics did not produce the intensity of interpretation evoked by Marley. Rastas consciously extracted the 'logic' of Marley's messages.)

Inspired by the Rastafarian afflatus in Marley's messages, the young blacks began to dissolve their own sense of powerlessness and isolation by building up walls around their own cultural confines and effectively excluded whites from participation in their own subworlds in much the same way as they thought whites had excluded them from entry into the mainstream of English society. The process of retreatism bred an antagonism towards and distrust of existing institutions and a longing to create alternatives. But the effects of Marley's influence are to be considered later; let me here concern myself with the influence itself.

It becomes something of an arbitrary exercise to try and isolate with any precision a specific date when Marley's Rastafarian pleas to recognise African ancestry, distrust white society and place faith in Haile Selassie really penetrated the consciousness of blacks in England. Quite obviously, there can be no single cut-off point. Rather his influence was cumulative and contagious. The issue of the album 'Natty Dread' and the national tour of England in 1975 did, however, appear to be a powerful combination of forces and one which was no doubt efficacious in provoking many uncommitted or unsure blacks to take an interest in Ras Tafari: 'When him say "Stand up for your rights, see the light" he talk to I and I, this was to be I's mission and his destiny, "see the light" ' remarked a Rasta.

There was, of course, a basis of organised Rastafarian groups in England, even before the release of 'Catch A Fire' and the development of such groups was not necessarily affected by Marley and his followers. More generally, however, the profusion of dreadlocks after

1975 would seem to indicate that Marley's influence reached something approaching a zenith at around the time of his 1975 tour. The proliferation of Rastas after 1975 was the product of sustained and contagious interest in the cult rather than increased enthusiasm for Marley the man. Ras Tafari spread like fever as young Jamaicans became privy to the meanings of Marley's messages. More articulate expansions on the Rastafarian philosophy were to come in 1976 with the release of 'Rastaman Vibration' an album which included a musical adaptation of Haile Selassie's 1968 speech in California at a time when Angola and Mozambique were riddled with war.

The album demonstrated Marley's musical maturity and his ability to produce a sound palatable to a mixed racial audience without dulling the sharpness of the lyrical invectives against white society. What his black followers were conveniently neglecting at this stage was that Marley, despite his strict separatist principles and condemnation of capitalism, was nevertheless compromising, however reluctantly, to engage in a multi-million dollar exercise in straightforward commercialism for the purposes of acquiring the despised gold of Babylon. The creation of Marley the product was well under way.

It had been realised that Marley was speaking for the black people of the world and the urban sufferers of Jamaica, in particular. This in itself was nothing new; hundreds upon hundreds of so-called 'protest singers' and 'social commentators' had expressed similar concerns. Marley, however, had the additional dimension of Ras Tafari; his music was soaked not only in political but also in religious dye. Here was a devoutly committed religious man, difficult to interview, controversial in his political black nationalistic views, notorious for his alleged inordinate consumption of drugs and wildly bizarre in his macabre presentation of self. Importantly, he had gripped the hearts and minds of a section of the world's population not merely with his music but with the form in which his messages were cast. In other words, the messages themselves were important but secondary to the vivid imagery of the idiom in which he communicated them. His was a rhetoric of defiance, and the language was that of Ras Tafari.

Advertising agencies often reiterate the truth of the apparent axiom: the package sells the product. Whether this was entirely true of Bob Marley is unsure, but one can plausibly speculate that the Rastafarian packaging created for Marley the kind of following usually reserved for prophets, seers or sages.

Some commentators have been severely critical of what they perceive to be a somewhat artificial projection of Marley. Linton Johnson, for example, has called the total Rastafarian image 'an instrument of capital':

This is the image that is used to sell Marley, the image of the rata rebel, and god only knows the eroticism and romanticism that this image invokes in the mind of his white fans. And this is where the ironies multiply. The 'image' is derived from rastafarianism and rebellion, which are rooted in the historical experience of the oppressed of Jamaica. It then becomes an instrument of capital to sell Marley and his music, thereby negating the power which is the cultural manifestation of this historical experience. (1975, p. 238)

Such scepticism is well taken and it would be naïve to ignore the powerful invisible interests at work behind the projection and representation of Marley as the ganja-smoking, uncompromising and irrefrangible champion of the world's black youth. There can be no doubt that after 1973–4 he became a highly marketable and exploitable commodity. His succession of sell-out concerts at the Rainbow Theatre, London, in June 1977 and at Stafford Bingley Hall in the following year amply illustrated his capacity to magnetise audiences.

But if the mechanics of promotion behind Marley may reveal a dull and unspectacular process of 'star production', his impact on the black audience of England was none the less immeasurable. Like David Bowie's immersion to the point of identification with his bisexual brainchild, Ziggy Stardust, Marley's intimacy with the Natty Dread folk hero cum devil established him as the archetypal Rastafarian menace, solidly entrenched in the mainstream of English–Jamaican mythology. Marley the Rastaman became the model for emulation by young blacks; the dreadlocks, the heavily slurred patios, the colours, the intention to live in Ethiopia, the anti-Babylon posture became clues for the suggestible black youth.

Perhaps I have erred in calling Marley a leader of Rastas, for in view of my treatment of Marcus Garvey the leader, the office of leadership might be thought to imply the spearheading of a physical movement to a specified destination (in Garvey's case, Africa). No such parallel existed in the English situation. Marley served as a guide for conduct, for posture, even for experience. I would draw the analogy of a wire between an electric instrument and the supply of electricity, with Marley constituting the vital link connecting the Rasta power supply to its vehicle in England (in this sense he might be considered a 'lead' rather than a 'leader').

He stubbornly resisted associations with comparably successful musical personalities who struck rich veins of support along social as well as purely musical dimensions. Unlike Bob Dylan and Stevie Wonder, who to a large extent transcended their roots and became institutionalised in the popular music establishment, Marley saw his role in a different light. He felt compelled to explain: 'Me hafta laugh sometime when dem scribes seh me like Mick Jagger or some superstar t'ing like dat . . . Dem hafta listen closeh to de music 'cause de message not de same . . . Noooo, mon, de reggae not de Twist, mon!' (quoted in McCormack, 1976, p. 39).

In other words, far from being the reluctant prophet, Marley understood himself as imbued with a sense of mission; he conceived of himself as a carrier of the Ras Tafari faith and his music as a vehicle for its dissemination. He made it clear that he firmly entertained the type of millenarian expectation characteristic of earlier cultists. In a BBC radio interview (Rock On, 4 June 1977) he dropped the tantalising hint that the apocalypse was near and that his fellow Rastas should prepare for the second coming of Ras Tafari. So, whilst acknowledging the greater importance of qualities and roles attributed to him rather than those of the man himself, one can nevertheless appreciate Marley's valuable contribution to the perpetuation of the mythology which grew about him. To a great extent his acceptability lay precisely in his ability to feed back the black youths' awareness of their disprivilege and emptiness and augment it with a means of at least transforming that awareness into a positive orientation. In his own words, 'Rastaman vibration yeah! *Positive.*' [Positive Vibration'.]

The English Rastafarian spread of affiliation was the product of conscious decision rather than the outcome of socialisation processes as in many religious and political phenomena. The family is often a principal, if not *the* principal vehicle in transmitting religious values to successive generations. Continuity of transmission in Jamaican families had been interrupted by abrupt disjunctures in material conditions, familial separation and profound changes in social relationships. In many circumstances, migrant parents were forced to abandon previous religious commitments and forge new religious patterns – as I have shown, Pentecostal churches were such a response. The transfer of primary allegiances by younger Jamaicans was central to the rise of Rastafarian values in England. Marley's alternative view of the world to that conventionally offered by first-generation migrants would have been hard pressed to penetrate had prevailing religious tendencies received constant reinforcement through strongly communicated parental affiliations. But such was not the case in West Indian families in England. Youths became culturally estranged from their parents; perceptions and attitudes changed as well as material conditions. As a consequence, they disaffiliated themselves from parental religious commitments and sought new avenues of experience set apart from culturally dominant modes of belief and action. The ideas and messages of Marley for many blacks provided access to such avenues lying outside traditional socialisation. His music fell on ready ears. On this view, one might see Marley as a paterfamilias as well as a leader.

The words of Bob Marley, then, reached a youthful black population whose prolonged stress in what was perceived as a hostile environment had made it sensitive to stimuli. My concern has been to show how depressions in living conditions, lack of a solid matrix of existing institutions and values, and systematic exclusions from mainstream institutional activities led blacks to a retreat into a subcultural existence where the need to develop a distinct identity went largely unsatisfied until presented with a persuasive set of guidelines as formulated in the music of Marley.

It would be a complex task trying to systematically link up the experienced deprivations of Jamaicans, both quantitative and qualitative, with the corresponding rises in receptivity to new ideas. A task I am not equipped to undertake. But, in a great many senses I feel the manifestations of Ras Tafari, its amazing popularity among young blacks and the stable basis which it consolidated in England, seem to bear out my argument.

Could the Rastafarian outbreak of the 1970s have occurred without the stimulus of Marley? Quite simply, no – unless, of course, a comparable figure in some public sphere could have been found to fulfil a similar function. Had he not appeared, it is likely that new patterns of thought and action would have occurred amongst black youth. Whether this would have been of a secular or religious nature is uncertain.

Marley proved a powerful agent, indeed, in the dissemination of Rastafarian values among the Jamaican youth of England, although he was, of course, not solely responsible for transmitting the faith. His influence was maximised by substantial commercial interests eager to promote the profitable image of the bizarre but attention-grabbing Rastaman for the purpose of economic gain. And, more recently, by the media, always ready to caricature a novelty in order to boost distribution figures, as the considerable exposure given to Marley's alleged affair with the 1976 Miss World and the attempt on his life in the midst of the Jamaican general election of 1976 attest to. The problem for many blacks was the enormous interest shown in Marley by white audiences which led to something of a shift in musical emphasis with his 1977 album 'Exodus', the 'Kaya' record of 1978 and the 'Babylon by Bus' album of 1979 revealing a pronounced western rock flavour and a seeming departure from his earthier sound of previous efforts ('Exodus' refers to the 'movement of Jah people' to their fatherland, Africa; 'Kaya' alludes to ganja, the popular theory amongst Rastas being that Marley received a visitation from Haile Selassie who instructed him to write such a song). Accusations of 'sell-out' abounded among the black community and he could have been in danger of losing his eminence in the eyes of many – though

I doubt it. The future of Marley, however, is of only marginal importance to the present book. My purpose has been to highlight the influence he has exerted over the Rastaman *nouveau* in England. Other musical exponents of Rastafarian sounds have been effective in collapsing Rasta themes into musical packages for English consumption and their sounds have been directed towards a much more racially exclusive audience, as opposed to the universalist Marley (e.g. Max Romeo; Burning Spear; Big Youth; Fred Locks); a Rastaman thought that 'Marley has been manipulated by Babylon, used maybe. But Fred Locks, Big Youth too: they're nearer the roots of the Rastaman.'

Undoubtedly pride of place must fall to Marley for he proved to be a *sine qua non* for the expansion of the Rastafarian posture. The large-scale transformations undergone during the mid-seventies explosion could not have been evoked simply by the doctrine. But they required, additionally, a human focus, in the person of a leader endowed with very special qualities. Marley came to announce and prepare for the final culminating events of history. He was no ordinary rock star, but in a world of his own; a world which thousands of other Jamaicans wanted to enter.

Most importantly for present purposes, Marley served as a role model, having himself gone through an enlightenment presumably at the hands of Mortimo Planno. His example moved others to imitation, making available the cultivation of new identities moulded on Rastafarian guidelines. But, crucially, it was the instability of some sectors of the context he was addressing which provided him with the responsive chords.

Bob Marley was arguably more important to many English Rastas of the 1970s than Marcus Garvey (though Rastas would never concede this). His profile was that of a prophet willing to extend his personal metamorphosis as a blueprint for others. Here is not the place to discuss Marley's own intentions or motivation for I am not interested in the man, but in the influence he exerted over thousands of English blacks. Marley's social relationship with his followers has been the focus of analysis; this is the critical nexus which broke down old loyalties and opened the way for new patterns of response to existing circumstances.

The impact of Marley on an already prepared black population triggered a new movement which was to find support rather than contradiction in the social environments of Brixton, Handsworth and other dense immigrant areas. After the initial Rastafarian outbreak, there were few significant barriers to prevent the contagion of enthusiasm which followed. Once doctrinal motifs and the disposition to adopt Rastafarian postures had been established, the movement spread like a rolling tide of lava through the black community. The figure of Natty Dread arrived in England.

Chapter 7

Creating Rastafarian Reality

> It takes severe biographical shocks to disintegrate the massive reality internalised in early childhood; much less to destroy the realities internalised later.
>
> *Peter Berger and Thomas Luckmann, 1972*

THE PROBLEM OF REALITIES

Rasta is not a *version* of reality, as you say; Ras Tafari *is* reality. (Dennis D., 1978)

I stated at the outset that this book was in effect an analysis of how a peculiarly Rastafarian conception of reality was possible in the context of late twentieth-century England. So far, I have looked at the reality's history, its transition and its transmission; in later chapters I will investigate how outside groups impinged on the Rastas' attempts to sustain their reality. For the moment, however, I want to examine more closely the internal mechanisms through which the Rastafarian reality was created and sustained.

Berger and Luckmann have produced an exhaustive framework for such study. Their attempt to demonstrate that 'reality is socially constructed' and that sociology should examine the process in which this occurs suggests that sociologists wishing to inquire into the reality prevalent in any group at any time must acquaint themselves with the sequences of creation, institutionalisation and transmission of such conceptions. In other words, studies of reality construction, whether within a rationally organised bureaucratic structure or within a millenarian cult, must commence with some appreciation of the subjective creation of that version of reality and then proceed through the phases by which it is maintained as an objective reality and taken to possess a 'taken for granted' character.

Under this spotlight, the social world consists of a plurality of versions of reality; some complementary, some competitive, but all essentially problematic: '*All* social reality is precarious' (Berger and Luckmann, 1972, p. 121) and in need of constant affirmation and legitimation. Just how precarious depends on the social position of the group espousing the conception of reality. Some versions have more purchase than others by virtue of their authors' right to appeal to an institutional power base, or, as Berger and Luckman express it: 'He who has the bigger stick has the better chance of imposing his definitions of reality' (1972, p. 127). So, groups controlling the principal legitimating vehicles of education, politics, the established church and, to an extent, the media have sufficient resources to make their definitions of reality 'stick' in society. Supporters of such definitions have resort to institutional power bases and, accordingly, have the conceptual machinery at their disposal to impose their versions in the most urgent and consequential manner.

On the other hand, groups creating and adhering to alternative – possibly more ingenious – forms of conceptualisation, but without institutional backing, are at an immediate disadvantage, for the resources available to them are generally insufficient for them to make any meaningful impression outside group members. These groups remain at the foot of a tier-structured hierarchy of realities. Where there is coincidence and complementarity, the chances of integration are good and the status of the marginal reality may be conferred; where there is conflict and competition, the issue of power will probably decide the future of the dissident reality.

Dropping from the theoretical realms, it is possible to see unorthodox religious movements as constituting alternative conceptualisations of the cosmos and, therefore, in a potentially competitive position *vis-à-vis* conventional definitions. The magnitude and intensity of their disagreement with established forms will determine the extent to which they will be subjected to institutional pressures. So, for example, the future of a potentially challenging and, in many ways, radical definition of reality, such as Scientology was hardly likely to be decided at the level of pure theoretical debate; it was perceived as inimical to extant realities and was punished accordingly (Wallis, 1976, ch. 7). More accommodating and innocuous were the Jehovah's witnesses who issued few challenges, stayed within acceptable boundaries and, therefore, made themselves available for integration without incurring the wrath of those groups wielding power (Beckford, 1975).

Despite the differing fortunes of these two movements, both were susceptible to institutional onslaughts because of their powerlessness. The vast majority of society did not share their beliefs, practices and perspectives and this fact alone cleared the ground for potential confrontation. If knowledge is, as Berger and Luckmann suggest, 'the certainty that phenomena are real and that they possess specific characteristics' (1972, p. 13) and that it is largely a matter of shared agreement rather than the outcome of a sensory imprint, then presumably the powerless group's body of knowledge of the world is technically open to disconfirmation. How, then, was it possible for tens of thousands of young West Indians to preserve and perpetuate a definition of reality, which was apparently susceptible to falsification, without resort to any kind of power to sanction such a definition?

It became imperative for the Rastas to develop and refine devices for coping with any attacks on their reality's core; they created conceptual machineries to maintain the continuity and logical coherence. Restriction of primary-group contacts facilitated the smooth working of such machineries (the Mormons also demonstrated the effectiveness of this). But sometimes such measures were unsuccessful and Rastas fell foul of the might of the police, courts and even the military (in Jamaica) and had their definitions subjected to pressure which threatened to force the movement underground (as, for example, occult movements were made to do).

The Rastas, as a group, presented a fundamentally different version of reality than that prevailing in contemporary English society, offering insights, theories and hypotheses quite alien to those contained in the stock of social and, in particular, religious knowledge. The Rastafarian movement's members in Jamaica were able to maintain a distinctive and, by conventional criteria, bizarre lifestyle and set of beliefs by severely limiting their contacts with actors outside the immediate collectivity and sometimes reinforcing geographical separation. Their English offspring had no such recourse to insulatory methods for they grew out of the urban centres of London, Birmingham and Manchester and had to tackle the ever-present hurdles of disconfirmation, illegitimation and other institutional pressures which threatened Ras Tafari's conceptual structure. Also, the original Rastas developed in a society which had encouraged and been conducive to the growth of deviant religious beliefs; the neoteric Rastas were something of an anomaly in modern industrial England. Even if the movement's members themselves did not feel their knowledge was open to disconfirmation, their lack of an institutional base, their minimal ideological coherence (due to epistemological individualism) and the constraints on them articulating their views posed serious problems to the whole movement's existence. Yet Ras Tafari became the most dominant and vital force to enter the lives of thousands of black youths and change their total lifestyles: 'Ras Tafari is not just a religion; it is a total way of life – it is my life,' affirmed a Rastaman.

There can be no doubt that the movement was an urban anomaly and a vulnerable one. Historically, millenarian phenomena flourish in relatively isolated agrarian milieux where their conceptual machineries remain unviolated by the iconoclastic forces of technology and science (see Burridge, 1969; Wilson, 1973; Barkun, 1974). Clearly, a movement worshipping Haile Selassie as its God and messiah and committing itself to taking all blacks to Africa was ill suited to the vortex of modern industrial life. But its members remained steadfast in their conviction that they had found the true path to salvation: 'The only truth is Jah. I can find truth only through Ras Tafari.' But there were few obvious mechanisms through which this reality was sustained; it becomes necessary to scratch deeper and analyse the processes and strategies at work in support of the Rastafarian reality. It is an exercise which takes as its starting point Berger and Luckmann's programme:

> in so far as all human knowledge is developed, transmitted and maintained in social situations, the sociology of knowledge must seek to understand the processes by which this is done in such a way that a taken-for-granted 'reality' congeals for the man in the street. In other words, we contend that *the sociology of knowledge is concerned with the analysis of the social construction of reality.* (1972, p. 15)

THE CONSTRUCTION OF AN ALTERNATIVE REALITY

The lack of any single leader forceful enough to impose an inflexible definition of what was to constitute the doctrine was contributory to one of the movement's central characteristics, that being what Roy Wallis calls epistemological individualism: 'the cult has no clear locus of final authority beyond the individual member' (1976, p. 14). The common stock of Rastafarian knowledge crystallised at only two points: (1) the divinity of Haile Selassie; (2) the importance of Africa as a physical entity and a spiritual, intellectual and cultural focus. These were linked by the fact that accepting Haile Selassie by implication meant that the believer also became convinced of his God's ability and intention to set in motion the African redemption.

Apart from these, the determination of what was to be accepted as the Rastafarian doctrine was largely up to individual interpretation and inference. The total belief system was available for adaptation by the individual brothers. So vague was the doctrine that little or no demands were made of the member, save for worshipping Haile Selassie and regarding Africa as his true home (this was, of course, part of the implicit appeal of the movement among black youth). But around these two principles a whole conception of reality was built, one which impelled young blacks to new modes of thought and action. While the Rastas shared an agreement as to the fundamental and ordered character of a factual domain independent of any mode of inquiry, there were certain accounts made by members which seemed to be clearly contradictory to empirical reality. For example, the Rastafarian claim that they were really Ethiopian would have seemed to be wide open to falsification; they were from England, or the West Indies and even their roots were not in Ethiopia but in West African coastal countries from where slaves were taken. Haile Selassie, it could be argued, was no more than a former Emperor of Ethiopia and never claimed any status beyond this. The expected transformation of the world and the return of all blacks to Africa would not happen and African countries would certainly not accept thousands of West Indians on any permanent basis. These were just a selection of the ways in which the critical observer might have brought off victories over the Rastaman and expose his beliefs as erroneous and ill-founded. And these were the type of allegations often levelled at the movement. So, it becomes interesting to ask exactly how the Rastafarian reality retained plausibility for its adherents; how its plausibility structure kept solidity.

Having accepted the divinity of Haile Selassie, the Rasta was subjected to a stream of reminders that the acceptance was genuine and correct, that the total rupture with the parental culture was an entry to the path to salvation. Responsible for reminding newer affiliates were those who had already drifted near the core of the movement to such an extent that they had unconditionally accepted Haile Selassie's divinity. The chief method through which the reminding was done was 'reasoning' procedures: the discussion and interpretation of virtually any topic had the effect of mutually reassuring the new acceptor and he who had already accepted. Michael Barkun summarises nicely: 'The individual who assures someone else that his act was right also assures himself. And when he sees the effect of his reassurance on the other, he is again confirmed in the rightness of his own position' (1974, pp. 114–15).

The implication of this was that during the late 1970s, when the movement's membership grew quite phenomenally, credence was constantly being lent to the belief system by virtue of the growing numbers: 'Each new person won over provides supportive evidence for those won over earlier' (Barkun, 1974, p. 117). So that the plausibility structure of the movement strengthened with each member. Given that reality is a matter of shared agreement (*pace* Berger and Luckmann), then, the growing volume of the cult itself functioned as a means of confirming the correctness or truth if its ideology. The mechanisms were summarised by a Rasta: 'Man, look around you; can all these Rastas be wrong?' First, then, the movement's growth was self-perpetuating and conducive to the consolidation of the Rastafarian reality.

Secondly, the disjuncture with the parental culture was completed with the acceptance of Ras Tafari; and this break symbolised the drift into a whole new reality, or the acquisition of new conceptual maps with which to comprehend the world. The endeavour to 'revive our true self and really know our ability by discovering our history' began in earnest once the rupture was consummated; they could then reflect back on how their parents were 'misguided' or 'brainwashed', or, as one Rasta put it: 'We believe that perhaps the majority of blacks in this country are still in a state of mind that can be described as not a conscious state of mind.'

Although there was no ritual accompanying the break with the old order as represented by other blacks, comparable to, for example, the Mau Mau initiation rites and oaths which involved extreme violations of Kikuyu taboos (cf. Corfield, 1960; Barnett and Njama, 1960, pp. 125–6), there was the suggestion of a total rejection of their past: 'I now look at myself as a proper person; I wasn't myself before'; 'I and I didn't know ourselves . . . now we're making positive steps to find our true selves', were retrospective remarks. The break with the old 'brainwashed' order and the entry into the new, meant that black youths attained not only fresh ways of looking at the world, but also a new way of cognising themselves: 'It's for I and I to revive the true self.' This realisation of the true self was conditional on the break with the old order and everything representative of it. But in doing this, the young blacks surrendered themselves to the new reality, a reality which contained an explanation of why they had laboured for years not knowing their true potentialities, why their parents were still labouring, and why they as the 'enlightened' people had cause to be optimistic about the future. Answers to all these questions were found in the Babylonian conspiracy theory.

THE BABYLONIAN CONSPIRACY

The black youth's isolation in the impoverished enclaves of urban England rendered him particularly vulnerable to a multiplying series of personal and communal traumas: familial fragmentation, unempolyment, crime and, of course, white racialism. Throughout the 1960s and 1970s the process was at work whereby visible differences were used as a basis for residential patterning: ghettoisation. Asian immigrants were, to a certain extent, prepared to draw upon their cultural traditions and organise communities around religious groupings. Early incoming West Indians turned inward to the passive and withdrawing Pentecostal-type churches. These were largely defensive strategies designed as buffers against the cycle of upheavals used by groups without sufficient resources to directly confront the sources of their anxieties. Over the years, the urban divisions became more institutionalised, creating the environmental conditions well suited to the formation of culturally different groups drawing into themselves sufficiently to maintain some degree of cultural autonomy. Combined with the motivation of group members to remain apart, the black ghetto became fertile ground for the growth of explanatory schemes facilitating the comprehension of current circumstances and ways of improving them.

All members of society house theories and ideas which help them understand present conditions; they may be drawn from the ideology of groups or they may be idiosyncratic, or a mixture of the two. But they are not always elevated to the level of consciousness where they can be critically debated in reasoned discourse. Where a group has, because of its weak social structural position, proved particularly vulnerable to upheavals and has experienced series of social crises, the problem of theodicy takes on paramountcy; the group has to search for reasons and ideas to explain adequately its continuing misfortune. The interpretation of evil may assume a strictly secular character or, as in the case of the Rastafarian movement, may blend the secular with supernatural themes to produce a formula not only for history but for future social transformation. The Rastas held to a vision of a radically changed social order in which they would ultimately travel to Africa and the grip of the white man would be nullified. But this vision was built on a steady theoretical foundation which explained the history and current circumstances of the black man and which incorporated a demand for the assuagement of present ills. Here I am interested not in the general Rastafarian theory of history *per se*, but specifically in how it functioned to defuse potentially disrupting events in the social world and explain them away within its own framework.

The appeal of the Rastafarian theory lay in the range of effects imputed to a single malevolent cause – Babylon. This was the source of all evil in the world and its destruction would presage the start of what Rastas called 'the new age', the entry into Zion. Like many other movements of dissidence, Ras Tafari saw the world as split into two distinct spheres, good and evil, the saved and the damned, Zion and Babylon. Only the dissolution of Babylon and its colonial machinery would suffice in clearing the path to Rastafarian salvation. This simple attribution of all blame and cause of anxiety to a single source established a theoretical thrust which served as the basis for a number of other important formulations. To summarise them:

(1) The Rastas were the reincarnations of the ancient tribes of Israel who had been enslaved and kept in exile by their white oppressors, the agents of Babylon.
(2) The entire history of the black man since his contact with whites should be understood in terms of a systematic denial of freedom, material and cognitive, and every event in the development of colonialism was a recycle of the same pattern.
(3) This pattern was the attempt of the white man to suppress the black's thought, his energies and potentialities.

(4) Haile Selassie was God, but white slavemasters and missionaries concealed this from the black man by force-feeding him mistranslated versions of the Bible; Rastas penetrated this and were cognisant of Haile Selassie's divinity and his efforts to transport them to Africa where they would resume their former dignity.

(5) Haile Selassie, though conventionally thought to be dead, was either in hiding, had assumed another form or was still as strongly present in all men despite his death.

The mechanics of colonialism were thought to perpetuate the obfuscation and militate against the black man's realisation of his own gifts and capacities. Because of their lack of resources, blacks had always been open targets for the military superior whites and could not withstand the impositions of Western religions which served the exigencies of Babylon and dimmed the black man's vision.

The contemporary Rastaman did not have to look beyond his periphery into history, to Africa and to the New World to find support for his theories: he saw and felt the oppression of Babylon in his day-to-day life, 'pressure' and 'suffering'. Giving his personal account of 'pressure', a Rasta said: 'I experience certain things: that a black youth cannot walk the streets at night without a chance of being picked up by the police, a chance of being beaten up by the National Front . . . we can't get a job because of our religion, the colour of our skin. Social-wise we can't walk the streets after certain hours . . . [the Rastaman] has to adapt himself to receive the pressure.'

What is more the Rastas' penetration of the workings of Babylon was seen to make their struggle harder; as one Rasta told me, he had to take 'oppression from men all because of what I stand for' but 'the faith is the strength to overcome the oppression'. They believed that every move they made was being noted and documented by the agents of Babylon: 'Babylon is a clever creature, very clever. It makes the black man fight it so that it can crack back at I.' This was an interesting acknowledgement of the black's impotence and the need to withdraw from any possible clashes with authority, the most obvious example of which was the police, though some were less emphatic about the need to avoid conflict and remained adamant that the Rastaman should 'stand up for his rights' and suffer the consequences; a Rasta asked: 'Why should I care if I get mashed and locked up? Jah is I and looking after I.'

Some projected from the Babylonian conspiracy theory and speculated that politics in England were moving inexorably to the right so as to oppress the black man even more. This view, it was suggested, was 'realistic' and not 'pessimistic' and the topicality of the National Front Party in the late 1970s was often cited as indicative of this trend. A physical remove was the only alternative to such oppression and members sharing this conception of the future tended to see the redemption as something to be encouraged and worked towards rather than simply waited for. In other words, the transformation process would have to be started by Rastas themselves and this would still be a manifestation of God's action because he was inhering in all Rastas.

Despite the conviction that the transformation was inevitable ('must come') there remained the ever-present threat that Babylon would retaliate and, knowing of the imminence of its fall, attempt to repress blacks even further. Asked for evidence of this, a Rasta replied: 'The existence of South Africa and Rhodesia is a perfect example of it being possible for us to be enslaved again because we have seen the hypocrisy of the West in condemning the atrocities committed in South Africa and Rhodesia. And these same people that condemn them are the people that South Africa needs to sustain its military supremacy in Africa. So we can see that we can and would be enslaved again – perhaps not in the way that has taken place in the past because man has increased his knowledge and therefore obtained more subtle means of oppression. But nevertheless it would amount to the enslavement of our people again.'

The 'more subtle' means of oppression were thought to lead to enslavement of a mental kind, a condition which only Rastas had escaped. A Rasta offered his view: 'They're [non-Rasta blacks] enslaved mentally because until one finds liberation of the mind then one can never hope for the body to be liberated. We believe that perhaps the majority of blacks in this country are still in a state of mind that can be described as not of a conscious state of mind.' (The words might easily have come from the lips of Marcus Garvey.) One of the most effective devices employed by Babylon to ensure this was conventional Christianity which had for years been the handmaiden of colonialism, 'the Imperial machine of the West': 'I and I now understand how the Imperial Machine of the West and the religions that served it were designed to oppress all the black peoples in the world. Because they realised this, they found it necessary to subscribe to a religion that was completely African in its origin.' Subscription to an English church was 'to submit yourself to exploitation and control'. Having been steeped in Christianity since childhood (and the majority of Rastas came from devoutly religious backgrounds) the Rastaman had to wipe out former conceptions in a process of mental erasure: 'These Biblical concepts we had to erase from our mentality.' Those still accepting them were derided as 'fools of Babylon' who had been duped into believing there was a white God when it was clearly written in Jeremiah 8:21: 'For the hurt of the daughter of my people I am hurt: I am black; astonishment hath taken hold on me.' The new conceptual maps which came with the acceptance of Ras Tafari provided for a reflective analysis of old religious forms in terms of the system they served and supported.

Like most conspiracy theories, the resolution was simplistic but comprehensive: the destruction of Babylon. The precise manner in which this was to come about was never clearly spelt out, but the Rastas were total in their conviction that it was inevitable and that it was God's will: 'It's written in the Bible already . . . this is the last days'; 'Must come'. Revelation was the most important book in the Bible for Rastas and this was seen to contain a foretelling of the transformation, which was preceded by, as a Rasta put it, 'the last days': 'According to the prophecy of Revelation the beast shall emerge in the last days. We now see the rise of the Common Market and we see that it is written in Revelations that my children are to leave Babylon.' (As an aside to this quote, I might add that some Rastas were convinced that the process of destruction was already in motion, while others thought the process would not begin until the grip of colonialism was broken.)

The Babylonian conspiracy theory made the world fully transparent to the Rastaman and gave him knowledge of the deceptions at work to discredit him; what might otherwise have been mistaken for damaging events (for example, the death of Haile Selassie) were reduced to epiphenomena: 'the lies of Babylon.' As such, the conspiracy theory strengthened the Rastafarian sense of reality through a process of revelation. By this I mean that as every new situation unfolded the Rasta was able to refer back to his encyclopaedic formula and make sense of it in Rastafarian terms. His ways of attending the world, in the manner of the self-fulfilling prophecy, conjured up its objective features: the reality of Babylon and its agents scheming and conspiring to subordinate the black man's body and mind as they had done for 400 years. Everything they said or did was to be comprehended within the framework of the conspiracy and, therefore, penetrated and decoded. It was for this reason that the status of the source of any information contrary to Rastafarian expectations was to be established before any judgement on it could be made; if the sources were of Babylon then its knowledge could only be construed as self-serving ideology perpetuating an artificial reality; as one Rasta put it, 'Imperial propaganda'.

The Babylonian conspiracy theory was a developed procedure to protect the precarious Rastafarian reality and reinforce members' convictions. It provided the theoretical support for giving a highly abstruse conception of reality an objective and ordered character and lent to it a subjective plausibility in the consciousness of the Rastas. It was the theoretical cornerstone of the whole belief system and as such legitimated the Rastafarian reality.

THE EXISTENCE OF A BROTHERHOOD

One of the noticeable features of the movement was its lack of formal social organisation which would have facilitated the establishment of channels of communication and the possibility of constantly recharging the beliefs with fresh infusions of information. The two institutional forms, the Ethiopian Orthodox Church and the Twelve Tribes of Israel, had somewhat rudimentary organisations and undeveloped lines of communication, but the vast majority of Rastas were affiliated to neither group. The consequence was an atomised Rastafarian population and no network of structured contact, save for the regular reasoning sessions, which was a limited intra-peer group activity. Opportunities to mobilise adherents and promote, for example, Bible-reading classes, instruction in the Amharic language or discussions on improving relations with police were created by informally organised groups (such as the Exodus group in Birmingham), but such meetings were sporadic and not well attended. As one baptised member of the EOC observed with slight resentment: 'Being Rasta is more exciting than going to church and doing constructive things.'

When groups did get together on a more organised level it was primarily for symbolic or expressive rather than instrumental purposes. The main point of contact was the reasoning session, but reggae concerts featuring Rastafarian outfits were also attended by Rastas (though they had to contend with the intrusions of non-Rastafarian reggae enthusiasts). Nevertheless, the crystallisation of members into smaller enclaves within the concert gave at least a short-lived opportunity to reinforce each others' convictions and draw sustenance from witnessing the performing artists whose allegiances fell squarely with Ras Tafari.

Reggae artists commanding status and prestige were important in exteriorising the movement's presence to the 'outside world' and convincing members of its currency. As such, it was taken as an acknowledgement of the all-pervasive nature of Ras Tafari and, therefore, supportive of the belief that linked Rastas together as a movement: the existence of the brotherhood.

Because contacts were infrequent or non-existent apart from small group constellations and reggae concerts, and no organisation existed even in an embryonic form some unifying adhesive had to be found, if only to hold the members together as a movement as opposed to a heterogeneous aggregation. The brotherhood functioned as a replacement for effective means of communicating and co-ordinating action; it served to promote the conviction that all black men were descended from common stock in Africa and that they had been scattered throughout the Western world by the fragmenting forces of colonialism. No extensive genealogical charts were needed to substantiate this belief for the relationship was clearly manifested in skin colour. Thus any black man was perceived as part of the African complement of the world's population, a perception which motivated Rastas to criticise assimilating blacks, particularly those adhering to conventional Christian beliefs, for failing to recognise their background; 'misguided' and 'brainwashed' were illustrative adjectives to describe other blacks. Ultimately, all blacks were Africans; but only the Rastas had realised this. Accordingly, they were an élite group, the chosen few who would be saved come the holocaust: 'I man realise his true self, his destiny.'

The brotherhood had defined boundaries on the basis of skin colour, but only Rastas were acknowledged as self-conscious members. 'Knowing one's culture' was a precondition to becoming aware of one's membership in the brotherhood. Once the black youth realised that Africa was in him, then he could embark on the voyage of discovery for the 'true self', the roots-searching process. Fellow Rastas were regarded as being closely and intimately related and this promoted a strong sense of in-group solidarity, or 'we-ness'. It also allowed for Rastas who may never have seen each other to enter into what an outsider might view as an intimate relationship without any suggestion of inquiry into background – the only background they were interested in was that they all came from Africa in the first instance; one Rasta expressed it in Bob Marley's terms: 'Rasta knows everything he needs to know about his brethren: we know where we're going, we know where we're from.'

An implication of this sharing of a belief in the brotherhood, or fraternity of brethren, was that it imposed restrictions on the Rasta's relationship to his environment by perpetuating the commitment to a world whose structures were predetermined by man's biological constitution. Because of the perceived commonness of birth-place and visible, physical similarities, the black man was seen as a creature of specific portions of the earth's surface, his relationship to which was fixed and unshakable (quoting Garvey's use of the Bible: 'The leopard can never change his spots; nor the Ethiopian his colours'). In effect, the black man was thought to belong rightfully in Africa, the centre of gravity of the brotherhood, and it was to this fatherland he should return. The displacement of blacks and the 'artificial' division of the continent of 'Ethiopia' into separate African states were seen as a strategies introduced by the colonialists to prevent the creation of what Garvey called 'a new world of black men'. Had nature been allowed to take its course, all blacks would still be living in Africa, Orientals in Asia and the rest of the world's population distributed spatially throughout the world. The Rastas believed that only a return to their fatherland would permit future development. The notion of a brotherhood encouraged the sense of rightfully belonging in a closed world, a culturally and biologically distinct section of the earth where the range of possibilities would be unhindered by the interference of outsiders. Only in this way could a proper African culture be developed and the 'true self' be revived.

Strengthening this subjective conviction in the existence of a black Rastafarian brotherhood was the principle of 'I and I', which, in the words of a Rastaman, 'expresses the oneness between two persons'. God was thought to inhere in all men; but only Rastas realised and accepted this; they were bound together, therefore, by this recognition. Subject–object dualisms were broken down 'because God is in man' and the 'bond of the Rastaman is the bond of God'. Not only were Rastas united by their common position in the relationship with Babylon (as those who were constantly subjected to persecution under 'pressure') but they were joined by the realisation that God was within them: 'Selassie I is in the hearts of man' (the recognition was more important in bonding than the actual fact that God was in men). So, in Rastafarian vocabulary reference to others was usually made in the first person: 'I and I feel the pressure each and every day.'

But the sheer belief in a common descent and the inherence of Haile Selassie and the concomitant existence of a uniting brotherhood was insufficient to hold tens of thousands of Rastas together; the structure was held not only by beliefs augmented by visible symbols but by the subjection to habitualised activities. The way in which blacks were regarded and treated by whites Rastas thought had been cast into a pattern over four centuries and, although the intensity and intonation of whites' relationships with blacks had altered at different times and in different contexts, the basic relationship between persecutor and persecuted had been reproduced consistently; enslavement took on many guises for the Rastaman. The Rastas drew on their knowledge of this pattern and used it as a background against which to make sense of their own experience and those of their fellow brothers. Revealed was a consistency subsuming a large variety of situations where blacks and whites had come into contact. Apprehension of this pattern implied that the unequal relationship in question would be repeated in the future in much the same manner as the past and the present; the 'Imperial machine of the West' of the Babylonian conspiracy would seek to enslave black men wherever it encountered them, whether it be on the African Gold Coast in the seventeenth century or on the streets of Brixton in the twentieth century. The meaning of slavery, of oppression, of marginality, of subordination was embedded in the consciousness of the Rastaman: 'It's all about suffering', explained one Rasta, 'the black man has been trodden on for 400 years and there's no reason why Babylon won't try to keep it that way!'

In other words, the way in which the black man had been treated and the Rastas' experience of whites in their personal history and day-to-day life provided proof of the existence of the brotherhood. The perception that all blacks were treated in exactly the same manner by whites suggested that there must be something similar about them which exerted a powerful influence on the thought of others and impelled them to action: 'For 400 years blacks have been dealt with by whites; brutalised and mashed; but now I and I can see the light – now we know why,' a Rasta informed. The conduct of whites towards blacks was seen as just the latest sequence of the historical process which was ineluctable and moving inexorably towards its climax; the destruction of Babylon and the black man's return to Zion.

THE REALISATION OF A NEW IDENTITY

The establishment of a mutual identification between Rastas through the nexus of a pervasive brotherhood, plus the formulation of a theoretical basis on which to interpret all events in the social cosmos allowed the members to not only live in the same subworld and to be subjected to the same treatments, but also to share each other's being, I and I. Consequently, the Rastaman was made to acquire a subjectively plausible and coherent identity which was based, first, on the acquisition of others' attitudes towards him. The process fed a congruence between objective and subjective realities because in appropriating his self-identity the Rasta, by implication, appropriated his specific location within an objective social world, a location which was filtered to him through the roles and attitudes of his other brethren. Expressed another way: the formation in consciousness of a self-identity coincided and congealed with the apprehension of the reality of which that identity was part; establishing a place in the world simultaneously established the reality of that world.

Most critically, the period of primary socialisation creates for and in the individual the most deeply embedded consciousness of the world and, however much this may be weakened by subsequent events, the basic interpretive platform for understanding and applying meaning to the world remains. The first learnt reality of childhood has a firmness or solidity which, to a large extent, precludes any possibility of doubt or suspicion. Becoming a Rastaman involved a secondary socialisation in which a great deal of what was learnt in earlier phases had to be interpreted in the light of Rastafarian concepts. Hence the process of mental erasure and the acquisition of new understandings, enriched by 'insight'. Socialisation into the Rastafarian subworld posed special difficulties which were not likely to be encountered in less embracing realities. It was a problem germane to any religious movement requiring its members to apprehend the world in a fundamentally different manner than the one they have been taught in later childhood and therefore to perceive themselves in a totally new light. Two Rastas' comments indicate the extent to which they transformed their self-conceptions after accepting Ras Tafari: 'I now look at myself as a proper person; I wasn't myself before'; 'Before I and I didn't know ourselves . . . now we're making positive steps to find our true selves.'

The modern Rastas of England rejected the world represented by their parents, by their schools and generally by white society ('Rasta don't want no part of that world'); and, concomitantly, rejected definitions of themselves as reflected in these groups and institutions. Theirs was a recognition that the world they had been presented with was a masquerade produced and orchestrated by the oppressive agents of Babylon: 'We were just blinded by the European thought' – but Ras Tafari brought new sight. If their parents had been duped into taking for granted the reality offered, then they would continue to suffer the consequences of humiliation and depression. Not so for the Rastaman: his effort was to detach himself from this conception and penetrate the mystique, at the same time envisioning himself as the forerunner of a different reality; he was a fugitive from the reality of his parents.

But there was no smooth transition from the reality sedulously cultivated by first-generation West Indian migrants and schools to the radically different Rastafarian conception of reality. The lack of continuity between the two suggests sequences of traumas, serving to loosen the youth's allegiances of his early childhood. The personal destruction of parts of reality internalised in primary socialisation was detonated by a series of identity shocks. Whatever degree of identification West Indian migrants or British-born children of migrants had possessed in relation to England had been relaxed during the later stages of secondary school. As I revealed in Chapter 5, every Rasta experienced the discrepancy between the expectation that he had been denied that participation on the grounds that he was black. The absurdity of being 'black' and being 'British' was rammed home to them and this constituted something of a milestone in their imaginations: the certainty of the first dawn of a racialist reality. To repeat a Rastaman: 'The leopard can never change his spots and the Ethiopian his colours; it is inevitable that we, as black people, were never and can never be part of this country where we do not belong.'

Subsequent exposures to the realities of racism and racialism at school and the workplace reinforced awarenesses of cultural vacuity; the feeling that they would never find acceptance in English culture, a culture which they saw as the sole property of whites and those blacks prepared to assimilate sufficiently. This sense of vacuity opened up the needs for explaining the reasons for such a condition and for providing some sort of nucleus of an alternative definition of the self other than that offered by white culture.

But, as I have made clear, the first stirrings of this awareness did not prompt an automatic 'search' for explanatory frameworks and alternative conceptions of the self. The interim period between the awareness of racialism and the acceptance of Ras Tafari – and, of course, the accompanying repudiation of white society – I characterised by using David Matza's concept of 'drift', to describe a condition of cultural limbo in which the youth escaped the control of the parental culture. Matza elaborates: 'Its basis is an area of social structure in which control has been loosened . . . Drift is motion guided gently by underlying influences . . . Drift is a gradual process of movement . . .' (1966, pp. 28–9).

To go over the scenario once more, it is my contention that the prospective Rastas, whilst conforming and adhering to what might be called the 'conventional values' of their parental culture in their childhood, experienced a series of biographical shocks, triggered by the discrepancy between what they expected out of society and what they thought they might get. These shocks served to loosen their attachments to the existing order in value terms. Whilst acknowledging that there is not a readily definable criterion with which to compare the disenchanted blacks' changing values, it seems plausible to allow some latitude for the co-existence of what Matza calls 'subterranean values', which emerged and might even have taken precedent when conventional commitments were weakened.

For the most part, Rastas' families had been avowedly intent on pursuing 'the British way of life'; they were prepared to forego some of the fuller benefits of participation in English society because of the memory of the worse conditions they had left behind in the depressed West Indies. Their children, if born abroad possessed only dim recollections of this and, as a consequence, expected a more rewarding life in England. When the realisation that they were to be denied full status and were doomed to remain second-order participants in society filtered through their imaginations, their allegiance to the legitimate moral order became strained and they came to exist in a kind of existential limbo, responding sometimes to the demands of convention and at other times to the demands of subterranean imperatives, 'the search for adventure, excitement and thrill'. Some Rastas had been in trouble with the police either before or after their involvement with the movement. The emergence of subterranean values as dominant motivating vectors of social action would, in all probability, make this understandable. Certainly, the lack of social control exerted by the West Indian family, due historically to the fragmentation of family structure in slavery, but exacerbated by migration, was permissive of this drift away from convention.

But, of course, this goes no way towards detecting the source of attraction inherent in subterranean values. I can only formulate the speculative view that the repulsion from wider societal values, initiated by the expectation of acceptance and the experience and realisation of rejection on what were considered racial grounds, stimulated an availability for any kind of activity which lay outside the realms of 'respectable' society. They were simply drawn to those modes of activity which were most freely available and which tended to contradict the definition of the self offered in childhood; thus exerting countervailing pressures on the internalised social identity of early periods.

The drift towards the Rastafarian movement is not to be regarded as inevitable or inexorable, but as a fluid affair in which growing familiarity with Rastafarian concepts, theories and ambitions produced a steady cognitive influence; appreciation of Rasta themes prepared the way for the acceptance of Haile Selassie. This is not to suggest that the prospective Rastas were propelled; the drift may have been deflected by external events, such as being offered a responsible job, or by personal adjustments such as the realisation that Christianity was the only road to salvation. (One black youth told me of how he had been initially attracted to Ras Tafari and was becoming familiar with its themes, when he experienced a vision in which Haile Selassie and Jesus Christ appeared before him and announced that Christ was the true Son of God; after this he joined the Seventh Day Adventists.) But, for the most part, Rastas suggested that their reasoning associations with interested friends and their intensifying familiarity with Rastafarian-inspired music fuelled a motivation to learn about and become involved with this new and alternative source of knowledge.

To summarise then, my suggested scheme for recruitment into the second stage of socialisation and the concomitant acquisition of a new identity proceeded through four phases:

(1) *The Apprehension* – of being denied full participation in society on the grounds that they were black.
(2) *The Loss* – of plausibility of their parents' beliefs.
(3) *The Drift* – to Ras Tafari in a phase of limbo.
(4) *The Acceptance* – of Haile Selassie as God and the changes in self-identity this brought with it.

The character of the secondary socialisation the youth underwent once drift to the movement was under way depended on the differing assumptions and perspectives he held, as well as his personal experiences throughout the process of drift. The transition was sometimes trouble-torn and laced with conflicts with the law, or relatively smooth and devoid of any serious conflict with authority. Such experiences coloured the individual's view of himself and his place in the Rastafarian subworld. Though all Rastas to a great extent internalised a rough calculus, the way in which they manipulated it varied with their own particular interests and circumstances. This was facilitated by the epistemological individualism which characterised the movement. Accepting that Haile Selassie was God and that all black men were originally from Africa, a continent to which they must some day return, did not furnish the accepter with stipulations as to his thought and behaviour; it provided only the nucleus for the apprehension of a different reality and a special place in that reality for the Rastaman.

The absence of directive was compounded by the anonymity implied in the existence of I and I. The Rasta was provided with new formulae for making sense of the world and himself; for instance, he received no formal assignment to 'spread the word' (though many said they had a 'mission' – without detailing what it was). Yet the lack of programmatic imperative did little to diminish the profound subjective impact on the individual in building up a high degree of recognition and identification with other Rastas and inducing him to manoeuvre thoughts in accordance with new, original insights. The Rastaman conceptually retranslated his world. The more he drifted to the core of the movement, the more subjectively plausible its world view became and, in turn, this affected the quality of his social relationships with fellow blacks. Some Rastas reckoned they had lost friends through their affiliation and relationships with the older generation were most assuredly aggravated: 'They can't see the world like Rasta and so think Rasta a bad thing; it's impossible for them to relate to us and I to them.' But the consequence of this experience was the increasing inability to segmentalise this portion of the Rastaman's life from others: 'Rasta is a way of life; it *is* my life.' The distance between his total self and the Rastafarian conception of reality was shortened with successive acquisitions of new knowledge, and the awareness that being Rastafarian was no role-specific activity sometimes produced crises. The most obvious manifestation of this was the break with families: disapproving parents sometimes ordered their children to leave home because of their new allegiances; less dramatic were instances of pure tension in domestic life. Accepting Ras Tafari broke the links with childhood realities.

There were no specific agencies nor predetermined sequences for the Rastafarian phase of socialisation. My view is that it was a self-intensifying activity in which the individual's appetite was whetted with a definition of reality which ran counter to conventionally accepted models and increased his awareness of its 'truth' through progressive reasoning and relevant reading; a stage arrived at when the acceptance of Ras Tafari as the only God became inevitable and the Rastafarian reality constituted the 'natural facts of life'. These facts were supported and reinforced by the theoretical premises contained in the Babylonian conspiracy which served to explain, and make meaningful, events in the world. In such a way, a congruence was achieved between subjective and objective realities. The process was never complete even after the acceptance: 'The learning never stops.' But, when doubts about the 'true' nature of the Rastafarian reality were quashed and the divinity of Haile Selassie accepted, the Rasta conception became less susceptible to displacement – it came to be taken for granted. After I had suggested that there were several ways of interpreting the 'facts' of reality and Ras Tafari was but one of them, a Rasta retorted: 'Rasta is not a *version* of reality, as you say; it *is* reality.'

Despite its status as the real world and as a product of activities in the real world, the Rastafarian reality was persistently open to challenge and so, therefore, was the Rastafarian self-identity. And here the ways in which the three elements combine become apparent: the theory of a Babylonian conspiracy giving an interpretive platform for making sense of external events; the concept of an all-pervasive brotherhood replacing and fulfilling the functions of formal organisation; and the transformed subjective reality. Given the enclosed nature of the cult and the restriction of primary contacts between Rastas, the onus was on significant others to maintain the congruence of objective and subjective realities and to confirm the subjective identity dimension of the enterprise. The identity of the Rastaman was at the nexus of objective and subjective realities; he conceived of a reality and located himself a specific place in that reality where he could cultivate a sense of selfhood and belongingness; where he could 'revive the true self'. In order to remain convinced of who he actually was, he looked to others for confirmation. If he looked to whites or non-Rastafarian blacks he would not have found the requisite support and probably have received ridicule, dismissal and disconfirmation. But, by reference back to the Babylonian conspiracy he could infer that these disconfirming statements were merely ploys or strategies in the wider plan to destroy the credibility of Ras Tafari and re-enslave its members in conceptual manacles; 'mental enslavement' as it was called. The disconfirmative responses were assimilated in terms of the conspiracy.

On the other hand, the Rastas were committed to the existence of a brotherhood, the enlightened members of which shared a penetrative understanding of reality. The Rastas were bound to look to these brothers, or brethren, for explicit confirmation of identity; and they received it. These significant others in the member's life were the principal agents in the maintenance of subjective reality; they supplied the day-to-day reaffirmation and, as such, occupied a privileged position in the process of identity sustentation. Non-Rastas also occupied a privileged position, but in the process of supporting the conspiracy theory. No amount of negative and antagonistic responses on the part of the wider society could outweigh the positive responses of other brethren; they could only confirm the conspiracy thinking. The two totally differing sets of responses were strange bedpartners in complementary processes, both of which lent support to and perpetuated the objective and subjective realities at the intersection of which resided the Rastafarian identity (see Figure 4).

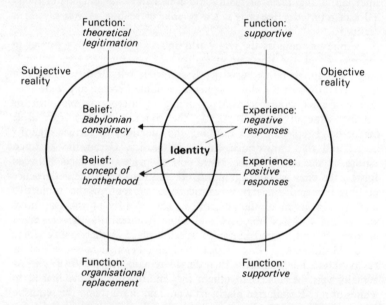

Figure 4   *Elements and Processes in the Rastafarian Reality*

The importance of social interaction between fellow Rastas in supporting conceptions of the self and reality should not be overlooked. Casual conversational exchanges in stylised patios which enabled them to communicate with Rastas in allusion rich in meaning but quite abstruse to outsiders, promoted the sense of kinship. It kept open semantic fields peculiar to the Rasta and maintained the flow of vectors of interactional reality-generation, whilst at the same time precluding too much opportunity for doubt about the definition of reality and concretising its plausibility. Effectively, the other members of the enlightened brotherhood mediated the reality of Ras Tafari to the individual. In this sense, membership to the movement implied a radical re-education and Rastas continually acknowledged this: 'Rasta is a form of education. It reveals the missing dimensions which European educations have concealed from us.'

But, of course, establishing a course for a new reality, whether borrowed as in Ras Tafari (i.e. from the Jamaican movement) or created *ex nihilo*, and following that course are two entirely different processes; and I am mindful of the exceptions which might be taken to my argument. To have contact with the ideas, messages, precepts etc. of the movement, to adopt its symbols, motifs, emblems and language and to assert one's commitment to the faith is one thing; to keep on taking it seriously as a new reality is quite another. Religious ideas *per se* lend themselves to manifold and often contradictory uses. They are ambiguous in the extreme and necessarily so. Accordingly, the concepts and categories of Ras Tafari were interpreted, manipulated and utilised in a variety of ways: sometimes as a sanction for criminal behaviour; sometimes as a basis for withdrawal or retreat from the wider society. Allegations that the religious commitment was little more than a justification for wanton misdemeanour ensued. But even if this charge was with foundation, it does not undermine my assertion that the individual's world found its cognitive and affective locus in the reality of Ras Tafari. The precise motivation behind accepting the faith of Ras Tafari could not be answered without resort to specifying individual circumstances and experiences, which is not my concern. I have attempted only a broad account of the shift in realities and the methods used for sustaining the Rastafarian reality. Ras Tafari was a Pandora's Box of symbols and ideas, most of which were discrepant with 'official' definitions of reality. The diversity of uses to which they could be put, guaranteed at least a spillover into the realms of disreputability and the consequent allegations of contumacy. Perhaps the 'bigger stick' might have been invoked more effectively to strain allegiances, for even the most devoutly religious individual has tolerance points. Such invocations, however, were interpreted by the Rastas as symptomatic of the reactive Babylon from which he had defected: 'We are prepared to struggle even harder when Babylon puts the pressure on; it knows its days are numbered and will try to crush the Rasta with whatever means it can,' claimed a Rastaman.

My work indicated that breaks were made with old realities and that the past, present and future were conceived of by reference back to the Rastafarian platform: 'I used to get involved in fighting and trouble like that, but then Ras Tafari came to I . . .'; 'I see now that all along I was wrong . . .' and similar retrospective observations suggested a biographical disjuncture after which the world could be seen through new eyes. What was previously cloaked in mystery was, after accepting Ras Tafari, self-evident; knowledge that was once unattainable was unavoidable.

The Rastas seemed to have evolved ingenious methods for the function of retaining the credibility of their reality at both objective and subjective levels. These were conceptual machineries for the maintenance of that peculiarly Rastafarian reality, which although never explicated by Rastas themselves, appeared to operate in a fairly systematic fashion. Whether these measures will ultimately fail and the precarious reality will crumble is open to question. The Rastas' beliefs may have incurred the wrath of Babylon, but the manner in which such a reaction was interpreted acted supportively rather than destructively. Having established a congruence between subjective and objective realities, and therefore the credibility of identity which cut through them, the Rasta prepared himself, conceptually at least, for his own future. Hence, the resources for the movement's self-perpetuation were in place. Since it was the new reality rather than the old which appeared overwhelmingly more plausible, the Rastas were unlikely to surrender clarity in exchange for opacity. As Robert Pirsig notes: 'no one is willing to give up the truth as he sees it' (1974, p. 68).

Rastas shared a conception of reality which was available to only those who had gained sufficient 'insight' to accept the divinity of Haile Selassie: 'Only those with insight enough to see the light of Africa will accept the truth of Ras Tafari.' For them, they were the enlightened ones, those who had seen the true and only path to salvation and would be returned to their fatherland, Zion, when the holocaust occurred. But, apprehension of reality in itself was no guarantee of the maintenance of the movement's distinctness and exclusivity. Lacking any authoritative locus and formal methods of social organisation and control, the Rastas had to develop strategies for maintaining boundaries around the movement and for hemming in the membership (and for excluding outsiders who did not accept their beliefs). In the Rastafarian reality the members themselves were the 'select'; it became necessary, therefore, to provide methods for perpetuating the subjective plausibility of that notion. To these I shall turn in the following chapter.

Chapter 8

In Search of the True Self

The battle for the maintenance of selfhood in the face of continuous subversive processes operating in society is one of the perennial problems of man . . . But men seldom face this continuing battle of selfhood entirely unassisted.

Abner Cohen, 1974a

A CULTURAL TRANSPLANT: THE BANYAN TREE

The cry of the Rastafarian, you know, is to get up and unite all our people under one banyan fig tree; which is not racialist but a vision of hope, a vision of redemption. (Brother Kinfe, 1978)

My treatment of the Rastafarian cult in England brings into relief the high degree of continuity between the Jamaican movement and its English counterpart. Emblems, titles, motifs, music and linguistic styles all survived the transition and remained largely unaffected by the migration. Collectively, they formed a rich symbolic tapestry into which the English Rastaman could weave his own personal experience. Ostensibly, the English movement was an extension of the original one into different social settings; a straight forward cultural transplant. The locks, the colours, the reggae were powerful Rastafarian symbols in Jamaica and they retained their efficacy in England, performing important parts in the maintenance of the notion of 'brotherhood' – and, therefore, in the maintenance of reality. Quite apart from the obvious ideological carry over, the persistence of symbolic forms in the English manifestation gave the strong impression that Ras Tafari was a survival from the past which had endured intact and had been extensively used by young blacks as a sheltering canopy of beliefs, ideas and styles. Hence, the accusation that the movement was an anachronistic phenomenon tinged with cultural conservatism and fated to extinction beneath the forces of urbanism; or at least pushed to the margins of insignificance.

Intuitively, it might be suggested that the bizarre and, in many ways, exotic patterns of social action were ill suited to the character of city life. But, if Ras Tafari was an urban anomaly, then there were others: the revival of occult activities in the 1970s, the mystical pursuits of Hare Krishna followers, the emergence of the Reverend Sun Myung Moon and his Unification Church (see Horowitz, 1978), the escalating popularity of Scientology (see Wallis, 1976), and the persistent fascination with UFOs were all indicative of the tendency to 're-mystify' the modern social world and incorporate myth into world views. All anomalous patterns of thought are subjected to debunking pressures from within and without yet somehow the preoccupation with the bizarre endures. Even within the secularised ambience of late twentieth-century England there was still time and inclination to indulge in the mysteries of the Bermuda Triangle (Berlitz, 1975), the puzzling assertion that 'God was an astronaut' (Von Daniken, 1971, 1972), the intriguing possibility of Atlantic rising (Steiger, 1977), and the terrifying macabre of demonic possession (C. Wilson, 1973). Alongside these, the Rastafarian insistence on the divinity of Haile Selassie and the return to Africa, and the adoption of long coiled hairstyles and Ethiopian colours seem less peculiar – though still enigmatic.

In Jamaica, the Movement slotted into a tradition carved out by the early thaumaturgical preoccupations impregnated with African elements, the Christian influences of Native Baptism and the refulgent visions of Bedward and Garvey. Against this backcloth, Rastafarian beliefs and programmes seemed almost logical outcomes of the incorporation of millenarian images of Africa into a basically Christian framework. It was well equipped to resist becoming another casualty as Jamaican society expanded industrially and, indeed, prospered by social and political advancements in the 1960s and 1970s. But, divorced from its original context, the cultural transplant was offered no guarantee of a future vitality in the new environment. The whole Rastafarian tapestry was transported to England, but it had to be rewoven in the changed context. Though the almost perennial problem of black subservience was fundamentally at the root of both movements, the English Rastas had to create their culture anew to suit their own purposes. In other words, whilst displaying obvious ideological and symbolic continuities, far from being a mere cultural survival, it was a continuous creation, a dynamic manipulation of concepts, programmes and symbols. So, although resort was made to existing cultural formations to articulate grievances and ways of alleviating them, the Rastafarian movement was not simply a reflection of its Jamaican progenitor but a recreation of it; and, while the movement was at all times regarded as part of a universal struggle, there were occasional acknowledgements that the English Rastas would have to perform independently: 'For the brethren in Jamaica total and complete political emancipation is a solution – at least for the time being. But for the Rastaman in English society, he must prepare for the redemption.'

In this sense, it is permissible to see the Rastafarian package as a set of resources utilised by West Indian youth in England as a means of establishing processes of inclusion and exclusion. Lacking in formal political and material resources – or, in Berger and Luckmann's terms, 'without sticks' – blacks turned to other available methods of articulating power by removing themselves from the main spheres of competition and insulating themselves in an enclosed subworld (though not necessarily of a geographical variety). This was possible because of the existence of a cultural formation which entailed the drawing of boundaries in such a way as to create new categories – including that of the Rastaman. While he might have experienced only limited success in the conventional sectors of, say, education, occupation or status, the Rastafarian member had recourse to a cultural realm and one which denied access to all other groups. So, although aspects of the traditional Jamaican culture were exploited by the new Rastas, the manner in which they were reformulated in the changed social milieu constituted a fresh creation.

The adaptation of existing cultural formations to suit new circumstances was in no way a passive acceptance of a pre-processed philosophy with implications for action, nor was it a regression into the past; but an active articulation of ideas, symbols, emblems and motifs to tackle current problems. As Raymond Firth has commented on such movements: 'They are not mere passive responses, the blind stirrings of a people who feel that they are being pushed around . . . they are creative attempts of the people to reform their own institutions, to meet *new* demands or withstand *new* pressures' (1955, p. 815).

Ras Tafari was an effort to erect boundaries, inside which the black British youths could cultivate their distinctiveness, transform their social identity and solidify their exclusivity; in other words, discover their 'true selves'. Adopting the visual appearance of their Jamaican counterparts, interacting in the main with fellow Rastas and speaking in only thick Jamaican patois, the youths attempted to intensify the contrast between themselves and the rest of society. But, importantly, not only were the physical and cultural differences made more salient but they also came to be seen by Rastas themselves as crucially significant in the long run; consciousness of belonging to a distinct and exclusive group rose to paramount importance. Rastas I spoke to perceived their allegiance to the movement as pivotal in both their own personal development and that of the black community. The tie to the movement was an almost primordial, physical and cultural bond and one which was unbreachable: 'I and I not only look different; but he is different – the man who has realised his past and future. Once this has been achieved nothing can shake him from the righteous path,' insisted a Rastaman; another Rasta pointed to history for evidence: 'Of course the Rastaman is different: 400 years have shown that; mashed down century after century.' (I should add that this view was subject to slight variation; for example: 'God is in all *men*; Rasta has realised this and accepted it.' All Rastas perceived their difference as salient though not necessarily immutable. And nearly all saw this difference as the critical variable which split them off from the rest of society. So, while the fact that God was inhering in all men was consciously entertained as a possibility, it was the Rastaman's realisation and acceptance of this which elevated him from the rest of the world and placed him in the enlightened position of having 'insight'. Hence, the apprehension of belonging to an élite group.) The cleavage instigated by the adaptation and recreation of Ras Tafari in England was apprehended as having self-evident relevance and overarching significance to members. Belonging to the movement was *the* critical divide which marked the Rasta off from the rest of society.

It was a perception encouraged by systematic exclusions from areas of educational attainment and occupational mobility for blacks; apprehension of commonality – the lowest denominator of which was blackness – was a necessary condition for immersion into the movement. The growing awareness that it was the quality of blackness that squeezed them into excluded positions prompted Rastafarian aspirants to use this characteristic as a basis for a new set of allegiances, selecting cultural traits from the Jamaican Rastafarian movement and elevating these to social prominence. So, a dualistic process went into effect whereby the awareness of inequality and injustice along racial lines fed a sharpened perception of group differences and a willingness to emphasise and, indeed, exaggerate them. As the involvement with the movement deepened and the allegiance intensified, the subjective reality of a significant difference became more cogent and liable to stimulate boundary-maintaining tactics. (Although this work attests to a degree of openness in the Rastafarian ranks, my initial approaches to groups provoked suspicion. Throughout my research I found no evidence to suggest that Rastas conducted sustained social interaction with non-Rastas. Primary contacts were restricted to fellow members or sympathising blacks. Associations with whites and Asians were reserved for intervals where such contacts were unavoidable, such as at work, on buses, in shops etc. Overall, the characteristic tendency of the Rastas was to close ranks.)

Strategies selected to maintain boundaries and so elongate social distances included the more obvious clustering together in tightly knit groups, minimising contact with strangers, cultivating exotic and bizarre appearances and the less obvious but enormously effective restriction of conversation to pure Jamaican dialect. These helped lash Rastas together and sustain a bounded social grouping. But they also engendered a response from other groups which was not altogether justified. The impression conveyed (not deliberately) from Rastas to, for example, members of the police force, Asians and unsympathetic West Indians was that of being racist in orientation. Nowadays, social scientists are generally agreed that racism is a fallacious belief in the ability to separate out groups of actors on the basis of phenotypical characteristics, such as skin pigmentation. Following on from this is the rather more pernicious second-order generalisation that such groups or races can be divided not only horizontally but vertically in terms of their inherent superiority and inferiority. Although I am not concerned with the influence of racism as a formal ideology nor its consequences for sociological theory (but see Banton, 1967, 1977; Rex, 1970, ch. 6) I am interested in why it was attributed to Rastas.

RACISM OR CULTURAL EXCLUSIVITY?

Rasta no hate whites; just expressing his differentness. (Brother Joseph, 1978)

Much of the Rastafarian movement's success in galvanising the hearts and minds of West Indian youth in the 1970s was due to its effective definition of membership through its identity and exclusivity. It was able to amplify its distinctiveness and preserve its insularity. One of the outcomes of this was that others regarded the Rastas as adhering to a doctrine of racial superiority. Their constant claim to being the lost tribes of Israel incarnate seemed to be a pretentious allusion to greater status with a smattering of American black power arrogance. Their apparent pretensions offended many groups: 'They're nothing but a bunch of racists' (middle-aged West Indian); '. . . racial lunatics' (Jamaican in his 20s); 'I think they're trying to get an American black power thing going' (police officer); 'Arrogant, racialist bastards' (white resident in Handsworth, Birmingham); 'They've got a chip on their shoulders' (Jamaican in his 20s); 'They think they're so superior now they've got this Rasta thing' (white London youth worker).

Certainly, there were elements in Rasta to suggest that its members were attempting to articulate a sort of counter-ideology to white racism or, as one Rasta put it, 'reflected racism': 'The only thing that gives one now the impression of us being racial is that reflection in the mirror of the practice that has been carried out by the European race. You know, because we knew nothing of racism in the sense of judging one by the colour and we've no apologies to make as far as preaching black equality and black identity. And it is not intended to be Fascist or racist, but it's for I and I to revive our true self and really know our ability by discovering our history.'

Even further, it brings little surprise to realise that such ideologies would appeal to black youth in the 1970s. The earlier efforts of de Freitas and Egbuna were aimed at redressing the stigmatic nature of racial definitions by the substitution of an alternative. Lack of psychological and social security aided and abetted the low level of commitment to the movement from first-generation West Indians in Britain. Their children, however, were much more readily disposed to articulate such an ideology as a way of resolving status ambiguity and associated anxieties. But, while black power drew upon the propensity of certain factions of the West Indian community to express overtly racial prejudice and condemn the evils of the white-dominated world, Ras Tafari had a more subtle appeal. It differed from black power in that it contained an enormously enriching symbolic dimension which was vital to its popularity; and it is for this reason that I am sure black power in its form of the 1960s would have failed even in the 1970s when blacks were gaining in confidence, commitment and frustration. Black power was, in effect, a conscious and positive manipulation of a racist counter-ideology imported from the USA and employed without serious alteration. It was engaged as a mandate for confrontation and overt conflict, sometimes of a violent type; and it was designed to inflame its perceived adversary, white society.

Like black power, Ras Tafari involved the extensive use of an existing ideology and therefore exhibited features of continuity. But, whereas black power was, to a large extent, inflexible and fused with dogmatism, Rasta was a much more fluid phenomenon, presenting a rich symbolic package enclosed in which were muffled and ambiguous political directives ready to be charged with fresh social significance in the new environment. Continuities and survivals were certainly there, but the way in which they were interpreted and manipulated was decided in the last instance by situational determinants. So ambiguous were the concepts and categories of the Rastafarian phenomenon that a straightforward carry over was impossible. Unlike black power, which was able to take root in England in a fairly uniform manner, Rastas were faced with a far more complex store of symbols and instruments in need of reinterpretation and rearticulation. There was no pure form of Ras Tafari available but rather two linked ideas around which revolved a kaleidoscope of differing beliefs, values, perspectives, commitments and assumptions, all directed towards the perceived, perennial problems facing the black man in a white world, but without any locus of authority to determine how they should be directed. And it is for this reason that I do not see racism as an integral part of the Rastafarian movement. Most certainly, there was an implicit potential for the articulation of racism through Rastafarian concepts and, superficially, much of the Rastas' thoughts and actions could lead the observer into believing that one of the fundamental implications of the movement's strain was a commitment to the superiority of the black man. The whole Rastafarian endeavour smacked of racism; and yet I will argue such a view is over-simplistic.

In Chapter 5 I outlined what I considered to be the three principal motivational routes to involvement with the movement. For purposes of analysis these were divided into the need for identity, the need for explanation and the need for mobilisation. Ras Tafari contained the elements for at least the partial satisfaction of all three. In the Rastafarian movement, blacks were to find the equipment for the achievement of a sense of personal and social identity, – selfhood; for the improved understanding of the way in which the world worked; and for the formation of a greater awareness of commonality and, by implication, the basis of political potential. Black power was also concerned with the solution to these three sets of problems but concentrated on using the first two as mechanisms in the promotion of the third. By contrast, the Rastaman was less instrumental in orientation, turning to clusters of symbols to establish his selfhood, tackle the perennial but largely irresolvable questions of existence and provide the foundation for a common awareness which might have brought a political alignment. And one of the ways in which he was able to do this was by fostering the belief of belonging to an exclusive group; the true Israelites, an enlightened people. In doing so, black youths created and developed boundaries around themselves and effectively denied access to non-Rastas.

Physical differences and cultural characteristics borrowed from their Jamaican forefathers were utilised in order to create a group by processes of inclusion and exclusion. Rastas drew on a variety of symbolic forms to define and emphasise their distinctness. Hence, the appearance of subscribing to a racist ideology. But, whereas the Rastafarian cultists were most certainly employing a range of strategies designed to enhance their distinctiveness and widen their distance from the rest of society, there were no suggestions that they believed their exclusivity was founded on such a superficial basis as physical difference. On the contrary, it was founded on a variety of social bonds expressing togetherness, a series of overlapping attachments which hemmed in some sectors and shut out others. These bonds were reducible in the last instance: 'The bond of the Rastaman is a bond of God,' explained a Rastaman.

Bonds were expressed through symbolic procedures and such expressions served to consolidate and reinforce the feeling of belongingness and unity. It was these bonds which held the Rastas together as a movement and not as an aggregation of individuals sharing similar social positions but without having the means to articulate their commonality, their belongingness under the one 'banyan tree,' as a Rasta expressed it: 'The cry of the Rastafarian, you know, is to get up and unite all our people together here under the one banyan fig tree; which is not racialist but a vision of hope, a vision of redemption.'

There were a number of ways in which the Rastas were able to demonstrate their exclusivity and thereby create it. My suggestion here is simply that by adopting and adapting the symbolism and organisation of the Jamaican movement the English Rastas not only developed strategies for expressing their distinctness, but also confirmed to each other the palpability of such a distinctness. They were able to display evidence of their exclusivity and therefore strengthen the belief in the efficacy of Rastafarian symbols. In effect, the symbols of the Rastaman did not merely reflect the wish to form an exclusive group; they created and recreated the foundation of that group's reality.

Before proceeding to delineate the methods used to create the exclusive movement of Ras Tafari, I should perhaps clarify some concepts. For a starting point I look to Abner Cohen:

> Symbols are objects, acts, concepts, or linguistic formations that stand *ambiguously* for a multiplicity of disparate meanings, evoke sentiments and emotions, and impel men to action . . . For the individual, symbols are fundamental mechanisms for the development of selfhood and for tackling the perennial problems of human existence like life and death, good and evil, misery and happiness, fortune and misfortune. (1974*a*, pp. ix–x)

Symbolism is ubiquitous in society; where human beings come together they construct endless arrays of patterned, symbolic action, whether in their interpersonal relationships, in their highly ritualised ceremonies, even in their formal contractual relationships. Though symbolism may be thought to manifest itself predominantly in pre-industrial societies, its existence and significance in modern complex societies attests to its social omnipresence. The work of Erving Goffman (1959; 1970) has indicated the extent to which symbolism pervades even the minutiae of social behaviour, but more evidently it is found in the stylised quasi-tribal rituals of soccer supporters (Marsh *et al.*, 1978, pp. 121–34), the esoteric pursuits of modern occultists, or the craft-like manoeuvres of high politics (Edelman, 1964). Even the movement organised under the rubric of 'black power' (an emotive symbol in itself), which was heavily instrumental in orientation, drew on a repertoire of emblems, such as the clenched fist, and slogans, the most obvious of which was 'black is beautiful'. The overall point is that within the most formally contracted and goal-directed set of human relations there can be found seams of symbolic elements; two of the key criteria separating the human being from the animal world are his symbol-creating capacity and his symbol-using proclivity.

For a second thread I turn to Kenelm Burridge's dictum: 'Indeed, all religions are basically concerned with power. They are concerned with the discovery, identification, moral relevance and ordering of different kinds of power' (1969, p. 5). Where there are minority groups to whom formal bases of power are not available, resort is often made to symbolic strategies in an effort to articulate expressions of dissent at their lack of material or cultural resources. In the case of West Indian Pentecostalism, disillusioned migrant blacks attempted to tackle their problems of existence through ritual and ceremonial activities, looking to other-worldly salvation as compensation for present distresses. The second generation was not in a significantly stronger position and had few, if any, opportunities to organise themselves along formal lines. Their solutions to problems facing them were different in quality to those offered by Pentecostalism, but were equally rich in symbols. Whereas Pentecostalists withdrew and retreated from white society, Rastas effected a repulsion of it (interestingly both Pentecostalists and Rastas conceived of themselves as the 'enlightened people'). In both instances symbols and symbolic activities were made use of for garnering the support of individuals and groups and calling their attention to their relatedness and joint interests. The symbols were powerful bonding phenomena, tying together blacks in a corporate endeavour to address what they perceived to be 'pressure' from the nefarious 'outside world', indexed by the Rastas as Babylon. The whole Rastafarian enterprise was seen as an element in the wider struggle of the black man. Most Rastas, particularly the more politically sensitive ones, considered themselves to be deeply involved in the more embracing problems facing blacks. Ras Tafari was seen as inseparable from the struggles in, for example, South Africa, Rhodesia and Ethiopia. A rather militant Rastaman asserted that: 'When Emperor Haile Selassie I was crowned King of Kings and Lord of Lords, the crowned King of the Lion of Judah in Ethiopia, to us we were stepping into a new era and this was a sign to us that our Kingdom had come, our King was ruling Africa. And this was a signal that our time had now come and that the time of all liberation and that whole freedom was here. And forty-seven years later we see there's only two places left in Africa that needs to be free'; another stated: 'My struggle has to be a universal struggle because it is to uplift each, everyone.'

Here, then, is the second key to understanding the Rastafarian imperative to erect boundaries and maintain exclusivity and uniqueness: the co-ordination of their corporate activities to combat perceived malevolence. Abner Cohen links the two together: 'Although they [symbols] can be said to be phenomena *sui generis*, existing in their own right, they are nearly always manipulated, consciously or unconsciously in the struggle for, and maintenance of, power between individuals and groups. They may be said to be "expressive"; but they are at the same time instrumental.' (1974*a*, p. xi). This is not to suggest that the articulation of symbols and the performance of symbolic behaviour, such as ceremony and ritual, can be reduced to an analysis of group interests, but that the 'two dimensions' of human relationships must be seen as having 'dialectical interdependence'. Symbols are created, mobilised and manipulated to aid groups in struggles for power. And, after all, the Rastas were involved in a struggle for power: power to define their own identity, to shape their own future, to establish their cultural autonomy, to escape the racialism they perceived and to overcome the material problems of existence. Rastafarian symbolic forms were by no means mechanical 'reflections' of these concerns but tangible expressions of the communion of West Indian youth confronted by the apprehension of evil, an evil that was stifling them as a group and, by implication, as individuals. Through symbolic strategies the Rastas were able to exteriorise their implicit *critique* of society. When asked about this, a Rastaman replied: 'I would say there is extensive and hostile criticism [in Ras Tafari] because we see how colonialism has stripped us completely of everything that has identified us as a people over the centuries and it has degraded us to an extent that we can no longer express ourselves as Africans.'

Ostensibly, Ras Tafari might have been escapist and possibly irrational, an attempt to dissociate the movement from the competitive world of Babylon and develop a separate culture; but the Rastas were, in a way, intensifying their struggle by articulating a series of criticisms and directing an assortment of nettles as the imperious wider society. Nettles which stung at the principles underlying the control and exercise of power to suit the requirements of Babylon, but which worked to suppress the black man's material and cultural capacities. The symbolic activity articulated a concern not purely with the incumbents of power positions but with the power arrangements themselves, or, as Burridge interprets them, the 'rules':

> Operationally, this concern is expressed in maintaining or challenging the rules which govern the use and control of power. And these rules assume the form of a set of moral discriminations which, in constricting animal man, also provide him with opportunities for realising his moral nature and potential. (1969, p. 7)

What a Rasta called the opportunity 'to revive our true self and really know our ability by discovering our history we know what we were capable of'. They were able to do this by adopting and rearranging an existing symbolic package, replete with emblems and slogans as well as theoretical expositions, and aligning this with different problems in changed circumstances.

Continuities between the Jamaican and English versions were

certainly maintained but their functions were altered to fit the new
social conditions. (Rastas themselves were aware of the similarities
and differences between themselves and their Jamaican counterparts:
'They are our brethren, but I and I must struggle independently
of they'.) Ras Tafari was sufficiently ambiguous and amenable to
reinterpretation without losing its underlying potency as a mobiliser
of emotions and sentiments in the effort to upgrade blacks in the
face of countervailing white ideologies which they considered down-
graded them.

Summarily, then, my suggestion is not that Rastafarian members
in England consciously adopted a prepackaged symbolic form and
actively used this to cultivate sets of social relationships to be used
instrumentally for the attainment of material ends (though I will concede a proportion of Rastas did take this stance). But that, without
deliberation, the Rastafarian symbols and activities, by necessity, inter-
penetrated and overlapped the more basic struggle for power over
material and cultural resources. Any attempt to understand the processes of inclusion and exclusion underpinning the creation of the
distinct and exclusive group of Ras Tafari which fails to account
for both dimensions is doomed to one-sidedness.

The Rastafarian enterprise was aimed at the resolution of an array
of felt problems confronting the black youth in England during the
1970s. Perceptions of rejection, of spirals of limited opportunities, of
restricted life chances, of having no cultural resources (as did, for
example, the Asian immigrants) stimulated a response organised
around the features of exclusivity and distinctness. A young Rasta
summed it up: 'We leave school and we go for a job; and can't get
a job because of the colour of our skin. Social-wise, we can't walk
the streets after certain hours. This is the aggravating situation that
society brings on us because they have rejected us . . . and time come
when he [the Rastaman] reject a society like that and that's what we're
doing, see . . . to check for a better way of life.'

Having been provided with a kind of blue-print – by reggae music
– they attempted to make use of it by familiarising themselves with the
basic Rastafarian ideology and developing objective signs of their
affiliation (though not necessarily in that sequence). Rasta was made
conspicuously visible through the cultivation of long coils of twisted
hair and beards, the adoption of garments and accessories in the
national colours of Ethiopia and the maintenance of a distinct style
of routine communication between the movement's members. The
significance of the first two can be appreciated without too much
recourse to historical significance but the mode of communication
was arguably the single most important symbolic including and
excluding device and warrants particular attention. To these I now
turn.

LOCKS AND COLOURS

Creating a unique set of observable group traits was of critical importance in the development of the Rastafarian distinctness. Not only did it facilitate the recognisability of fellow members of the brotherhood and therefore generate the formation of primary group relationships between them, but it also provided an inhibiting obstacle to the development of relationships outside the brotherhood. The somewhat exotic appearance of Rastas provided evidence of their disaffiliation with the wider society and served to solidify feelings of belongingness to a small but exclusive movement. Hair presented possibilities, as Firth notes: 'It is striking to note how out of this sluggish, physiologically almost functionless appurtenance of his body, man has imaginatively created a feature of such socially differentiating and symbolic power' (1973, p. 263).

According to Michael Smith and his colleagues (1967, pt. 1, p. 9) Rastas had worn beards and allowed their hair to grow long since the early days. But when some photographs of Ethiopian warriors became available during the 1940s some Rastafarian followers twisted their hair into long coils in emulation of these warriors. Negroid hair grows naturally into dreadlocks once the coils have been formed – not plaited as popularly believed – and left unkempt the appearance is not dissimilar to that of Medusa, the mythological gorgon with hair of snakes. Old Testament sanction was found for the cultivation of locks; to cite three instances:

They shall not make baldness upon their head, neither shall they shave off the corner of their beard, nor make any cuttings in the flesh. (Leviticus 21:5)

And in Numbers 6:5 the Lord instructs Moses to 'speak unto the Children of Israel' telling of the vows of the Nazarite:

All the days of his vow of separation there shall no razor come upon his head: until the days be fulfilled, in the which he separateth himself unto the Lord, he shall be holy, he shall let the locks of his head grow long.

I Corinthians 11:4–6 gives instruction for women:

Every man praying or prophesying, having his head covered dishonoureth his head. But every woman praying or prophesying with her head unveiled dishonoureth her head: for it is one and the same thing as if she were shaven. For if a woman is not veiled, let her also be shorn: but if it is a shame to a woman to be shorn or shaven, let her be veiled.

Accordingly, Rasta sisters always wore their long hair covered, usually by a headscarf or turban, in anticipation that they may be called upon to pray without notice. In Jamaica, the locks were used to consolidate the exclusivity of the early cult and later to signify affiliation to the growing movement. Similarly, in England the growth of dreadlocks spread during the mid-seventies. Aided by posters and record sleeves of Rastafarian reggae artists, in much the same way as the Jamaicans had been by the pictures of Ethiopian warriors, young Rastas in England cultivated unkempt manes to enrich the distinctness of the emerging movement. This external distinguishing sign of the dread-locks was vitally important to the growth of the English movement; it provided members with tangible evidence of their own special identity.

The locks were part of the more general process of discarding allegedly significant attributes such as the desirability of straight, well-groomed hair and white skin. Hair straightening and skin lightening were strategies available to black women in the Western world wishing to rid themselves of their stigmatic appearance (Garvey was particularly ferocious in his condemnation of these). For the Rastas, however, possession of coarse, curly hair and a black skin was given new meaning. Instead of constituting the occupation of a stigmatised place in society, it allied the Rastaman to constellations of others bearing similar attributes and belonging to the new élite, those who had taken 'vows'. In this sense, the sight of others wearing locks fostered the formation of a new consciousness of being 'in' society but not 'of' society. The locks signified that the Rasta recognised that the blacks were encased in a society which attached negative values to negro characteristics and that he rejected that world and those values. During the process of exaggerated estrangement from the world, a new élite was authenticated; the dreadlocks were a visible reminder that the Rastaman had arrived and intended to assert his presence, or to the Rasta, 'the fulfilment': 'A Rastaman is a Nazarite. There are certain vows set aside for the Nazarite . . . we are just fulfilling what was spoke unto our fathers and we are in the faith and spirit of the Nazarene. This is the cause of the locks.' (The reference is to the Fourth Book of Moses.)

But the locks were important in another sense: not only symbolising the rejection of Babylon and its definitions, but in morally upgrading the black man's self-image. Stigmata attributed to blacks in Jamaica, and for that matter in England were not merely attachable and detachable labels, but were internalised by blacks themselves. Blackness was widely regarded as a sign of inferiority and blacks themselves were likely to feel that their downgrading was legitimate. Hence, the acceptance of restricted opportunities, barriers to progress and material and status deprivation by Jamaican blacks and, most strikingly, by first-generation West Indians (due to the twofold process of first, becoming aware of white definitions and observing the reality of black disprivilege, and, secondly, linking these in a causal manner, i.e. 'the blacks are in a position of disprivilege because they are inferior, so the whites' definition of blacks as inferior is well founded,' the demonstration effect). Hair straightening and skin lightening were indicative of the extent to which blacks despised their own blackness and longed to rid themselves of the stigma. As a Rasta put it: 'They still believe they are perhaps inferior.' The growing of hair in untamed corkscrews was a feature peculiar to the negroid physical makeup. This part of the Rastafarian enterprise was designed to elevate negro traits by emphasising features traditionally connoting inferiority and giving totally transformed meanings to them; concomitant with this process was the riddance of old self-conceptions. The American Black Muslims were engaged in a similar catharsis:

> The 'real' rather than 'ostensible' enemy of the Nation of Islam or of the Negro masses in general, is not the white person *per se*, but the Negro himself – his subculture, his image of himself and of his 'place' in society, his attitude toward white people, and his idealisation of all that is white. From the point of view of all black nationalists, the Negro can never be really free until he has purged from his mind all notions of white superiority and Negro inferiority and thus ceases to despise himself and his group. In doing so, he may have to shed the outward appearances of white culture and, most importantly, the 'old time' religion. (Essien-Udom, 1962, pp. 335–6)

(When I asked about Ras Tafari's connection with the Black Muslims and other black movements, a Rasta answered cogently: 'Ras Tafari supersedes all movements.')

Locks were an element in redefining the black man to himself; to demonstrate that Rastas were prepared to go against the ideological grain and respond to white definitions with counter-definitions. So, rather than succumb to the degradation associated with blacks and blackness the Rastaman used his hair as a tool with which to degrade his degraders. Locks were for the enlightened few, the true 'Nazarite' who could transcend conventional white definitions and aspire to the spheres of the black élite, 'the lost sheep of Israel', as one Rasta put it.

My point is that dreadlocks were expressive phenomena but also instrumental; used to marry blackness to positive attributes and so upgrade the black man and align him with élite groups – and so render white stigmatic conceptions of blacks impotent.

The locks were elements in the dire struggle to reclassify Rastas as a spiritual and moral élite, the 'true selves'. Deprived of material resources, they took cognisance of their oppression, identified their oppressors and attempted to undermine their credibility and, by implication, the credibility of their definitions of blacks and black attributes; not only for the sake of white society but for the sake of other Rastas – to totally convince them that the white-oriented association of blackness with inferiority was incredible; another component of the Babylonian conspiracy to repress blacks: 'There was also things done to make the slaves believe that their culture was inferior,' reasoned a Rastaman, who found agreement with one of his brothers: 'Ever since slavery the white man has tried to teach the black his unworthiness; but this will soon end.'

The appearance of locks celebrated blackness: made its quality and possession esteemed and positively valued. In no way was the growing of locks an element of black racialism, but a strenuous effort to cleanse the black man of white-defined self-images and to instil in him self-confidence, pride and dignity in being black. Dreadlocks were not so much a sign of superiority as a rejection of inferiority: a reformulation of the labels of the white world by 'cleaning up one's own back garden' and determining the 'true self': 'We're trying to clean our back garden up first before we start to speak about integration and these things. We're trying to solve our own problems, first, which is self-determination. It is not racialist, no way: we hate no one.' Here then is the clear recognition that the evil besetting black people lay not only outside them but inside them; Babylon had entered them and, like a demon, had to be exorcised – an observation first made by Garvey.

It was Garvey also who instigated the use of the Ethiopian national colours to signify his allegiance to Africa (which he considered synonomous with ancient Ethiopia). The inspiration for the UNIA's official flag came from Garvey's reading of the Book of Psalms: '. . . methinks I see the Angel of God taking up the standard of the Red, the Black and the Green, and saying "Men of the Negro race, Men of Ethiopia, follow me" ' (M. Garvey, 1967, Vol. 1, p. 73).

After the demise of Garvey's movement, the Rastafarian cultists adopted the colours as if to stress the continuity between Garvey's enterprise and their own. Garveyite slogans, such as 'Africa for the Africans' and 'One Aim! One God! One Destiny!', were also preserved. Gold was added to Garvey's colours and they were incorporated into clothing, badges, paintings and prayer sticks or 'rods of deliverance' to signify the determined effort of Rastas to impress upon the world the presence of Garvey – if only in spirit: 'The colours show that we are truly Ethiopians.'

But the colours also served as readily recognisable distinguishing signs. Like the uniforms of the American Black Panthers, the lapel buttons of the Gay Liberation Front, the safety pins of punk rockers and even the ties of Old Etonians, the red, black, green and gold of the Rastas visually marked them off from other groups and convinced members of their own special identity. Easy identification of fellow Rastas was facilitated and this eased the way for deepened in-group interaction and more involved reasoning.

Originally, Garvey interpreted the colours as significant with the red representing the spilled blood of blacks, green as nature, and black the colour of Africans' skins; but to modern Rastas they functioned differently. On the surface they symbolised the connection with Garvey and, by extension with Ethiopia, but at another level they articulated a rudimentary organisation by intensifying visual distinctiveness which in turn fed informal patterns of interaction. In other words, the adoption of the colours by individuals helped define the movement's members clearly and unambiguously and unite them into a single social structure, or what Abner Cohen calls an 'invisible organisation' (1974*a*, ch. 6). The Ethiopian colours worked as a 'membership' card for the Rastafarian brotherhood. (The wearing of colours was especially important in the English movement's nascency but, once established, members could afford to don tams of other colours without denying their affiliation and in 1978 the tall, peaked cap of corduroy or wool with a ribbon appliqué in the colours came into vogue.)

A subsidiary item of appearance which had symbolic importance was the narrow-legged trouser worn very short to emphasise poverty and the necessity of wearing 'hand-me-down' clothing. This was a hangover from the rude boys whom Hebdige reckons 'went out of their way to embrace the emblems of poverty' (1975, p. 148). Another little style was the towelling face cloth hanging from the back trouser pocket, which also seems to be a variation of the rude boys' characteristic of displaying a coloured handkerchief.

I do not feel the dreadlocks and the Ethiopian colours were consciously manipulated as strategies in the struggle for power with the wider society; they were, however, symbolic responses to the perception and feeling of powerlessness and cultural anonymity. They were means of controlling what limited resources they had available and one way in which this could be achieved was by creating distinctiveness, enriching identity and exclusivity and sealing this with cultural boundaries. The cleavage the Rastas initiated may well have looked to be organised along racial lines, but, on examination, it was multidimensional.

External signs were important in establishing distinctness and solidifying exclusivity; but also in providing a base from which to articulate a critique of the distribution and exercise of power, a critique underpinned by what I call the Babylonian Conspiracy theory. Being equipped with the symbolic devices of locks and colours stood as an index of the member's affiliation to the movement, adherence to the critique of Babylon and co-operation to the common cause of the black man in the white world.

So far, then, I have described how visible cultural traits were selected and mobilised by West Indian youths who used them to typify or characterise their own particular social group, thus operationalising processes of inclusion and exclusion. Whether, in fact, cultural differences existed between blacks and whites in England was irrelevant; the conditions of resource competition and structured exclusion constituted the main cleavage and the Jamaican cultural items fused with new social significance as a response to this rejection. Differences of culture grew more apparent and became perceived as relevant by blacks as they gained awareness that blackness could be – and was – used as a basis for rejection.

But, peculiarity of appearance alone was insufficient to deepen the cultural distinctness of the Rastafarian movement. Looking different worked well in establishing presence but did not consolidate the processes of exclusion necessary for the maintenance of what I earlier called a 'subworld'. A limit on communication was needed to hermetically seal the Rastafarian world; a way for members to communicate with each other without the risk of outside interference; a codified form of intra-group verbal exchange which shut off channels to non-members. Again they only had to look to Jamaica for ready-made modes of communication. Here was a form which sealed in the Rastas from the rest of the world. Only other Jamaicans would find their tongue intelligible and even so they stylised and refined it in such an esoteric way so as to make it their exclusive property. Language was probably the most important symbolic device in enriching the Rastas' distinctiveness and elaborating the members' special sense of identity. For this reason I will dwell on it at some length.

JAMAICAN PATOIS

. . . a strong and tasty pepperpot of language. (*Frederic C. Cassidy, 1961*)

Enslaved Africans would have experienced nothing like a well-lubricated transition from one reality to another when undergoing the traumatic jolts from capture to seasoning. Stanley Elkins has analysed the transition from tribal life to slavery in terms of a series of 'shocks': 'We may suppose that every African who became a slave underwent an experience whose crude psychic impact must have been staggering and whose consequences superseded anything that had ever happened to him' (1963, p. 98). He breaks them into the shock of capture; the long march to the sea; the sale to European traders; the middle passage; and the shock of the introduction to the West Indies (Elkins, 1963, pp. 98–100). In other words, the Africans were conscious of the world as consisting of a series of realities, but, when confronted by the white men, previously not encountered and the measures they sought to impose, they had to come to grips with a completely unexpected and devastatingly new reality. The move from the composite 'African reality' to the inchoate 'slave reality' was experienced as a sequence of shocks caused by the shifts in attentiveness that the transition entailed.

The new reality of slavery came to be the reality *par excellence*, subordinating previously experienced African realities to the peripheries of dreams, memories and reminiscences. Slavery imposed itself in the most violent and oppressive manner; it was impossible to ignore, insurmountably difficult to escape from and hard to rationalise. What is more, its grip of presence was given ultimate strength by the raw edge of coercion. Slaves did not need to pinch themselves in order to gain reassurance that they were wide awake; they had the whip to remind them.

Not only was the geographical location different but so were tools which they were taught to use, shackles which they were made to wear, food which they were given to eat and accommodation they were made to live in. Apart from these main material changes, the slaves were thrown into a totally new order of social relationships; they were provided with a category of differently coloured superordinates for whom they were made to toil and sometimes die, but also an array of other Africans, most of whom were as alien as the Europeans in all except their appearance. Though the Europeans would have apprehended and oriented themselves towards the New World slaves in a fairly uniform manner, in much the same way as they would work horses, the variety of tribal backgrounds among the slaves would have made the formation of common, patterned senses of experience extremely unlikely. Customs, practices and beliefs were diversified throughout the African continent and the only recruiting bias Jamaican slave traders demonstrated was a preference for the tribes of Ghana and Southern Nigeria. This made for a lack of common co-ordinates of life and, most crucially, the lack of a common language.

Communication, then, was kept to a minimum; a situation reinforced by talking being forbidden during working hours for fear of conspiracy. Even if the slaves desired to cultivate some kind of stock of shared meanings, the structure of the slave system virtually compesced this possibility. During the early periods vocal expressions were no doubt kept to the level of snarls and grunts conveying subjective postures. Slave drivers could always reduce the ambiguity of their instruction by using brute force to consolidate the intention of their gestures; slaves had no such recourse.

The diversity of background of the slave populace of Jamaica militated against the development of any shared meanings. By far the most oft-heard and loudest language of the time was English. This was the tongue of the superordinate, the possessors of greater knowledge and military strength which had enabled them to wrench the African from his homeland and plant him in a strange and perplexing environment where he was made to work for no reward – except for the skin on his back. Misunderstanding the white's instructions had often fatal consequences, so it was unwise to escape the imperatives of the English tongue. The magnetism of English lay in its capacity to communicate meanings in the most massive and conclusive manner. Its power originated in the face-to-face experience where its comprehension was positively reinforced with approval and negatively sanctioned with consternation and punishment. The ongoing production of English vocal signs gradually came to be synchronised with subjective intentions of whites, giving rise to a basis for the fostering of the new tongue. The acquisition of English terms and phrases, therefore, came not as a result of any aesthetic curiosity, but principally as a matter of expediency: the pragmatic impulse to avoid punishment.

Not surprisingly, the situation proved largely to strike against the survival of African languages. While fresh infusions of Africans to the island fed the continuance of tribal exclusivity, the creole blacks and the more seasoned African-born slaves were made to adapt and adjust their sights, thoughts and actions, not to mention their tongues, to the requirements of the new environment. After the end of the slave trade the adaptive process was accelerated unhindered by African influences. There can be no doubt, however, that African elements permeated all attempts to imitate the English-talking whites. Indeed, Frederic Cassidy's exhaustive study of *Jamaica Talk* (1961) cites numerous examples of African words and intonations filtering into the emergent language of African Jamaicans. Pronunciation, grammatical structure and pitch, or tone, are all seen as affected to some degree or other by African influences, though the difficulties of precisely connecting up exact sources make many of Cassidy's theories, thorough as they are, at times speculative.

Slaves were brought over speaking many African languages and utilising local dialects, so they simply had to pick up English as best they could without the guidelines of instruction or formal example. The original arrivals would have been exposed to only white exponents of the tongue, but later incumbents of slave positions were in contact with other blacks who had fashioned their own versions of the language. From, say, the 1700s blacks came to be the first models. Immediate exposure was to an incomplete English language spoken through the mouth of an African and the persisting influence of Africanisms in negro speech was to be expected in the absence of correct instruction.

But the African shadings were unquestionably offset by the pre-eminence of English which the blacks' discourse sought to imitate. Conditions made for the emergence of a distinct creole Jamaican language; a provincial form of speech which was to be adopted and refined by successive generations of slaves and their offsprings without ever losing its roots in the slave system. This I take to be part of what Dick Hebdige alluded to when he opened his article thus: 'The experience of slavery recapitulates itself perpetually in the everyday interactions of the Jamaican black' (1975, p. 135) (though he had other elements in mind as well as language).

Quite clearly, the Jamaican slave underwent very singular experiences and the pliantly expansive nature of creole language allowed him to subsume them into categories in terms of which they had meaning only to himself and his fellow slaves, thus excluding non-slaves from the subuniverse of meaning. Even in the late 1970s Rastafarian brothers in England repeatedly stressed: 'It's impossible for a white man to understand what suffering means; it just makes no sense unless you're Rasta.' Though the word itself anonymised the actual experience of suffering it remained available for use by anyone falling into the requisite category of language-users, the Rastas. In this way, the biographical experiences of slavery were subsumed under general patterns of meaning which transcended the layer of experience of any one single generation of Jamaican blacks. It is quite remarkable that black youths in the seventies constantly harkened back to the critical concept of suffering; it was as meaningful to modern Rastas as it was to seventeenth-century slaves. Through the employment of this solitary concept the whole world of slavery could be conjured up in a moment. As I was told by a Rastaman: 'Suffering? It's *all* about suffering, man. Since Africa came under European rule, the black man has been oppressed, starved of his culture and his religious and ethical values; mentally as well as physically oppressed. You see the black man's history is a history of suffering.'

And 'suffering' is by no means a unique example of an English word whose meaning was slightly distorted and grossly personalised to embrace an exclusive order of experience. Creole language originated in and had primary reference to the day-to-day life of the slave. (Similar tongues grew elsewhere in the West Indies.) It was designed to slice up the vast accumulations of meaning and experience peculiar to the slave. As such, it successfully became the repository of past experiences which it could preserve and transmit to following generations. Its longevity attests to this. The blend of linguistic components created originally by African slaves was born amidst the conditions of life on the plantations; but it was carried and preserved for almost 400 years without considerable dilution.

All this is not to suggest that this linguistic syncretism was the special preserve of enslaved blacks, for Jamaica's native whites were in later years to acquire a similar tongue. No doubt the process of absenteeism, whereby plantation owners returned to England, bore responsibility for emptying the island of 'pure' English speech influences, leaving attorneys, bookkeepers and agents to adopt forms of communication already existing amongst slaves. Ease of conversation between blacks and whites would have been enhanced by the white's cultivation of a creole tongue as opposed to a strictly standard English one. Whatever the motive behind the development, the creole whites' language was virtually identical to that of the slave and as such became very offensive to some Englishmen of the period. Major Chambre felt compelled to declare: 'Sometimes they even adopt the barbarous idiom of the negro, thinking to make themselves understood. The consequence is their pronunciation is abominable, and the rising generation, notwithstanding the pains taken to educate them, retain the villainous *patois* of their parents' (1858, p. 129).

It is taken, then, that by the time of the termination of slavery a distinct language unique to Jamaica had emerged which, to a large degree, cut across racial barriers. Cassidy begins his analysis with the idea of a scale at the one end of which is the 'inherited talk of the peasants and labourers, largely unaffected by education and its standards' and, at the other, 'the London standard' or 'educated model' (1961, p. 2). At the emancipation, it would have been those whites and privileged coloureds who, having enjoyed the benefits of an Anglicised education, would have reflected most closely the 'London standard', with the uneducated mass of blacks retaining the 'barbarous idiom'. The general pattern persisted.

For the moment I am unconcerned with the actual content or structure of Jamaican language (but see Cassidy, 1961, ch. 3); suffice it to say that Jamaican patois was an amalgam of different elements mixed to produce a unique and often confusing sound. The confusion caused by the first significant waves of incoming Jamaicans during the 1950s was quite obviously compounded by the immigrants' use of this strange, unfamiliar and un-English-sounding language. Quite apart from their obvious physcial differences, the linguistic differences could have served to confirm the great gulf which seemed to separate blacks from whites.

Problems associated with language were threefold: first, the reinforcing function whereby beliefs in racial differences were supposedly confirmed; secondly, the hindrance to immigrant–native communication, which whites might have taken as signifying a reluctance to enter into social relationships; these two led quite logically on to a third multifaceted problem of social disadvantage in which the inability to communicate on what would be considered an articulate level would impose on the immigrant and his children a considerable handicap in the spheres of employment and education.

Obviously, language was but one of a welter of variables which gave rise to the patterns of rejection experienced by immigrants to England. Quite often a variety of factors, such as cultural background, education, class, motivation, appearance, residence and, of course, the central criterion, racial difference, complicate any clear conception of the problem and, in all probability, these variables were intertwined. Obviously, language cannot be convincingly separated from education, cultural background, country of origin and class position. Linguistic competence was, nevertheless, often at work as a strong disadvantaging factor in employment and housing and this had strong repercussions in terms of loss of long-term opportunity.

In relation to the first generation of immigrants, research in six areas in 1967 confirmed and elaborated the findings of several local studies that there was 'substantial discrimination', largely based on colour, against coloured immigrants applying for jobs, seeking housing and obtaining services in shops, hostels, insurance, banking etc. (see Daniel, 1968). Linguistic ability was isolated as one of the several factors influencing the non-acceptance of the first generation. The creole vernacular of Jamaica and other British West Indian islands proved to be something of an unexpected stumbling block for hopeful blacks, whose contact with English-speaking whites would have been confined mainly to the small minority of Jamaicans (or island natives) who spoke with a creolised emphasis (and, of course, some tourists). Jamaicans were not misled in their understanding that English was the spoken language in their future residence but they would not have foreseen the markedly different vernacular as a preventive barrier to acceptance by the majority.

But the immediate concern is with the second generation – those migrating as children or teenagers or those born in England of West Indian parents – from whose ranks the Rastas were drawn. Most of the Rastas completed their secondary education at English institutions (though most of them found it an unrewarding experience). Consistent with the major contrast in orientation between the first and second generations, the younger West Indians would have been less inclined to respond readily and obediently to English norms in an effort to gain some degree of acceptance and stability in the new environment: 'Man, you see some of these older folks trying to straighten their hair, dress like Europeans, even talk like them to get accepted. We want no part of that, you see; we want to find ourselves,' insisted a Rastaman.

It might be supposed that the massive increase in exposure to standard English, particularly the working-class dialects of London and Birmingham would have led to a gradual diminution of the more pronounced features of the patois and a certain alignment of vocabulary, pronunciation and grammar. This was most certainly the case for many, particularly the older members of the community. For them, comprehension became easier and many came to speak fluently in local accents untainted by patois.

Interestingly, however, Jamaicans conversing with each other were able to retain their past language and resort back to a rich and thick creole form which would be largely unintelligible to the uninitiated Englishman. Clearly, the migrant was resourceful, tailoring his accent to suit the company; talking to whites his speech was glossed to make it more palatable to the English; talking to other blacks he utilised unabashed patois. This tactic was no doubt an expedient measure to facilitate social relationships rather than a conscious attempt to emulate British accents in admiration. (It did, of course, alleviate many of the linguistic problems relating to employment which troubled immigrants in the fifties and sixties.)

It was not a policy employed by most Rastas: theirs was a language of thick and treacly patois, seemingly untouched by local influences and emphatic in its repudiation of standard English. Rastas talked to each other in a concentrated and almost caricatured Jamaican parlance and refused to dilute it when in contact with whites or other groups, sometimes adding expressions peculiar to Rastafarian vocabulary, the most obvious being the confusing 'I and I.' Speech was part of Rastas' panoply which insulated them from the wider society – at least subjectively. The refusal to transfer to an English idiom when in conversation with whites must have been symptomatic of the desire to alienate the host community, to perplex its members and deter them from attempting communication. (Communicating with Rastas could be a taxing exercise. Few concessions were made to the insensitive English ear and I was conscious of having to gear up to new organisations of vocabulary, grammar and syntax.) Language was one of the blades used by the Rastaman to cut his links with the encompassing Babylon. It aided maximal detachment from the everyday experience of white society and encouraged insularity and the development of in-group solidarity.

Here was the attempt to crystallise into small enclaves of meaning where the experience of being black in a predominantly white world could be made to serve as a cement for cohesion and brotherhood. Jamaican patois was a language of kinship, albeit a fictive kinship. By submerging the polished tones of standard English and engaging themselves exclusively in Jamaican parlance the Rastas (even the minority from other parts of the West Indies) could retain their links with history and their roots. Jamaican language, like any other, was capable of eliciting visions highly abstracted from everyday experience and also of presenting them as objectively real elements in everyday life; it was capable of making present a variety of experiences which were spatially, temporally and socially absent from modern life. The Rastaman, through his language, was trying to actualise the entire world of slavery and remind himself and his brothers of their 'real' position in history as opposed to their present one. In doing so, they built up zones of meaning which were superficially irrelevant to the condition of the migrant Jamaican, but which for the Rastaman were essential elements in the black man's biographical experience. Jamaican patois bridged the gap between current circumstances and situations of slavery. Synchronised were the biographical time sequences of the late twentieth-century English Rastas and the seventeenth-century West Africans. It was a language born out of slavery, and served as a continual reminder of the reality of that phenomenon: 'As well as taking away our African culture, the white man stripped us of our native tongue. How we speak reflects what Babylon has done in the past.'

The Rastafarian revival of patois as the sole linguistic form as opposed to most other Jamaicans' dualism represented a return to a reference point – a province of meaning which might have seemed somewhat irrelevant to the contemporary West Indian in England. But, to the Rastaman, ambiguous and sometimes meaningless concepts such as integration, gradualism or assimilation were alien and strangely out of stride with the real ambition of the black man – to develop his culture without interference from whites, a point reinforced by a Rastaman, thus: 'Rasta don't want no help or sympathy from Babylon. All I's progress will be made within our true culture. Don't want them to understand us.'

It becomes very difficult not to glean a statement from the rejection of a vernacular acceptable to whites and the embracing of the idiom of forefathers. Its functions were multiple. Distancing whites and discouraging them from contact which was neither valued nor required except in necessary circumstances was an important one. But at the deeper level the engagement of Jamaican language simultaneously recapitulated the entire history of the black man, his origin, and his experience in Babylon; it became a persuasive cohesive force tying Rastas together almost as Hebrew functions to help maintain the Jewish community. This led to the attempted elimination of insecurity, uprootedness and overdependence on white society; it communicated a sense of unity and power; the unity which provided the platform for the creation of a special indentity, the 'true self'.

Here, then, was the integrating power of Jamaican language: the ability to draw its users together into a common enclave and to generate the kind of awareness necessary for the cultivation of new identity. But simultaneously it asserted the ferocious insistence of severing links with the white society. As Alan Little commented (in a lecture, London School of Economics, 14 February 1978): 'The young West Indian speaks Brummie or Cockney quite fluently; his dialect is a blatantly political phenomenon, signifying his rejection of the system.' Jamaican patois was the language of the English Rastaman; not his exclusively but in his hands an instrument as much as a mode of discourse; a means of prising open gaps between him and white society and building bridges to link him with his African heritage. It was part of his attempt to articulate an objection to extant power arrangements by pulling away from any connection with the perpetuation of them. The Rastaman was involved in constructing immense edifices of symbolic representations which towered over the reality of his everyday life in England, casting a gargantuan shadow for him to stand in. Patois gave him one of the means to make this venture possible.

I have pinpointed three basic symbolic strategies employed by the young West Indians to make the presence of the Rastaman visible and audible; they were dimensions of social bonding which brought the Rastas together in a series of attachments and took them further from the wider society in a series of detachments. The whole enterprise was underpinned by complementary processes of unity and division, inclusion and exclusion. Awareness that they were 'in' but not 'of' Babylon promoted the all-important consciousness of belonging to a social group that was somehow separated from the rest of society and would remain untainted and not infected by the evils of Babylon. The members could comfort themselves with the assurance that non-Rastas could not penetrate their exclusive subworld: 'Only those with insight enough to see the light of Africa will accept the truth of Ras Tafari.'

And much of the problem of inpenetrability surrounding the movement could be seen as a manifestation of the strain to conserve this enlightened position and shut out those without insight; when questioned on this very point a Rasta replied circumspectly: 'If I reveal to you everything about I then I lay myself open; this is not good for a man,' a Rastaman warned me.

The locks, the colours and the speech form were strategies in the creation and maintenance of distinctiveness and exclusivity. They were adopted and refined by a group lacking in material and cultural resources but aware that the distribution and exercise of power was not in their immediate or long-term interests, but in the interests of the oppressive system which they thought continued to subordinate them – mentally if not physically. But the critique was not expressed overtly and articulated along formal political channels but in symbolic forms. In the modern political context, conditions militated against young blacks organising as formal interest groups (not just external conditions, but dispositions and motivations within the second-genera-

tion West Indian community). The symbolic formation of Ras Tafari
presented a persuasive attraction for co-ordinating the corporate
activities of blacks and providing the integrative forces of a rudimentary informal organisation, worked out with the vital concept of
a Rastafarian brotherhood.

In this sense, the adoption and reinterpretation of Rastafarian
symbols and theories were not merely ephemeral indulgencies of a
bored section of the black populace but creative attempts to articulate
a number of criticisms and functions: criticisms of the white colonial
world which had stripped them and their ancestors of their culture
and material possessions and perpetuated a system of 'slavery', known
by some as 'mental enslavement'; functions of mobilising awarenesses
of commonality and the need to co-ordinate together at some level
in order to realise their true potential. In the process, the individual
could identify himself in terms of his membership of the group,
an impermeable élite group, the boundaries around which ensured
cultural distinction and the preservation of the Rastafarian identity.

The Rastas were not consciously engaged in a struggle for power;
in a great many cases they regarded themselves as opting out of such a
struggle. But they were articulating their discontent at the extant
ordering of resources and their distribution; or, as Burridge put it,
the 'rules' underlying the distribution and exercise of power. Their
peculiar, bizarre and exotic appearance and sometimes incomprehensible, almost codified mode of communication set them up as targets
for ridicule, dismissal and blunt criticism. But for the Rastaman
they were all elements in a common enterprise aimed at establishing
a culturally unique and élite movement propelled by the interests of
the black man (or at least the perceived interests of the black man).

It is my contension that once the Rastafarian allegiances had
been forged the meaning of affiliation took on rising importance for
the individual member; he came to see himself as a member of a
vanguard movement; one who had pierced the rhetoric and mystification of Babylon and seen 'the light of Africa'; one whose enlightened
insight would enable him to struggle more effectively and prepare
for the coming holocaust which would wipe out current evils and
restore power to the blacks. In other words, he came to perceive his
membership as a critical allegiance. Abner Cohen captures this:
'Selfhood becomes identified in terms of membership of the group.
The group and the self become parts in the scheme of the universe and
are thereby validated' (1974*a*, p. 81). And a Rastaman also: 'I and
I are one people. I have this sister here and this brother here and we
are all one. Ras Tafari is in all of I.'

Being a Rasta was regarded as the salient divide between himself
and the rest of society. The overwhelming majority of Rastas regarded
their membership in Ras Tafari as *the* most important aspect of their

lives: 'It *is* my life.' Accepting Haile Selassie constituted something of a breakpoint with the rest of society: 'Time come when he [the Rastaman] reject a society like that'; he disengaged himself from the involvement with Babylon. After the break was made, however, changes in orientation facilitated fresh perceptions of society and the self: 'I now look at myself as a proper person; I wasn't myself before'; 'The world became clearer for I after Ras Tafari come.'

The relevance of Rasta was heightened through intensifying interaction with fellow Rastas, increasing familiarity with Rastafarian concepts and theories and deepening immersion into the total enterprise, the drift to acceptance.

I have attempted to abstract what I consider to be the most important symbolic elements of the movement and trace their background with a view to showing how they related to the more general responses of the young black population to conditions of powerlessness and cultural vacuity. The key to understanding the processes underlying the Rastafarian movement is not racism, cultural conservatism or indulgent escapism; rather it is the dynamic process of creating cultural exclusivity, a process consisting of an interplay of symbolic and power relations; the invocation of symbols charged with new meanings to accommodate new social circumstances of resourcelessness, the attempt to 'revive the true self'.

Chapter 9

Encounters in Babylon

This is not where Rasta belong; this I feel and know – in
my body and my mind. Every day I man can look around
him and see Babylon all around him. Rasta want no part
of that world.

Brother William, 1977

THE PERSONIFICATION OF BABYLON: POLICE

While the Rastafarian movement had no active programme of
involvement with other groups in the wider society and, indeed, sought
to restrict primary relationships to in-group members as part of the
effort to maintain exclusivity, contact with outside groups was inevitable. One prominent objective of the whole enterprise was to develop
and perpetuate the feeling of belonging to a distinct and, in many
ways, élite movement and the processes of inclusion and exclusion
discussed in the previous chapter were intended towards this aim.
Once boundaries had been created, their penetration by non-members
became extraordinarily difficult: 'I man want to keep some of his
mystery; don't want nobody to know all that about us; we are our own
people.'

But the movement was an urban phenomenon and, as such, had to
live amidst a multiplicity of different groups, including interest
groups, racial groups, subcultural groups, control groups; the whole
complex of contrasting social groups whose interaction makes up the
vortex of urban life. Rastas for all their pretensions to exclusivity
did not live in a social void but in a world populated by individuals
and groups, each with their own beliefs, values, perspectives, ambitions and conceptions of reality. Despite the strategies utilised to
insulate members from outsiders and their conflicting realities, the
Rastas were compelled, if only by virtue of their geographical location,
to conduct relationships (however tenuous) with other groups which
fell outside their parameters. These relationships can be characterised
as ranging from antagonistic to indifferent to compatible. My purpose
here is to run along this scale, selecting four groups with whom the
Rastas were in immediate contact. Beginning at the former end it

becomes apparent that, although the Rastas' central gripe was with the total system of Babylon, their attentions in the immediate environment were trained on what they regarded as the front-line enforcers and defenders of that system, the police.

For the Rastas, Babylon was the ultimate evil; much more than an emotive symbol but an everyday reality, something tangible, the effects of which could be experienced through day-to-day 'pressure'; a Rastaman declaimed: 'Each and every day pressure bears down on the black man: racism, unemployment and I would say injustice in the courts.' It was not a convenient synonym for abstract categories of colonialism, institutional racism or capitalism but a palpable and urgent reality which surrounded and encapsulated them. Even the early Jamaican Rastas who tried to separate themselves from the rest of society by setting up the Pinnacle commune under the leadership of Howell had to contend with periodic interference from the police who eventually closed down the settlement and arrested many of its members. The police more than any other group personified the Rastafarian conception of evil; they were the living proof that Babylon was alive, active and waiting for any opportunity to suppress them; they constituted empirical referents to the Babylonian conspiracy theory.

Like their Jamaican predecessors, the English Rastas perceived the police as a perpetual threat to their existence. Every encounter with them could be interpreted as the apocalyptic confrontation between good and evil. Of all their contacts with outside groups the relationship with the police was the most conflict-riven; one illustrative comment on this was: 'Conflict with the police? Huh! Police themselves are conflict.'

The police regarded the majority of Rastafarian members as inimical to the 'community interest'. (These observations are based on interviews with police officers in 1977–8.) Siding with the John Brown distinction between 'true Rastafarians' and 'the criminalised Dreadlock subculture' (1977, p. 7), they refused to concede the legitimacy of the movement as a religious phenomenon and saw only the Ethiopian Orthodox Church as the genuine wing of the movement. Police opinions on the Rastas (although not of direct relevance to this study) I found to be fairly consistent and in line with Brown's findings. A representative opening remark from an interview with a Superintendant I took to be revealing: 'The first thing you've got to do when you're talking about Rastafarians is distinguish between the real followers and these kids who stick a few posters of Haile Selassie on the wall, grow plaits and call themselves 'Rastas'. Most of them don't know what the hell they're on about and they're the ones who cause all the trouble for us.'

The situation parallels the early development in Jamaica when leaders were constantly intimidated, jailed or committed to the Bellevue lunatic asylum, thus discrediting the movement as having any legitimate religious content and relegating it to the margins of disreputation. But in England sanctions were not so severe, though allegations and counter-allegations of police brutality and Rastafarian attacks on police permeated the atmospheres of such areas as Brixton and Handsworth.

Consider the following three examples of police over-zealousness provided by Rastas:

I was just getting ready to close the shop – I'd turned out the lights – when this car went by and shot the fucking window through. They didn't have no uniforms on but I recognised the ras clots. Shot me fucking window straight through here (pointing to bullet hole in shopfront). (Rastafarian owner of West Indian takeaway food store)

I and I [pointing to two other Rastas] were just walking along this very street, about 12 o'clock – when Babylon just come up and threw us against the wall. Said to shut our mouths or they'd shut us up. Then they hammer us, man – fucking sticks and rods – really mash us. For nothing! I never did nothing, man, fuck all!

They [the police] were coming to the house – said they wanted to ask some questions about thieved radios. Then they really turn the place over, man . . . threaten to kill us. Then they took Ras Joseph away and brutalise him. Man, them real pressure.

The police were certainly apprehensive about the growth of the movement and the perceived deterioration of police–black relations, as the commission of Brown's *Shades of Grey* study (1977) indicated. The West Midlands police force called in an academic from the Cranfield Institute of Technology to compile a report on what was considered to be a volcanic situation in Birmingham's district of Handsworth (discussed in Chapter 10). The principal finding was that

The most serious police problems relate to crimes of violence against persons and personal property – notably robbery, thefts from the person, burglary, woundings and assaults . . . mainly committed by a particular group – some 200 youths of West Indian origin or descent who have taken on the appearance of followers of the Rastafarian faith by plaiting their hair in locks and wearing green, gold and red woollen hats. (J. Brown, 1977, p. 3)

Whilst reserving my comments on this allegation for a later chapter, it is as well to note that police in Handsworth seemed to be in agreement with such a conclusion. Brown's work, for all its faults, brings into focus some interesting perspectives of police officers based in the high immigrant area of Handsworth. He extracts from his interviews some telling comments such as:

And where Rastas are involved, there's always a risk of violence . . . I've seen too many of the lads done over. And I've suffered myself. Look, there's the scar still on my arm where a Rasta bit me last year.

The girls are often more vicious, stirring the boys to violence, and violent themselves. We've just had three cases of assault by girls. A copper hit with a steam iron. Another attacked with a knife. The third kicked in the testicles.

They've said they'll [Rastas] take a WPC, gangbang her and return the bits to Thornhill Road . . . I've been followed by groups of Rastas out on patrol, and involved in incidents that really frighten me. (J. Brown, 1977, pp. 9–10, 11, 16)

The validity of these statements is not in question for it is irrelevant to present purposes: what is relevant is the way in which they had incorporated the popular stereotype of the Rastaman into what Jerome Skolnick (1966, ch. 3) calls the police's 'working personality', a sort of perceptual shorthand which enables the policeman to deal with the exigencies of routine policing. If the above comments are to be accepted (and my own findings bear a similarity), then the police were prone to associate Rastas with open hostility. And, where danger is perceived, the police can summon mandate for a wide range of decisional latitude directed towards the maintenance of civil order (see also Skolnick, 1966; Bittner, 1967; Chambliss and Seidman, 1971, chs 15–17).

Now, I am neither suggesting that the police's accusations are incorrect nor that they used them as rationalisations for differential treatment of some sectors of the community (such suggestions would be improper, given the more limited task of this work). I am merely indicating that the police, by virtue of their work role, staked out a vast and unmanageable domain much of which was fraught with danger and ambiguity. It has been suggested by others that to facilitate their enterprise they collapse their working worlds into more graspable categories of where situations are liable to be typically dangerous, which areas are likely to exhibit most unrest, where conditions are likely to lead to disorder and what type of people are likely to involve themselves with violence or robbery and so on. They divide the world up according to its typical features so as to derive clues, suspicions and intuitions – more generally 'hunches' – about how to tackle their jobs most efficiently. And these typical features constitute the prisms in what Skolnick calls the policeman's 'cognitive lenses' through which he 'sees situations and events' (1966 p. 42). Such lenses are ground to suit the central variables of the police role, danger and authority, and the constant of efficiency. Skolnick's view has it that the police, by virtue of their role as upholders of civil order, see themselves as continually facing situations of potential physical violence which must be dealt with as efficiently as possible. They are required to exercise authority over other social actors whether it be arresting ganja-smokers, apprehending urban terrorists, or merely issuing speeding tickets to motorists. These in-built features of the role tend to make the police see the world through lenses which are more conducive to the efficient enforcement of the prohibitive norms of criminal law than the religious adherence to the dictates of due process. In other words, the most important function is the repression of criminal conduct, or the maintenance of order, and not an inflexible commitment to the rule of law (cf. Bittner, 1967).

Skolnick's work has been seminal in the field of police-work studies and I feel it provides insights into the tension-fraught relationships between the Rastas and the police in the late 1970s. Assuming that the police operated with these cognitive lenses, it is possible to draw out some statements of what was seen through them. For example, it seems that members of the Rastafarian movement were a threat to the order of the community, that they had scant respect for the law of the land and had no compunction in breaking it. Theft and robbery were their principal methods of gaining income, they preached peace and love yet practised violence and generally constituted a hazard to the community – and one which had to be checked (see Brown, 1977, sects 3–7). The elements of danger and authority were important. Because Rastas were regarded as potentially violent people ('where Rastas are involved, there's always the risk of violence') there existed the perception of danger. In particular, police in Handsworth and Brixton were 'very wary indeed' of black youths wearing dreadlocks or Ethiopian-coloured garments; it was this feeling that all such men were potentially dangerous to the policeman's safety that compelled the latter to maintain the upper hand at all times. One consequence of this might have been that the police were more likely to use force and be overly intimidating when arresting or questioning young blacks of Rastafarian appearance. (Certainly, the introduction of measures in Handsworth following the publication of *Shades of Grey* indicated the police's general concern and their effort to instigate a system of repressive measures rather than being purely reactive (i.e. to particular incidents.)

Again, my work was vitiated by the lack of any tangible evidence to corroborate or invalidate such allegations. The atmosphere of certain areas of London and Birmingham were so thick with accusations, denials, counter-accusations and counter-denials that, as Philip Knights, Chief Constable of the West Midlands Police Force noted, 'myths and realities' were 'woven together' (in Brown, 1977, p. 1). But it would be naïve not to extricate some strand from this web, if only by resort to James Baldwin's dictum, 'the only way to police the ghetto is to be oppressive': 'Their [the police's] presence is an insult, and it would be, even if they spent their entire day feeding gumdrops to the children. They represent the force of the white world' (Baldwin, 1962, p. 65).

The relevance of this is that for Rastas the police personified the nefarious system of Babylon, it was its front line, policemen were the puppets responding to the string-pulling politicians, bureaucrats, financiers and industrialists: 'Them just respond to the needs of Babylon; wear "the badge of brutality"' argued a teenage Rasta. Irrespective of what they actually did it was what they represented that was seen as so inflammatory. Their visibility was a continual reminder of the argus-like existence of Babylon, casting keen eyes on the Rastas' activities and seeking to suppress their attempts at carving out a cultural tradition of their own. Rastas were convinced that the police were engaged in a deliberate and orchestrated attempt to suppress them – on behalf of Babylon. Police were not seen as 'just doing their job', but were thought to be consciously directing their efforts towards the suppression of the Rasta population. Rastas were almost oblivious to any other duties of the police apart from what they considered to be the organised persecution: 'That's what they're there for, man: to keep the black man down; they see I as a threat.'

The police for their part were well aware of the contempt in which they were held and organised their role in accordance with the exigencies of the ghetto. Even the most passive, well-intentioned and virginally innocent policeman would soon discover he was the object of abuse and revile, not because of himself, but because of what he stood for. Under the accumulating hatred conferred upon him, he would be forced to adjust his sights, or lenses, and align his postures with the pressing circumstances confronting him in his elemental role as the maintainer of order.

In other words, the two sets of typifications would have been mutually re-inforcing, almost self-fulfilling. The Rastas were contemptuous of the police because of the oppressive system they considered they represented, the police were wary of the Rastas because they perceived them as disorderly troublemakers and had their perceptions enhanced by the bitterness they encountered: their postures and activities were forged with a view to controlling a hostile and disruptive group; the consequence of this was seen by the Rastas

and indeed by other young blacks (Troyna, 1977*a*) – as further
evidence of the attempt to suppress them and so naturally regarded
the police as agents of this attempt. In one notable incident at which
I was present four Rastas were apprehended by two police officers
springing from a panda car. Within seconds a group of 12- or 13-year-
olds emerged and started to revile the police with shouts of 'Babylon'.

The tension was further tightened by two factors. First, the Rastafarian refusal to recognise the institutional legitimacy on which the
police stood, and secondly, the police's attribution of organisation to
the movement. As members of Ras Tafari, blacks sought sanction for
their actions from a higher authority than English law; they looked
to 'God's law' which was founded on the principle of 'basic human
truths and rights'. The law as implemented by the police was regarded
as 'artificial', a man-made law, or 'the law of the Queen of England'.
Rastas were looking to a superordinate reference point for moral guidelines. So, for example, 'thieving' was not intrinsically wrong if the
culprit was without food and income, there was nothing improper
about trespassing, provided the trespasser had no other form of
shelter and, of course, smoking ganja was permissible because it was
a practice ordained by Jah (this accounts for the reluctance of the
majority of Rastas to condemn other members who might have continually brought the movement into disrepute in the public eye). Not
that they were prepared to flout the English law flagrantly for they
were sharply aware of the ingenuity and stealth of Babylon, 'a clever
creature' as it was once called. Working the system was a requirement
of survival; to oppose Babylon at its every manifestation was to
commit oneself to extinction. The soundest policy seemed to be in
cultivating a posture of non-contact and therefore minimise situations
of potential conflict; as a Rasta pleaded: 'Rastaman want nothing to
do with them, man; just want to be left alone and let the pressure
drop.'

The perceived lack of legitimacy in English law was certainly an
exacerbating factor in the Rastas' relations with the police which was
after all engaged in the affirmation of that law, but in many ways it
served to immunise them from the consequence of breaking that law.
As a Rastaman, the young West Indian was appealing to a higher
authority, that of Jah, and as such he was prepared to endure the
hardships, or 'pressure' ensuing from his ignorance of English law.
The law might 'mash' him and the police could 'brutalise' him
intensifying his 'suffering', but the Rastaman could comfort himself in
the sound knowledge that he was one of the Jah people, the
enlightened few obeying God's word and not that of others. The Day
of Deliverance when Babylon would burn out would prove them right
and, in the meantime, as one Rasta put it: 'The faith is the strength
to overcome the oppression; He [the Rastaman] has to adapt himself

to receive the pressure; but once he has his faith in God, then God will help him through.'

A second factor contributing to the decayed relations was the police's attribution of too much organisational sophistication to the movement. The police seemed to assume that the Rastaman was part of an enclosed and secretive organisation which was capable of co-ordinating effective acts of criminality. It was assumed that because Rastas associated with each other and interacted in the main with only fellow members, they were knowledgeable of each others' names, addresses, whereabouts, and so on. So that when they were questioned their failure to offer such information was a deliberate obstruction of justice. My findings concur with the observation that Rastas did interact frequently and regularly with one another (not only within specific territories: a Birmingham-based Rasta could easily strike up *ad hoc* relationships with London Rastas without prior meetings), but this is not evidence that they were privy to any personal information beyond that of belonging to the same brotherhood. As I have shown in the last chapter, the concept of the brotherhood circumvented clusters of organisational problems and facilitated the spontaneous establishment of interpersonal relations without the necessity of previous introduction. The brotherhood was the organisation; without its recognition the Rastafarian enterprise could not have functioned as a movement and would have dissolved into an unstructured aggregation of individuals and therefore cease to exist as such. However, the police, I sensed, regarded the movement as much more highly organised than it actually was (as one Rasta – seriously – suggested: 'Them think I and I like the Mafia'). As a result inquiries and questionings were conducted on the assumption that contacts between Rastas were less impulsive, more deliberate and purposeful, that each member of the brethren knew details of the biographical background of others and that failure to respond to such inquiries was due to lack of co-operation or downright recalcitrance. This observation was reinforced by conversations with police officers who seemed to detect that the Rastas really knew each other quite intimately and deliberately refused to co-operate for fear of breaking rank. Rastas themselves, when asked of their relations with the police, often complained that the police interrogated them in the belief that they really knew a great many other brothers on a personal basis; when in fact nicknames or baptismal names were often the extent of their knowledge of each other.

The lack of dialogue which characterised the relationship between the Rastas and the police fostered the mutual suspicion and contempt. At a general level it could be stated that since high crime rates are demonstrably correlated with poverty and deprivation, the police are always drawn to poor and resourceless groups, including minority groups; where a group exists that makes apparent its loss of affinity with the wider society and all its ramifications, then the police will, in all probability, operate with increased severity in regard to them. Such actions serve to underscore the initial minority group distrust and reinforce their conception of the police as oppressors. Bearing in mind the police's preoccupation with controlling or maintaining order rather than strict adherence to rules and the potential for wider ranges of discretion this breeds, it becomes obvious that the police's conflict-torn relationship with Rastas was rooted in the structure of the ghetto where the perceived legitimacy of the law was at its lowest and the urgency to use repressive policing tactics at its highest.

The Rastafarian relationship with the police was a particularly sour one and one which simply could not be sweetened. Attempts to improve relations were ill-founded and inevitably doomed to failure. Once the mutually unfavourable typifications, which were products of ghetto exigencies, had been concretised, the antagonistic processes were impossible to arrest. For the Rastas, things were happening to them, that is 'pressure', and, armed with the apprehension of how the world worked (the Babylonian conspiracy) they needed to look no further than their immediate environment for identifiable persons causing these things to happen. Living in the ghetto imposed narrowly circumscribed horizons and produced ranges of broadly similar experiences for young blacks. Being equipped with the theoretical skeleton for comprehending the world was of limited usefulness if no flesh for the bones was at hand. The police became the visible personification of the forces of Babylon which constrained and entrapped them: 'Where is Babylon?' a Rastaman reiterated my question, 'Babylon is everywhere, man, everywhere you see!'

On the other side of the relationship, the police in their zeal to exert complete control over potentially disruptive situations helped themselves with typified conceptions of where and from whom disturbances were likely. The Rastaman and his dwelling fell into this category – a position which was reinforced by the *Shades of Grey* findings. One probable consequence of this was the tendency of the police to hold circumspection in abeyance when approaching or questioning Rastafarian suspects. (In Birmingham the local police force of Handsworth embarked on an open campaign to stem the perceived menace of the Rastaman. See Chapter 10.)

The anatagonism with the police was a constant feature of the Rastafarian movement in Jamaica; it became possibly the most widely publicised feature of the movement in England and was influential in cultivating the popular association between the Rastas and violence. My impressionistic evidence, backed by theoretical support from elsewhere, provides some sort of framework for appreciating more fully the sets of hostility and how they were grounded in the structural conditions of the ghetto. But less obvious were the antagonisms vented against another group which was ostensibly separated from Babylon and in many ways more akin to the Rastas themselves. While the hostility to the police was in some measure a 'logical' outcome of circumstances, the aggravated relations with Asians require a little more perspicacity regarding the activities of this other minority group.

THE DISTURBING ASIANS

Asian migrants to Britain in the 1950s and 1960s came from a variety of geographical backgrounds, carrying with them their own particular cultural traits, different religions, languages and to an extent different aspirations. Once in Britain they coalesced into separate communities residentially and socially according to their characteristics.

Their presence in England was nearly as old, if not as celebrated, as that of West Indians. As early as 1873 Joseph Salter was to document the establishment of a group of Asian seamen in London's East End (Ballard and Ballard, 1977, pp. 22–3) though it was not until the 1950s that large-scale emigration from the Asian continent to Britain became a reality. The pull factors facilitating this movement stem from basically the same conditions as those working in relation to West Indian migration: a swelling economy and insufficient indigenous unskilled labour supplies. Together with the incoming West Indians, Pakistanis and Indians converged on Britain to satisfy the requirements of industry. Without going into detail, it seems fair to suggest that they experienced the sharp prongs of racialism as painfully as blacks and settled in social positions akin to those of their fellow immigrants.

Like West Indians, they retreated into enclaves, forging self-sufficient networks of involuted relationships which were by and large untouched by the white world. But, unlike West Indians, they crystallised into regional and village groups in English cities, helping each other in supportive endeavours to create businesses, property holdings and other commercial ventures. (The West Indians did utilise a system of 'partners', but this was aimed at basically existing rather than building commercial enterprises.)

For present purposes it is unnecessary to detail the exact reasons for this tendency, for this would require a documentation of values, dispositions, motivations, class and caste backgrounds etc.; suffice it to quote Badr Dahya: 'Since the motive for migration is economic, and since the immigrant regards his stay in Britain as temporary, he is keen to deploy his time to his best end' (1974, p. 92).

The view is perhaps simplistic but for the moment I need only record that one consequence of it was the emergence of a commercial structure bearing marked Asian characteristics. Pakistani bingo halls, Indian travel agencies, clothes manufacturers and retailers, banks, estate agents, grocery and fruit shops became evident in northern and midland towns as well as areas of London, and their presence was rammed home by Urdu signs on facias and windows and Hindustani posters on hoardings. What success the Asians had in the commercial sphere was rendered conspicuous by their concentration in particular geographical areas of cities such as Leeds, Bradford and Leicester; the profitability of their ventures was no secret to the ghetto resident.

Significantly, the advancements of Asians brought no resentment from their less socially mobile fellow migrants. Neither group, it seems, had any initial ambition to settle permanently in the new environment, though, of course, attitudes probably changed after periods of orientation (see Davison, 1966; Foner, 1977). If West Indians did begrudge Asians their successes, however limited, they certainly did not convert this into open hostility. For the most part, they shared a common position of overcrowding in decaying areas of the inner cities, having to bear the brunt of racialist practices in employment, housing, services and seeing their children socially disadvantaged at school; generally living amidst a hostile climate – sometimes hotter, at other times cooler.

Not only did Asians value commercial independence, but also cultural autonomy. They brought with them rich, historical, religious and cultural traditions, replete with customs, ritual and ceremony and sought to transplant them in the new environment. Obviously aware of the difficulties and contradictions this would impose, Asians settled for a type of 'Jekyll and Hyde' existence, compartmentalising their involvements at work and at home so that the reciprocal interference was minimised. Occasional spillovers, such as the Sikh's insistence on wearing turbans at all times and the Muslim's obligation to pray to Allah at junctures in the working day, caused flashpoints, but in the main the two spheres were kept separate and conflicts were contained. As such, traditional cultures proved a valuable resource for Asians who might have faced ill conditions and tension-fraught social relations during their working days, but once home could retire into a rich cultural complex comprising historical, religious traditions around which webs of social relationships were formed.

First-generation West Indians, as I noted, also took refuge in religious forms, but these started very much as makeshift institutions to tackle the immediate problem of religious vacuity and were in this sense not cultural extensions (though, of course, similarities were maintained in West Indian churches).

Asian religions were all-pervasive, providing not only a basis for social organisation and networks of relationships, but guidelines for practices, norms, customs, obligations, social behaviour and generally what is known as 'a style of life'. While they may have overtly suspended their religious adherence for the pragmatic purposes of earning a living, the Asians had deeply embedded cultural resources to withdraw into and find social support.

Generally, then, the Asians worked at establishing self-sufficient networks of relationships based on traditional principles which were shielded from the wider society and, at the same time, very effective in promoting cultural alternatives and commercial bases. Throughout the 1960s, these networks strengthened and evolved into what might warrantably be called Asian community structures, including the features of social organisations and control, cultural values and norms, principles of inclusion and exclusion, religious ideals and practical objectives; semi-autonomous sub-societies – hence the attribution of labels such as 'Little India' to parts of urban centres.

West Indians demonstrated only limited zeal in both commercial and cultural spheres. They brought with them little or no experience in establishing and running businesses and nothing resembling the Asians' cultural and religious legacy. The consequence was that they were commercially unsuccessful and culturally vacuous compared to Asians. If the blacks had chosen to use Asians as benchmarks of their success in the new environment they would have been drawn irresistibly to the conclusion that they were failing. And yet the differential in success between the two sets of first-generation immigrants did not translate into hostility or even resentment. Presumably West Indians were less inclined to view Asian's achievements as criteria of success; and more likely to use their past existence in the West Indies as a basis for comparison with present circumstances. The upshot of this was a condition of 'peaceful coexistence'; the two groups, whilst living in close proximity, interfered with each other only minimally, restricted social relationships and remained unconcerned about each other's respective activities. West Indians and Asians formed two distinct and separate enclaves, bulked together as 'immigrants' by observers, but sharing little common awareness of their shared position and joint interests.

First-generation West Indians had experienced concentrated hostility during the Teds' 'wog-bashing' episodes of the 1950s, but were not slow to retaliate once they realised the commonality of their position. Asian immigrants came to their turn slightly later, in the 1960s, when they were forced to take the bitter medicine of 'Paki-bashing' once the skinheads had set their sights on selected targets. A feral combination of skinheads and rude boys was the source of extreme anxiety to the Asians who were subjected to frequent and unprovoked attacks for no reason other than that they carried the visible features of the Asian, or 'Paki' stereotype. This *accouplement* was charged with the imperative to challenge authority wherever it existed; in the school, at the soccer match, at the discotheque or at the police station. It was a marriage of convenience designed to extract maximum excitement out of a loosely articulated directive to destroy or damage anything which impinged on the skins' traditional, reactionary working-class values; deviant groups and all manifestations of authority.

The spate of attacks on Asians in the sixties lends a useful insight into the pattern of West Indian–Asian relations for, although the working-class skins' antagonisms can be understood in terms of their general ethos which Clarke (1975) characterised as 'the magical recovery of community', and their efforts to eliminate the perceived threat of, to them, deviating groups, their temporary alliance with the adolescent West Indian rudies brought forth a stituation in which the sons of black immigrants were engaged in a stylised – almost ritualistic – violence directed at a group of fellow immigrants who, in a great many ways, faced exactly the same problems of existence as themselves.

The rude boys' aggression had an almost paradoxical element to it; but one which was to endure in second-generation West Indian social patterns. Superficially, it could be dismissed in terms of a 'follow my leader' policy in which the excitement-seeking blacks simply tagged on to a group with whom they shared a number of characteristics and unthinkingly trailed along into the battlefield, striking up similar postures and advocating similar tractics. It is more likely, however, that the adolescent West Indians had cultivated a genuine dislike of Asians and found in the skinheads ready partners; together they formed a dirigible vehicle favourable to the commission of violence against very specific groups, one of the chief targets of which was the Asians.

Whatever the rude boys' motivations there can be no denying that they were at least, in part, responsible for the establishment of institutionalised second-generation West Indian–Asian hatred. During the course of my research, I encountered several allegations from Asians that younger West Indians were, at one extreme, abusive and, at the other, terroristic. Asian shopkeepers were (on their own account) perpetually disturbed by threatening behaviour and almost systematic thieving; accusations of accosting in the streets abounded and police officers I spoke to were recipients of regular complaints of harassment. During the late 1970s it became apparent that there was no love lost between the two migrant groups.

Ostensibly, Rastafarian members were not interested in Asians; in their own words they were 'impartial' (meaning quite literally that their feelings towards Asians were neutral). Their relations with Asians were allegedly minimal and not valued and therefore not encouraged; but, because of their attitude of total indifference, relationships never involved the element of conflict. Apparently, they did not even think about the Asians enough to cultivate any posture of hostility towards them. But Asians claimed that Rastas were intensely antagonistic, in many ways symbolising the second-generation West Indian's unkindly stance. Tales of street attacks and violent robberies as well as the more mundane verbal abuses were no doubt penetrated with a substantial dosage of hearsay and mythology, but confirmation from the police of Asian complaints lent some credence to the Asians' claim that they bore the brunt of the Rastas' wrath. Irrespective of the validity of such a charge, the Asian conviction that they had become the new 'whipping boys' for the Rastas fed an anxiety and concern for their own community existence. They became vigorously critical of the Rastas, calling for disciplinary measures from the police and insisting that they heralded the latest spate of intimidations of Asians. Clearly mindful of the Paki-bashing activities of the sixties, Asians perceived the growth of the new West Indian youth culture, structurally apparented to the rude boy complex (though vastly different in content) as severely inimical to their own interests.

During 1977 and 1978 Indians and Pakistanis indicated a rising concern with the Rastafarian movement, attributing to its members disgraceful motives, condemning them as irreligious and generally castigating the movement's principles as socially harmful. Their complaints (which I base on informal interview notes) came under the following headings: street attacks; shop-lifting; accosting in the street; verbal abuse; protection rackets (though not run exclusively by Rastas); and deliberately playing loud music to disturb neighbours. Rastas themselves were thought to be racialist; violently motivated; criminally inclined; lazy and indolent; and some even suggested they were mentally unstable. As such, they were thought to be bringing inimical influences to bear on the younger West Indians who were vulnerable to 'indoctrination' and to Asians whose existence in England was thought to be 'hard enough without more dangers from within the immigrant community'. Generally, the whole immigrant community was perceived to be threatened by the disrepute engendered by the Rastas.

Rastas may well have been wrongly branded as Asian antagonisers, and faced with such an accusation they responded by denying any acrimony. There was, however, sufficient formally and informally transmitted evidence to suggest that at least some elements of the movement were averse to the Asian presence. Apart from the evidences of the police and Asians' remarks about the Rastas' dislike of them, I gained some interesting insights from non-Rastafarian blacks who were very concerned about the conflicts (Rastas themselves talked about Asians only after much cajoling). On one occasion I was present with a non-Rasta West Indian in the immediate aftermath of an incident in which an Indian grocery store owner had his shop window smashed and some of his products stolen by black youths wearing Ethiopian coloured tams. The picture I pieced together from all the scraps of evidence supported the view that considerable anti-Asian sentiments existed in the Rastafarian movement. Rastas' dislike of Asians in many ways brought into the open a simmering bitterness felt by second-generation West Indians. Since the rude boy escapades, no real systematic pressure had been imposed upon Asians: but no significant improvements in relations had ensued either. During the interim, the Asian community had worked fairly energetically at improving their material and cultural conditions with a degree of success: West Indians had made little impact in either sphere. And in this difference lies the key to understanding the apparent hostility, or at least 'virulent indifference' of some Rastas in relation to Asians.

My argument rests on the concept of resentment of the British Asians' material and cultural advancement relative to the modest achievements of West Indians. Rastas saw Babylon in every social sphere where the black man experienced exploitation. As I have stressed before, the whole history of blacks' relations with whites could be explained by reference to the Babylonian conspiracy, the theory which accounted for the persisting suppression of black people's potentialities. In their immediate environment, blacks were accustomed to buying from Asian-owned stores and paying rents to Asian land-lords; evidence that Asians had fully integrated themselves into the structure of Babylon, the exigencies of which were to maximise profit at the expense of the black man. To young blacks the fawning Asians had gained a degree of acceptance by white society and were seen as ready partners to the conspiracy. Babylon was a palpable and available reality to Rastas, not a pure theoretical elaboration of the workings of the world. 'Pressure' from the forces of Babylon impinged on their everyday experience squeezing them into positions of powerlessness and cultural anonymity. As well as having the analytical equipment provided by the legitimating conspiracy theory of the movement, Rastas had tangible reminders of the reality of Babylon – as was noted in the previous section. Asians emerged as a manifestation of another tentacle of the Babylonian octopus (a warrantable metaphor): they aspired to power and wrested it admirably, accepting the ultimate domination by whites but working steadfastly within the system to achieve their aims.

Knowledge of the Babylonian conspiracy gave Rastas the abstract categories of thought to analyse their conditions but they could also perceive what I call the immediate idiom, apprehending their local environment and relating this to their theories. In this sense, the servile Asians came to look like augmentations of Babylon. This grew from the resentment of the Asians' gradual but perceptible assumptions of power over material resources; the inroads they had made through their commercial enterprises had taken them to positions of material superiority over the West Indians and they were regarded as utilising their power to exploit blacks further (through high rents and inflated shop prices, for example). One Rasta held the extreme and provocative view that the Asians were organising their own conspiracy in which they would eventually swallow up the whites' supremacy: 'They [Asians] are a growing threat which must be destroyed before they achieve the monopoly they are after.'

If Africa was to serve as an exemplar – and young West Indians were certainly directing their attention towards this continent for inspiration – then the cases of Uganda and Kenya were helpful reminders of how Asians should be disfavourably treated. If Jamaica was to serve as one, then their parents could supply stories of the small minority of Asians on the island, most of whom had established themselves on sound commercial footings.

But there was another aspect to this resentment which was of a different quality. As I have said, the Asian immigrants brought with them a rich cultural tradition based on the religious principles of Islam, Hinduism and Sikhism. They extended these in the new environment establishing social relationships on territorial and religious bases, and constructing their own temples for worship, and, of course, as sources of community foci. They demonstrated their culture almost arrogantly wearing turbans, Muslim fezes and saris made of imported silks; and they communicated in their native languages. There was almost an élitist tinge about the way they restored their culture in England, especially where religious points clashed with constitutional laws, and the issue could be promoted as a political event, such as the wearing of turbans on motorcycles or the polygamous practices of Muslims. (The sense of élitism was probably redoubled by the fact that Asians would have been familiar with a stratification system based on culture as opposed to the more obvious criteria of power, wealth or race.)

Rastas, I detected, resented the Asians' possession of this deep-seated cultural tradition and their own lack of anything comparable. It enabled Asians to ride out the problems of racialism much more effectively because they could always content themselves with the satisfying conviction that they belonged to a separate, distinct and, in many ways, exclusive culture the paths to which were barred to whites. Moreover, they practically held a mirror to whites by containing and preserving those characteristics so highly prized by 'conventional' white society. For example, the Asians' retention of their own religion imbued them with cultural conservatism or traditionalism, affording their community stability and tight internal controls, leading in turn to highly principled practices of morality, minimised deviation from norms and respect for authority and age. Such community traits were regarded as virtuous by whites and so allowed Asians the contentment that they were in a very real sense superior to the rest of society – by its own criteria (!) – thus dispelling any doubts about their own élitism and offsetting the negative perceptions held about them by the wider society (I am grateful to Percy Cohen for this point). So, whereas the West Indians would have been hard-pressed to find counter-definitions offering different conceptions of themselves to those offered by white society, Asians had continual recourse to traditional elements as a kind of buffering culture.

As I have emphasised, the dynamic impelling the whole Rastaferian enterprise was the effort to upgrade blackness in the face of prevalent stigmatic conceptions. Central to this was the establishment of a distinct and separate culture; the focus on Africa to dig out 'roots' and 'the way of the Ancients' (Ethiopians) was a desperate search for a meaningful cultural nucleus around which to build improved social lives. The locks, the colours and the language were important symbolic strategies in promoting this sense of cultural discovery among blacks. 'Rasta', it was repeatedly stressed, was not just a religion but 'a way of life' – a total cultural experience. But while the Rastafarian attempt to resurrect a cultural heritage was an arduous, often painstaking task, fraught with obstacles of non-acceptance and disconfirmation, Rastas saw the Asians as facing no such difficulty. And here the resentment surfaced.

They saw the Asians holding similar positions to themselves (as non-white immigrants) yet coping much more successfully thanks to their cultural independence. Looking to their parents, they found no parallel: blacks devoid of any socially significant contribution, only bastardised versions of Christianity which drove them to the margins of 'conventional' or orthodox religion and encouraged them to accept passively the patronising whites' definitions of blacks and their corresponding social roles. Rastas were cautious when criticising their parents outright but intimated that they were generally disappointed with the limited progress made by first-generation West Indians. They had little to be proud of in terms of cultural achievements and nothing of note in the commercial sphere. These failures were seen as attributable to the passive modes of posturing adopted by this generation due in the main to the 'brainwashing' influence of colonialism. Effectively, the only route available to first-generation blacks with their limited cultural resources was to assimilate and aspire to white ideals which led to their 'mental enslavement'; to repeat a Rasta: 'They're enslaved, they're enslaved mentally because until one finds liberation within his mind then one can never hope for a body to be liberated. We believe that perhaps the majority of blacks in this country are still in a state of mind that can be described as not a conscious state of mind. They still believe they are perhaps inferior.'

By stark contrast, Asians possessed their own religious institutions and languages, replete with symbols and symbolic activity which owed nothing to white society (and was not even connected to Christianity). What is more, they had used these conspicuously to create their own semi-autonomous 'ethnic colonies', incorporating elements of internal politics, social organisation and social control. Rastas, of course, were vehement in their outright condemnation of assimilation of English cultural goals as irrelevant to the black man and a retardation to his overall development; and it was for this reason that they held a grudging admiration for aspects of Asian communities. Often Rastas would compare their own position to that of the Asians, usually expressing the wish that Ras Tafari be recognised as a viable religious enterprise and therefore (theoretically) amenable to integration. This was regarded as a phase in the more comprehensive redemption plan: 'Understand I and I as religious people'; 'Rasta is trying to form his own community, just like the Muslims and the Sikhs have done over here'.

The two sets of Asian achievements, material and cultural, jelled into an interesting paradox: for the Rastas they had become accomplices of Babylon through their commercial, exploitative ventures; yet they retained cultural separation, almost aloofness and preserved their own distinctness from white society; whilst participating in Babylon they drew short of actually being of that system. Rastas, I sensed, were disturbed by both halves of the paradox; the first because Asians were parties to the exploitation of the black man, the second because they had possession of something akin to what Rastas themselves aspired to. And it was these two disturbing features which prompted the rather uneasy tension (to put it circumspectly) between young Rastas and the whole Asian community.

The Rastas were not interested in the particularities of Asians, their cultural diversity, the fact that most of them were fixed at the bottom of the occupational hierarchy or the conflicts they had to contend with. They oriented to an Asian working his way into the rotting structure of Babylon, yet holding on to a set of exclusive cultural preserves which gave him the edge over the rest of the immigrant population.

What was for the Rastas a paradox, was for the Asians a resolution of conflict between two cultures: working the system and sustaining the culture. They were bemused by the Rastas' often overt hostility and held no malice against the elder West Indians for the attitudes and practices of their offspring (except that they were perhaps too lenient with their children).

The antagonism, then, was not reciprocal: Asians on the whole respected the West Indian community and were tolerant of the youthful exuberances without ever comprehending the reasons for them. But for the Rasta, the Asian presented a disturbing, inconsistent feature of his immediate landscape. Feelings among Rastafarian ranks varied between disinterest and despite, but none openly sympathised with Asians as fellow migrants. Asians had grappled with the contradictions of switching to a new environment, adapting to it, yet retaining a rich cultural tradition; but the manner in which they had achieved this was totally unacceptable to the Rasta. In many ways, the Asian symbolised the accomplice of Babylon, but one which was artful enough to engineer its own cultural continuance as a separate and autonomous entity: 'Them real cunning: make up to Babylon but keep their own secrets.' (It might be interesting to compare the Rastas' feelings about the Asians with the American Black Muslims' feelings about the Jews. See Lincoln, 1961 and Essien-Udom, 1962.)

Apart from the police and the Asians the ghettos from which the Rastas emerged were populated by other blacks. Their relations with Asians were tense, often spilling over into conflict situations. But then again they were forced into encounters with Asians because of their geographical location; social ties were practically non-existent. On the other hand, ties with black residents of the ghetto were multifaceted and therefore warrant attention in their own right.

OTHER BLACKS

In Jamaica, the black reaction to the Rastafarian movement had ranged from fear to indifference or even sympathy. Without assuming a complete homogeneity of attitude and opinion, certain patterns can be discerned which indicate changing relationships between the black majority and the movement. During the 1970s when the spread of Rastafarian ideas and imperatives penetrated even party politics with Premier Michael Manley's adoption of Haile Selassie's Rod of Correction, it seems that many blacks were generally in sympathy with the problems and ambitions of the cultists and liable to lend their support, if only passively. But, of course, by the late seventies the Rastas had toned down their more extreme and bizarre insistences on a supernaturally wrought remove to Africa which characterised the early cult, and abandoned ideas of usurpation entertained by at least some factions during the 1960s. By 1978 the Rastas in Jamaica had achieved some degree of acceptance and legitimacy amongst other blacks without really cleansing themselves of the stigma associated with earlier phases; cases of crossing the road to avoid Rastas were still commonplace (reported by Roger Frankland in personal communication, January 1978).

At the same stage in the development of the English movement it was difficult to determine with any precision the reaction of other West Indians not affiliating with the movement, for in many ways they were still recovering from the initial shock of witnessing its rapi growth in the urban areas of London, Birmingham, Liverpool, Leicester and Manchester. Many were startled by the sudden appearance of dreadlocks and colours and tended to view the movement as an ephemeral indulgence of youth. But as the Rasta phenomenon took root it became apparent that Ras Tafari was arguably the most exciting and vitally important force in the lives of second-generation West Indians. Even those black youths who did not accept Ras Tafari themselves were implicated by their relationships with members. So, as the movement grew to prominence the black community was made to recognise the presence of a distinctly English manifestation of the Rastafarian movement and therefore to take some kind of stance towards it.

Overall, younger blacks were *en rapport*, while the middle-aged and older members of the black community were dismissive. A degree of sympathy from others of the same age bracket was perhaps understandable; the Rastas were, after all, articulating an expression of dissatisfaction with the treatment of blacks generally, not just idiosyncratic grievances. The response of the first generation was more interesting, resulting, I would argue, from the different life experiences of the two groups. The older blacks, it should be remembered, had to cope with a formidable disjuncture at the situation of migration, or, to dilute Elkins' formulation, a sequence of 'shocks', compounded by the encounter with rejection once in England. They had to grapple with the totally changed social and geographical environment without the assistance of any tangible resources. The intention of returning home after a period of anticipated prosperity and the memory of the awful conditions they left behind in the West Indies were effective in enabling new arrivals to adjust to the new conditions. It was noted in Chapter 3 how they kept a low profile, retreating into Pentecostal-type churches and looking to other-worldly salvation as compensation for hardships in their more immediate situations.

By the mid-seventies most of those intending to stay permanently or at least semi-permanently had achieved some kind of stability and security of position; they had a stake in England. Alarm crept in as they saw their sons and daughters drifting into lifestyles and appearances of a group whose notoriety was probably at its peak in Jamaica at the time they had left. (My research indicates that most Rastas, about 85 per cent, came across with their parents between 1960 and 1968, aged between 6 and 14.) The incidents involving Claudius and Ronald Henry and the episode at Coral Gardens (see Chapter 2) had prompted an island-wide panic and the government's anti-ganja programmes were topical themes during the sixties when as far as the public was concerned the Rastaman awoke from his delusional daydreams of an African redemption to assume the more threatening role of a folk devil. Jamaicans in England were no doubt fearful that their children would incline towards similar postures as their frustration mounted.

As it became apparent that the English movement was of different quality and tone to its Jamaican equivalent, parents buried early fears and became more concerned with the difficulties their children would face when trying to 'fit in' to society whilst retaining the bizarre appearance of the Rastaman: 'How do they seriously hope to fit in this society looking like that?' a Rasta's father asked.

Those blacks without children were concerned with the more pragmatic problems of how the Rastas' appearance and supposed misdemeanours could bring the whole West Indian community into dire disrepute. They trivialised the young blacks' complaints of white society by referring back to the problems facing blacks in the British West Indies and called for a more disciplined approach to social control from within and without the community. In particular, the Rastafarian claims of police brutality were scoffingly dismissed. Brown's *Shades of Grey* study, despite its flaws, brings out this sentiment rather well; he quotes: 'Harassment, they don't know what the word mean. If any of these boys go back to their own country, then they really find out. Then they go suffer harassment. If the policemen there say "Keep moving", then he keep moving. If he don't move, bam, bam, bam. Then he keep moving . . .' (1977, p. 32). And he goes on: 'they [the police] are pressed – by West Indians – to take stronger action against West Indian youth' (p. 33). These observations agree with my own; older West Indians showed concern at the apparent lack of discipline in the second generation and sometimes regarded the police as contributing to the problem by 'taking too soft a line', as one middle-aged Jamaican put it. (One senior Rasta once confided in me: 'Rastas over here complain about police brutality but truthfully they don't know its meaning; in Jamaica police use their clubs first – and then don't ask questions at all!')

At a theological level, West Indians found the Rastas' belief system abstruse, perplexing, or just 'illogical'. An otherwise sympathetic black, Anglican vicar (himself from Jamaica) informed me: 'I think the general ethos of the movement is very positive for young blacks in this society; but I personally find it theologically illogical.' A Roman Catholic church-goer (also from Jamaica) observed: 'I think this society [as he called the movement] is confusing because they [the Rastas] have got hold of a philosophy without achieving a full knowledge of the doctrine of Ras Tafari. As a consequence they are making fools of themselves.'

Christians regarded the movement as somewhat heretical with the young blacks bringing a slur on the whole West Indian community. As nearly all Rastas came from conventional Christian family backgrounds it was inevitable that parent–child conflict over beliefs would arise. In practically all cases tensions had caused either temporary or permanent rifts, with the youth leaving home after disagreements had grown to a head. Sometimes, the younger members returned to their parents after a reciprocal modification of attitudes in which the parents adopted a more accommodating stance and the youth exercised a greater degree of tolerance; a kind of depolarisation. Considering the religious tendencies of early migrants, the lack of sympathy was understandable. Rastas were, in many ways, the antithesis of their elders, eschewing conventional church-going activities, disbelieving mainstream interpretations of the Bible, refusing to accept passively existing circumstances in the hope of other-worldly compensation, as well as turning their sights away from Britain, or indeed the West Indies, as their focus of identity. It constituted a complete rupture with the religious beliefs and practices of the first generation, agreeing at only a limited number of points such as the acceptance of a single deity (though differently conceived of), the recognition of the Bible as the sacred book (though differently interpreted), and sometimes the self-commitment in being the 'enlightened people'.

But doctrinal particulars were less important to the Rastas themselves than the postures they prompted. They saw in their parents models of deprivation and debasement, people who had uprooted themselves from their homeland in anticipation of a new life only to find severe limitations on their opportunities due in the main to their skin colour. Rather than retaliate against this rejection they had adapted to it, retreating into black communities and adopting hardly visible profiles. They saw their parents passively withdrawing from the world instead of trying to transform it: 'Fooling themselves; they're never going to be treated as equals in this society.' As the second generation, they had spent at least the later sections of their childhood in England; they had been schooled here, learnt to interact with white children in a great many spheres and were led to believe that they faced the world on an equal footing with their native, white counterparts. As a consequence, their expectations and aspirations were buoyant and likely to feed discrepancies when they were not met. The bitterness and resentment felt by young blacks after the frustration of their ambitions impelled them to take fresh cognisance of their parents' outlooks and stances, asking the question: 'Were they appropriate to the situation?' With no tangible hope of improvement on the horizon, they formulated a rough calculus and concluded that their parents were sadly misguided, hopelessly deluded or simply duped by society into accepting erroneous beliefs. Ras Tafari was a way of rectifying these. 'Misguided by European Christianity', 'blinded by Babylon', 'possessing an inferiority complex', or just 'brainwashed' were some of the phrases used by Rastas to describe their parents' subordination.

Drifting into the Rastafarian movement reinforced these views; Rastas, after a period of outrage with the first generation's attitudes and postures, became convinced that the whole phenomenon could be explained by reference to the Babylonian conspiracy framework. 'Misguided' was the key word; voluntarily misguided but led by the persuasive forces of Babylon. No anger was expressed by the Rastas at their elders' failure to take up more challenging postures because they did not doubt their sincerity nor their intention; their vision had simply been obscured through over-exposure to white religion and its ideals. On the other hand, they perceived themselves as the enlightened ones; those who had pierced the rhetoric and obfuscation of Babylon and would aspire to new, higher ambitions and objectives, guided by new ideas untouched and unpolluted by white influences. First- and second-generation blacks may both have been searching for God but the paths each took and the postures they cultivated were in striking contrast.

Rastas were not antagonistic towards their parents because of their beliefs and attitudes (although in the initial period of drift, many said their family's intolerance and repudiation of the movement had led to situations of conflict). Once it became apparent that the Rastas had stabilised their beliefs and were deriving support and inspiration from them, attitudes of hostility dissolved and dialogue between parent and child reopened; asked about this, a Rasta replied: 'Yes, my parents had great difficulty understanding I's faith. But they had to get to terms with the fact that it is my life. Once they get this then they accept more. My relationships with parents are even better than before.'

Rastas emitted an interesting response to the presence of West Africans, a comparatively small minority group in England, migrating either temporarily or permanently from, in the main, Nigeria, Ghana and Sierra Leone. Considering that the Rastas constantly drew inspiration from Africa, their spiritual homeland, and quixotically neglected their immediate interests in England in the hope of an ultimate redemption in that continent, it is perhaps surprising that Rastas did not find some sort of affinity with black Africans. They did not: on the contrary, Rastas found little or no common ground with Africans and, in some circumstances, despised their presence. Conversely, Africans tended to be rather perplexed by the Rastafarian insistence on a 'return' to Africa; the claim to be of African descent was clear enough, but the synonymity of Ethiopia and the whole of Africa, the divinity of Haile Selassie and the obsessive urge to migrate to Africa were puzzling elements. Beyond this, West Africans were incredulous at the Rastas' somewhat politically naïve conception of the continent and astounded at their conviction that African countries would be so accommodating as to entertain the immigration of West Indians. (These observations are based on interviews with

Nigerians, some of whom were studying and some settled permanently.)

The Rastafarian lack of any type of attachment to Africans in England was simple to understand. The Rastas had, by and large, internalised the popular image of the West Africans in England: here for university degrees or technical qualifications not available in their own countries; members of the aspiring middle class, reaping the benefits of a family wealthy enough to send them to England for education; self-oriented with their almost mercenary approach and caring little for the millions of other less fortunate blacks. Characteristics stemming from this type were the propensity to assimilate if necessary, adopting conventional white ideals (for example, educational attainment, professional positions), European styles of dress. English accents (as far as possible) and generally approaching the pejorative role of 'black Englishmen'. Apart from all these negative traits imputed to West Africans in England, there was the one irrefutable reality that while Rastas were trapped in England and wished to go to Africa, Africans had left their birth-place to go to England!

Here I am unconcerned with the extent to which the Rastas' images measured up to the patterns of West African migration to Britain and the dispositions of those migrating (but see Goody and Groothues, 1977); it was a subjective reality and one which Rastas organised their relationship around. They saw Africans in England as somehow anomalous, a misplaced presence. They were not to be regarded as 'true' Africans, otherwise they would not have broken fidelity and left for England. Whether they intended to utilise their skills and expertise for the benefit of their country was secondary; the immediate reality was that they were prepared to foresake their homeland in the quest for personal advancement. In a great many respects they symbolised the corruption of Africa by the Europeans: seduced into abandoning his culture and acquiring white characteristics, the African was enticed by the lure of Western ideals; as a Rasta pointed out: 'Africans over here are good examples of how colonialism can work: to split a man from his fatherland and make him think he is doing a rightful and worthy thing.' Considering the Rastas valued English education lightly, the idea of leaving Africa to pursue that very target seemed absurd and self-defeating. The educational system was seen as structured around white precepts and integrated into the Babylonian programme of suppressing blacks. Africans willingly entering into it were tantamount to 'lambs to the slaughter'; gullible recruits to the structure of white domination: 'Some of them practically white themselves; briefcases and that.'

One group of blacks who were clearly not parties to the perpetuation of white domination were black power organisation members. In the 1970s they drew their recruits mainly from West Indian immigrants but also from settled West Africans. As I mentioned in Chapter 5 many affiliates of black power turned to Ras Tafari in the hope that the cultivation of awareness of commonality, or 'black consciousness', would lead on logically to mobilisation at a more overtly political level. Many were disappointed at the way the movement developed after its promising genesis. Members seemed to lack interest in conventional politics, eschewing any connection with Babylon. Further, the emphasis on the implicitness of Haile Selassie and the doctrines of 'peace and love' were at variance with the more militant proposals of black power which sought to 'stir up racial hatred': 'I can't take this "turn the other cheek" philosophy: if someone pushes me, then I go to war with him whoever he is,' claimed a black power adherent.

Even those black power members who enjoyed good relations with Rasta groups exhibited disappointment with the failure of the movement to articulate a more political critique of society. The more militant blacks displayed a marked ambivalence about the movement, seeing in it the glimmer of hope for a mass political mobilisation, yet expressing disappointment and almost disgust at its failure to peel away the 'transcendental' elements to reveal a starker form of protest: 'Sure, the potential was there; the whole deal was a consciousness-raising exercise. But they can do no good the way they are. What good is it going to do sitting around contemplating Haile Selassie and peace and love for all men?'

Some Rastas, of course, were drawn from the ranks of black power groups in much the same manner as many original Rastafarian adherents were former members of Garveys organisation, the UNIA (Vincent, 1976, p. 227). But while some drifted more deeply, involving themselves in the concepts and themes of Ras Tafari to the point of accepting Haile Selassie as God, others grew dissatisfied at the failure of the movement to metamorphose into a political organisation; one militant described the Rastas as 'slightly wayward brothers'.

Apart from these disagreements, Rastas retained good relationships with black militants. Both housed a fundamental critique of Western society and both sought a comprehensive and radical change. A Rasta told me: 'It's good that they want to change society, but I just can't accept the ways it has to come. Where is the plan?' The modes of expressing the critique and the manner in which the change should occur were largely incompatible, but these were 'mechanical' rather than 'kinetic' issues. The two were tied by the underlying imperative to free the black man of his subordination in the white-dominated world and to allow him to realise his full potential. They entertained forceful visions of how this disentanglement from white society could be achieved and it was these visions which constituted the dynamics energising both movements.

Black power was unpalatable to Rastas, as was the form of

Christianity practised by the first generation. The one lacked religious significance and preached a racism which was unacceptable, while the other lacked any critical impulse aimed at extant institutional power arrangements. As I showed in Chapter 8, the Rastafarian movement was characterised by an interplay between these two dimensions of symbol and power; it combined elements of both in such a novel and imaginative way as to capture the minds and hearts of great chunks of the West Indian second generation.

Overall, the Rastas' relationships with other blacks were not nearly as tension-fraught as their relationships with the police and Asians. But it took a white group to really arrest the Rastafarian attention and forge the only meaningful link the movement had with an out-group. For the most part the Rastas restricted their primary contacts to other members, relaxing them at only selected intervals; but in late 1977 and 1978 at least some members struck up an interesting relationship with another young movement whose aims and ideals, whilst not the same as the Rastas', were intriguingly compatible. The remainder of this chapter will be taken up with an account of this coupling.

THE PUNKS : POGO REVOLUTION

We're on the same side as the Rastas. People think they're as luny as us. But it's because they're their own people, projecting their own image. (*Willie, 1978*)

An interview on Thames Television's news programme, 'Today', heralded the beginning of the eccentric, and, in some ways, primal subcultural phenomenon of punk rock. Thames' interviewer, Bill Grundy in November 1976 invited what he considered to be a representative sample of devotees of a nascent musical form to a general discussion about their aims, merits, values etc. and instead was subjected to a battery of verbal abuse from members of a band called the Sex Pistols. Literally overnight punk rock became the source of a new moral panic. The media seized upon the episode as indicative of an emergent new cult which menaced societal values and threatened to corrupt British youth with its inherent evils (*Daily Mirror*, 3 December; *Sunday Mirror*, 5 December, *News of the World*, 5 December, *Sunday People*, 5 December). Capitalising on their new-found notoriety, the Sex Pistols and other bands loosely subscribing to punk, or, more euphemistically, new wave music, used every opportunity to gain media exposure, incurring bans from record companies and concert venues for alleged indecency and disruptive behaviour – on and off stage. To a greater or lesser extent, the subculture was associated with vandalism, vulgarity, violence, vileness, venereality and intellectual vacancy. Moral entrepreneurs, including editors, politicians, even members of the clergy, spoke out against the punk rockers and the moral degeneration they seemed to symbolise. Yet, paradoxically, it was the massive overdoses of media exposure which unwittingly contributed to the phenomenon's spiralling popularity in 1977.

The media's stylised and stereotypical presentation prompted pronouncements and diagnoses from accredited 'experts' but simultaneously provided models for youths of a like mind to fashion their appearance and conduct around. The two reactions were complementary to the rise of punk rock and the evaluative status conferred upon it. As Stanley Cohen observes the media's creation of a parallel subcultural phenomenon, the mods and rockers to whom negative evaluations were also applied: 'The media have long operated as agents of moral indignation in their own right: even if they are not self-consciously engaged in crusading or muck-raking, their very reporting of certain "facts" can be sufficient to generate concern, anxiety, indignation or panic' (1973, p. 16).

Careful relaying of events at punk concerts, such as vomiting, spitting, destroying, and sexually suggesting, intensified the attribution of stigma and enhanced the subculture's reputation among youths wishing to indulge themselves in such disreputable pleasures. Reports of attacks on punks, first by offended loyalists after the Sex Pistols' anti-monarchist record, 'God Save the Queen', and then by the Teds, a recycled, reactionary version of the immigrant intimidators of the 1950s, whose presence was commonplace throughout the Summer of 1977, abounded.

As 1977 drew to a close, the panic seemed to be subsiding and the previously outcast bands were making incursions into the best-selling record charts as well as making television appearances on 'respectable shows'. The punk label looked to be losing its stigma. Of all the successful new wave bands who turned into *cause célèbre*, including the abstractly named Generation X, the Jam, the Clash and the Stranglers, only the Sex Pistols resisted integration into the mainstream of pop culture and retained their stigma which was enhanced by the release of their first album, provocatively entitled 'Never Mind the Bollocks, Here's The Sex Pistols' and intensified by the murder accusation followed by suicide of the by then disbanded group's member, Sid Vicious, in 1979. Nevertheless, many of the negative connotations had been removed from the music and its followers, who had in the meantime constructed rudimentary communication channels through the production of 'fanzines', modelled after the science fiction mimeographed news sheets. The process was an example of what George Melly (1970) called the 'revolt into style': 'what starts as revolt finishes as style – as mannerism'. As Mark Kidel observed at the time: 'The punks are busy ranting, spitting and vomiting their way to the top; rock's latest wild bunch, sworn enemies of the establishment, have been lapped up by the music business with almost indecent haste' (1977, p. 862).

An interesting by-product of this genesis was the tenuous but discernible bond forged between punks and Rastas, who were to become subjects of a moral panic in their own right at the end of 1977 (see Chapter 10). Stemming in the main from a musical affinity, the links strengthened as both groups became aware of similarities in their respective critical postures. They were further reinforced by the perceived threat of reactionary adversaries; namely National Front members and Teds, both of whom in their own ways symbolised the forces of nationalism and conservatism. One obvious ramification of this affinity was the introduction of reggae bands into punk clubs – especially in London where bastions of new wave such as the Vortex and the Roxy offered black bands the opportunity to perform and, in one case, installed a Rastafarian, Donovan Letts, as resident disc jockey. Birmingham's Rebecca's extended a similar facility. Growing numbers of British, black Rastafarian-inspired musicians such as Matumbi, Delroy Washington and Steel Pulse appeared in front of mixed audiences and the nucleus of the first really stylised *rapprochement* since the skinheads and the rude boys was in the offing.

(This section is based on observations and conversations at punk clubs during 1977 and 1978.)

Like the skins, the punks were drawn to blacks by their music which, by 1977, was saturated in Rastafarian concepts and contained streams of invectives against the evils of Babylon. Through their familiarity with the music the punks were able to identify Babylon as another way of expressing contempt for the same social order that they were criticising. Though they phrased their critique somewhat differently, the basic imperative informing the punks' 'philosophy' was very similar. Lacking a formal and coherent character, the punk phenomenon nevertheless communicated a fairly explicit attack on existing circumstances; but no constructive alternatives were ever offered. The songs of the new wave generally articulated the despair of youth augmented with demands for a comprehensive – if ill-defined – series of social and political changes; a music of symbolic revolt delivered loudly and tenaciously by groups which, as the *Sunday Times* (17 July 1977) correspondent put it, played as if they 'wanted to punch holes in your knee-caps'.

Musically, its aspirations were limited – necessarily so – and, in many cases, the songs were vehicles for lyrical exhortations to 'destroy' and 'change' and panegyrics to violence. The nearest thing to a political position came with the Sex Pistols' controversial 'Anarchy in the UK' in which it was announced:

I am an anti-Christ,
I am an anarchist,
Don't know what I want
But I know how to get it.
I wanna destroy.

Performances by bands, punk or reggae, were occasions for scenes resembling mass tribal rallies with the principally young working-class audiences assembling to spit and throw drinks at each other and the band, an action which was sometimes reciprocated to symbolise the intimacy between the performer and the listener. Their dance was the 'pogo', a frenetic sequence of vertical leaps performed with delirious energy and as little bodily co-ordination as possible. Torn clothes, adorned with chains and straps signified the bondage out of which the punks sought to break. Plastic garments and safety pins, or paper clips worn through the ears and lips, projected the punk's awareness of belonging to an environment characterised by increasing artificiality and cultural desertion. It constituted an arena for fighting authority and 'the establishment' through symbolic gestures, in much the same way as the reggae concert had worked for young blacks.

In sum, the phenomenon was non-didactic but urgently oppositional, catching perfectly the infectious mood of frustration and transforming it into music, symbols, emblems and fashions which exteriorised the rejection of extant social conditions. Its comments were blunt and unambiguous; it offered no solutions; but it was seductively appealing. Appealing because of its magnetic attraction to working-class youth faced with the prospect of leaving school and joining the army of one million unemployed (Summer 1977) and pessimistic about their own life chances amid the seventies depression. Peter Marsh compared it with the previous phases of musical history: 'In contrast to the rock and roll, which grew up in the "You've never had it so good" 1950s, this is the music of the unemployed teenager. It's dole-queue rock' (1977, p. 114).

Punk rock protested, but revolted only at a symbolic level; it produced little in the form of constructive enterprise and was ultimately rendered impotent with its adoption by large-scale commercial interests, whose property it became. If the punks rejected society, the attention afforded them by the media, and the music and fashion industries indicated that society certainly did not reject them.

The link between new wave and reggae and the sentiments they conveyed is apparent: both reflected outright rejection of the social order and neither offered anything like tangible alternatives short of total transformation. The adnascence was easily understood as Donovan Letts confirmed: 'They're both underground musics, made by young people in the same position – people of the streets, people in poverty, people feeling pressure, and in a way they're both protesting against the same thing' (in Brazier, 1977, p. 38).

During the latter half of 1977, more and more Rastas and punks started congregating quite harmoniously at venues where reggae and new wave was played. The music became a potent lever in raising each group's awareness of the other's discontent and ways of confronting them. Unlike the rude boys and skinheads who came together in a reactionary alliance with the purpose of confronting the perceived menace of alien and deviant elements, the punk-Rasta connection fostered efforts aimed at the furtherance of black–white relations through the elimination of groups threatening them (in particular, the National Front was an object of much vituperative comment and, sometimes, attack). An organisation called Rock Against Racism worked to promote relations by setting up concerts in which reggae and punk bands played to mixed black and white audiences. Even Bob Marley acknowledged the communion with the release of his awkwardly titled single record, 'Punky Reggae Party' in December 1977; and, in January 1979, I noticed a piece of graffiti in a Birmingham subway, which seemed to capture the mood of the liaison: 'Punk Tafari'.

The punks' disaffection with 'conventional society' and its values served to cleanse them of the taints of Babylon. Their critique was equally as vehement as that of the Rastas and their weird appearance ensured that the disenchantment was made visible. Safety pins and shorn hair functioned in much the same way as prayer sticks and locks. Though initially suspicious of the punks' purity of intention, the Rastas, through the bridge-building musical enterprise, came to identify more with the *nouvelle vague*, though they found the punks' lack of vision dangerously nihilistic: 'Rasta don't just want fall of Babylon; he seeks the new age.'

Affinities were strongest among the young Rastas, to whom the punks presented fellow travellers along the road to social change; ('like us, the punks want to change society'): older members (say, 20 upwards) were rather dismissive, viewing the whole phenomenon as ephemeral, superficial and unrelated to the serious pursuits of the Rasta. As an older member of the movement told me: 'Yes, there are certain similarities, I suppose. But you can never seriously talk about punk in the same way as Rasta. Rasta is life itself; punk is a fad or fashion answering the needs of youth. But it will eventually die its death.' Punks welcomed the rich Rastafarian musical input and respected the movement's aims without really comprehending in any greater detail than was provided in the songs: 'Some of the best sounds around today come from the Rastas in Jamaica,' a punk told me.

The coalescence illustrates once more the force of music in sensitising sectors of the population to new ideas and possibilities. Jamaican music of one form or another had united white and black youth, divided them and brought them back together again. When coinciding with favourable social circumstances the 'echoes of suffering' exerted powerful integrative influences on the black and white communities. It transmitted problems, moods, usually of despair and sometimes ways of overcoming them; it elicited the vicarious sense of suffering and pressure so vital to the experience of the Rastaman. On reflection, it is doubtful whether the punk rocker's apprehension of reggae was etched with so much significance as the Rasta's, but he was most certainly aware of the luminary effect it had on the black populace.

Both Rastas and punks were, in their own ways, subjected to the labelling process of stigmatisation, activated by media exposure and societal reaction, and contributed to a period of moral panic. Their efforts to find avenues of release from a restrictive day-to-day existence generated sufficient concern for them to be branded as social problems to be addressed, diagnosed and dealt with. The lack of insight and empathy of the wider society's response to these adolescent groups worked to create conditions under which the two groups banded together, in the face of adversity (bad publicity, police supervision, stigmatisation, and so on). Both external pressures of exposure and reaction and inner processes of affinity and similarity of critical profile have to be understood as variables in the relationship between the Rastas and the punks. The processes of inclusion and exclusion which laid the basis for the construction of boundaries around the Rastafarian movement were without doubt a central feature of the movement's organisation. Its claim to exclusivity and distinctness stood or fell by its ability to promote internal cohesion and severely restrict contact with outsiders. However, the Rastafarian activity of the 1970s took place not in the geographically isolated wastelands of North Wales or the hippy paradise of Glastonbury, but amidst the heterogeneity and complexity of urban–industrial areas such as London, Birmingham and Liverpool. More specifically within the confines of the ghetto. Whilst attempting to maintain well-bounded enclaves in the ghetto, the movement was quite literally forced to make contacts with the fellow residents. For the most part, Rastas cultivated stances of hostility towards other inhabitants of the ghetto, particularly to the police, contact with whom was avoided, but also to Asians who appear to have been the objects of extreme resentment. On the other side of the 'balance sheet', relations with those blacks in sympathy with the general concerns of the movement flourished and the *modus vivendi* achieved with the punks, though stemming from a musical affinity, was perhaps the most impressively good set of relations with an outside group in the movement's entire history.

The Rastas were a culturally self-conscious group which had deliberately turned inwards and carefully regulated its transactions with the outside world. But their geographical and social position dictated that they confronted their environment and the other groups populating that environment. Faced with such a task, some early cultists in Jamaica fled the city and took to rural parts where they established communes; but even they dissolved under police pressures. The same pressures might have militated against the survival of the English movement, but Rastas possessed a theoretical bulwark against this type of force and, indeed, used their perceived differential treatment as confirmation of their distinctness: 'If Rastaman just the same as anyone else, how come he always treated different?'

Their ghettoised existence threw them into encounters with other groups, most of which were not valued but none of which were significantly disruptive. One exceptional circumstance, however, placed the movement under extreme criticism and commentary from outsiders. It served to force the Rastas as a group further away from the mainstreams of respectability and made them the focus for considerable attention from the police. Relations with outsiders were exacerbated as the Rastas became central figures in a moral panic sweeping first through Birmingham and later filtering into other major cities.

Chapter 10

The Handsworth Panic

> It is appropriate to make distinctions between true Rastafarians and the criminalised Dreadlock sub-culture in Handsworth.
>
> *John Brown, 1977*

> People now look at a man of dreadlocks and think 'there is a bad man, a threat'. Now every I man with locks is thought of in this manner and we must feel the pressure even harder.
>
> *Brother Tessfa, 1977*

THE RASTAMAN TYPE

Any understanding of the Rastafarian movement would be incomplete without some consideration of the societal reaction engendered by its presence. The manner in which the wider society reacted to the sight of strange-looking West Indian youths, their hair piled up into braided corkscrews, carrying makeshift prayer sticks and adorned with the national colours of Ethiopia, had a crucial impact on the development of the movement in England.

In Jamaica, the vicissitudes of the cult were to a great extent determined by the ways in which it was defined by institutional authorities holding big-enough 'sticks' to impose their definitions in a most convincing and urgent fashion. Shortly after emerging, the movement was treated as an anachronistic fringe phenomenon, a curious throwback to pre-slavery days in that its members insisted on their African origin through lines of direct genealogical descent and their need to return there at some future stage. Rastas were regarded as participants to a large-scale *folie à deux* in sedulously cultivating this conception of Africa as their rightful birth-place and Haile Selassie as their God and messiah; but, for the most part, they were harmless creatures sharing delusional ideas.

When its leaders became more visible and vociferous in their insistence and made known their condemnation of the evils of Babylon and the inevitability of its destruction, the cult became redefined as a potential threat to societal values and interests. Accordingly, pressures were brought to bear in the form of sanctions. Hence, the various punitive measures imposed on Howell, Hibbert and Dunkley served as exemplary cases. The Rastaman was publicly held up to be a demented demoniac whose presence, if left unchecked, could have a deleterious effect on the prevalent moral order. Howell, in particular, symbolised the Rastafarian progress of early years, being jailed for twelve months in 1934 for uttering seditious language 'calculated to cause disturbance and violence amongst the ignorant people of this country' (Chief Justice quoted in the *Daily Gleaner*, 17 March 1934); later to be jailed for two years for assault offences; and eventually admitted to the Bellevue lunatic asylum in 1960.

Writing in the early part of the 1950s, Simpson observed:

The attitude of middle-class Jamaicans, as well as of Englishmen and Americans living in Jamaica, toward Ras Tafarians is one of contempt and disgust. There seems to be no fear of a Ras Tafari uprising, but it is widely believed that the members of this cult are hooligans, psychopaths and dangerous criminals. Ras Tafarians are often referred to as 'those dreadful people' and at least some police officials believe that the Ras Tafari movement includes the 'worst' residents of West Kingston (1955a, p. 144).

After the events of 1959–60, climaxing with the discovery of the Henry arms cache, Jamaicans were warned by prominent official, Edgar Bryan Rogers that: 'They are malleable material for Communism, and we had better do something about these people before Communists start working on them' (in *Newsday*, vol. 4, no. 8, August 1960). In this *Newsday* article the police alleged that an American black terrorist organisation 'tried to use the discontented Rastafari element to start political trouble'. The *Sunday Guardian* front-page headline claim that 'Jamaicans Live in Fear of Rasta Men' (1 May, 1960) seemed to be reflected in the death sentence passed on Ronald Henry and four of his accomplices. Frantically, the Government commissioned the University College of the West Indies to investigate the movement and make suggestions on action to be taken towards it (Smith *et al.*, 1967). A mission to explore the possibilities of a mass emigration to Africa brought forth sets of contradictory conclusions (Report of the Mission to Africa, 1961).

During the 1960s decade the so-called militance seemed to decrease and the movement was variously described as 'a cult of outcasts' (H. O. Patterson, 1964b), 'a religious cult and protest organisation' (Kitzinger, 1969) and, more vividly, a group of 'lazy, dirty, violent and lawless scoundrels mouthing religious phrases to cover up their aversion to work and their ill habits' (*Daily Gleaner*, 30 April 1960)

– a description that would be consistent with later characterisations of the English version. But, in *Public Opinion* (29 April 1966) it was announced that the cultists 'can no longer be regarded as outcasts'. And in 1971 it was speculated that the movement's offspring would become 'the dynamic standard bearers of a new Jamaican society' (Bowen, 1971, p. 50). Rex Nettleford agreed:

> Yet the role of the Rastafarian movement has been a dynamic one in the wider society of which it is really part. Many of the ideas and much of the mood of this group have seemingly passed on to the younger generation at large. What would have been regarded as peculiarly Rastafarian in 1959–60 was to be assimilated ten years later into the mainstream of thought on black power and majority control. Many of the views have since developed a cogency partly because they were to come from persons who had passed through the established educational institutions of the country and could no longer be seriously dismissed as the escapist indulgencies of an economically worthless and lunatic fringe. (1970a, p. 46)

More recently, Leonard Barrett has gone so far as to write:

> The message and visions of movements like the Rastafarians point the way to new patterns of society. Though often unheeded, new movements generally have clear visions of where society should be going . . .
> . . . The Rastafarians must be seen above all else as the champions of social change on the island. (1977, pp. 225 and 174)

Clearly, then, the Rastaman weathered the changing fortunes of almost fifty years and emerged with flying colours. At various intervals he was decried as a criminal menace and the object of a national panic, one ramification of which was the mass destruction of the ganja crops; and, at others, addressed as having a legitimate proposal, one which deserved investigation. (The Mission to Africa signifies the extent to which the status of the Rastafarian had been elevated to the realms of legitimacy and the spread of Rasta ideas in the seventies seemed to consolidate this status.) During the latter half of the seventies the sense of fear and panic produced by the cultic activities was pushed into the background of folklore and the Rastaman was perceived as a valuable addition to the island's cultural pattern – particularly with his artistic endeavours. The association of Rasta and violence was broken and he became amenable to cultural integration.

The way in which the movement was reacted to and its members defined had important consequences for the cult itself and, of course, its relationship with the social context (which is, after all, what this book is about). Punitive stances brought forth inimical influences on the members and polarised them as an outcast group, thus undermining any claim to legitimacy they might have held and undermining the validity of their religious stand. Recruitment would have been difficult, as new members would be automatically consigning themselves to a position of marginality and possible intimidation. Problems of co-existence spurred a tendency to geographical isolation and the consequent formation of communes which were periodically subject to police surveillance. The identification of the Rastaman as a certain social type – say a demonical menace to morality – would have generated new self-conceptions; the recognised status assured that Rasta of a place in the social cosmos by imposing on him an identity and a role which would have been hard to escape. In other words, the Rastaman, in the manner of the self-fulfilling prophecy, came to internalise others' negative conceptions and orient his thought and behaviour accordingly. As a consequence, socialisation would have been phrased in terms of these conceptions.

The impacts of social typing on both the group structure and the individual identity were multifaceted, and, suffice it to say, they were massively consequential in their effect on the genesis and development of the movement. Parallel reactions from society were experienced at different junctures by the Maroons, Sharpe, Bogle, Bedward's movement and Garvey's organisation. But, whereas Sharpe's abortive revolt, Bogle's attempted insurrection and (to a lesser extent) Bedward's fantastic scheme were identified in terms of particular events or sequences of events and disapproved of actions, the Maroons, Garveyites and Rastafarian brethren were cognised as types – they were literally type-cast. As such, they were amenable to gross generalisation and multiple associations with other phenomena (for example, the Maroons with terrorism, Garveyites with racism and Rastafarian cultists with delusion). The members of such movements could be classified according to their particular social category and not in terms of isolated episodes for which they could be remembered. They occupied positions which, although not static, were fairly enduring and manipulable only within prescribed limits. These groups were made accessible to the wider society through typified characterisations which ultimately shaped the general pattern of societal reaction. Additionally, they functioned as specific reminders of what constituted 'undesirable elements'.

In a similar fashion, the English Rastas were subjected to typecasting which informed popular and general societal reaction. During its infancy, no definitive pattern of response from the wider society emerged and public opinion was moulded by fragments of information gleaned from newspaper reports telling of a 'Mafia-style secret society' (*Reading Evening Post*, June, 1976) and a 'black power move-ment on the warpath' (*Birmingham Post*, 8 June, 1976), a television programme on a mysterious Jamaican cult, whose members were waiting in vain for the ships bound for Africa ('Everyman', BBC 1, 26 June 1977), or even the cryptic tales of Marley in which Babylon was to be destroyed and the black man restored to his rightful Zion. At the start of the 1970s the English movement had hardly been heard of outside the West Indian community and those groups specifically concerned with race relations. Only a handful of groups in England identified themselves as Rastafarian and they were well screened from the public eye. The concept of Rasta was totally mean-ingless in England. Seven years later a series of national and local newspaper reports on the movement spoke in terms of 'Streets of Fear', 'Wave of Terror', '20 Bobbies Lead Race Peace Bid', 'Terror Gangs Shock', 'attacks on elderly (*sic*) or defenceless people' and 'knives drawn and blood spilt'. (*Birmingham Evening Mail*, 6 December; ibid; *Sunday Times*, 11 December; *Birmingham Evening Mail*, 25 November; *Guardian*, 5 December; *Observer*, 11 December. All 1977.) Twenty extra policemen were drafted into an area of Birmingham where Rastafarian members were allegedly creating havoc, new mercury vapour street lighting was installed in the area so as to discourage 'mugging' and vandalism, and two members of the police force were sent to Jamaica to gain a 'better understanding between blacks and police' (*Birmingham Evening Mail*, 10 January 1978).

The panic generated in late 1977 was to have repercussions for the English Rastas and impose on them a typification they had previously avoided. By 1978, the stereotyped conception of the Rastaman as a racist thug, lurking in the ghettos of big cities and waging war with the rest of the community – especially Asians and the police – had become cemented in the public consciousness; a social problem evolved; hysteria and panic followed and ways of coping with the Rastafarian menace were debated and operationalised. If any single event was responsible for this process of labelling the Rastaman as the villain of the piece it was the publication of a report on police–community relations in Birmingham's high immigrant district of Handsworth. The media reaction to this was of sufficient proportions to magnify its content and present it as a definitive statement of the real nature of the Rastafarian. Its publicisation generated a sense of sudden threat, not only amongst the Handsworth community and the wider society, but among the Rastas themselves who foresaw the damaging consequences the report would have on their already dented reputation.

THE PARADOX OF REACTION

How, then, was a report such as this able to stimulate and sustain a panic which led to a new apprehension of the Rastafarian as a symbol of black racism? A relevant framework for the analysis of this process is found in the work of Leslie Wilkins (1964, ch. 4), an adaptation of which Stanley Cohen (1973) used in his study of mods and rockers.

Wilkins' amplification spiral theory takes as its starting point the contention that the nature of information about some deviant phenomenon fed into the public sphere can serve to increase the amount of deviance or normative diversity by magnifying it, thus prompting further reaction, further increases in the deviance, and so the cycle continues. As the majority of society does not come into direct contact with the deviance, it depends for its information on secondhand sources – primarily the media. Press and television present pre-processed and highly typified images of the subject of the deviance and it is to such images that its audiences react. Usually the initial act of deviance is disapproved of and considered to be undesirable; the response to it is highly negative and this tends to polarise the group or groups committing the defiance from 'conventional' society. In turn, they begin to perceive themselves as deviant and congregate with others of a similar position, where the commission of more deviant action is facilitated. The swelling volume of normative diversity, plus the vulnerable position of the deviant engenders more resolute reactions from agents of social control attempting to suppress the phenomenon and the imposition of further penalties.

Wilkins's systemic phraseology gives the deviance cycle a tinge of mechanistic inevitability and leaves some of the links between phases untheorised. Other writers (for example, Lemert, 1951, 1964; Becker, 1963, 1964; Matza, 1966), however, have provided rich insights into how the process impinges upon the cognitions of the individual, influencing changes in self-conception and consequent changes in dispositions to act in certain ways. During the process, the individual has attached to him the label of being a deviant, a highly anonymous typification, but one which in time he is forced to take notice of – if only because he is oriented to by others in terms of that label. His identity becomes opaque, sometimes 'transparent' so that he comes to see through his personally held conceptions and view himself as really deviant, as opposed to purely going through the motions of acting as the deviant. This recognition calls for a readjustment of perceptions of the self; he adopts a new identity as defined by the more powerful institutions of social control (police, courts, academics, psychologists, probation officers, etc.). The propensity to behave in a deviant manner is enhanced from the 'inside' as well as 'outside' forces. He faces a spiral of limited opportunities to assume roles and act in ways contrary to deviant expectations and becomes inclined to act out his part.

This is by no means a deterministic approach to the study of deviance for the labelling sequence is meant to be illustrative of the role of societal reaction as an independent variable in the creation and perpetuation of deviant behaviour; how the attribution of a deviant label, or 'branding' can cause the actor to respond in ways which maximise the possibility of him engaging in further deviance. Its importance to present purposes is in its emphasis on the ways in which properties conferred on groups by audiences witnessing them (whether directly or indirectly) affect the development of those groups in an almost paradoxical manner: the reaction to deviance works to produce it.

Cohen extends Wilkins' cycle to the study of the mods and rockers phenomenon which grew up during the 1960s. The two groups involved were young and controversial, dressing in unorthodox fashions and engaging in attention-grabbing episodes of violence with each other. The mods were drawn to West Indians because of the attractiveness of their original and obscure music, ska. They drove motor scooters, dressed expensively, spent plenty on entertainment and generally symbolised the 'age of affluence', as the fifties and sixties were known (see Bognador and Skidelski, 1970). Rockers, by contrast, were direct descendants of the Teddy Boys and so inherited many of their postures, disliking all black and coloured immigrants and modelling their lives on the James Dean/Marlon Brando motor cycle-adoring prototype with the suicidal thirst for daring and adventure. Fights between the two groups were frequent, especially the large-scale ones which took place at English coastal resorts over a two-year span beginning in 1964.

Extensive coverage was given to these events and the various court cases which followed and stereotypical images of the deviants were presented by the media for public consumption. Reports, according to Cohen, were generally exaggerated and distorted, frequently containing misleading passages and lurid headlines such as 'Day of Terror by Scooter Groups' and 'Wild Ones Invade Seaside' – a similarly melodramatic vocabulary was employed with regard to the Rastas in 1977. An implicit assumption present in virtually every report was that what had happened would inevitably repeat itself, and this predictive element had the effect of the self-fulfilling prophecy in sensitising the communities to expect trouble and the deviants to provide it!

The communication of specific typified notions of mod and rocker brought with it evaluative connotations; the categories came to be symbolic of a certain status (for example, delinquent or pill-taker), as did the hairstyles and fashions of 'modism' and the motorcycles and leather jackets of the rockers. Eventually, the terms mod and rocker acquired a wholly negative status and, of course, phenomena which can command such statuses have an inbuilt appeal for the media; like the old chestnuts of sex, drugs, violence, vandalism, etc., the mods and rockers were eminently newsworthy. Auxiliary status traits were introduced to complete a composite stigma attributable to those groups performing certain acts and dressing in a particular manner; immaturity, arrogance, irresponsibility, lack of regard for the law and the property of others were often cited (Cohen, 1973, p. 55).

Causes were discussed, solutions were entertained and punishments were intensified in a series of public dramatisations. The deviants were not only labelled, but seen to be labelled, setting into motion a veritable 'moral crusade' designed to eliminate them, but in fact creating images that maintained them. Incidents which would not under normal circumstances (i.e. not in times of panic) be interpreted as manifestations of the mods and rockers phenomenon were brought into sharp relief as acts of stylised deviance after the press and public had been sensitised to the original themes. Warning cues were assimilated within new frames of reference and classified as being signs of mod and rocker activity. Thresholds of tolerance were lowered, with police and local authorities becoming 'jumpy' at any semblance of trouble, fearing more mod and rocker outbreaks.

With the escalating beliefs in the dangers of mods and rockers, measures were developed to combat the threat in a fairly systematic and routinised way. The sum of this organised reaction constituted what Edwin Lemert has called 'the societal control culture' which includes 'the laws, procedures, programmes and organisations which, in the name of the collectivity help, rehabilitate, punish or otherwise manipulate deviants' (1951, p. 447). Not only formal social control, but informal community reaction was geared to the amplification of the phenomenon. Members of the public brought pressure to bear on authorities for more effective action by control agents, sometimes exposing inadequacies in existing security arrangements. But the whole amalgam of societal reaction, contrary to its anticipated effect, amplified the deviance.

Equipped with the foreknowledge of coming disasters, seaside towns prepared for the worst: 'stage-setting ceremonies', as Cohen (1973, p. 147) calls them. Elaborate plans were made well in advance and even national institutions such as the Home Office began to take a co-ordinating role. Further, these preparations were well publicised in such a way as to issue warnings to potential deviants.

The incidents which did occur over the span did not measure up to the stereotypical image of two highly structured opposing groups, each exhibiting a high degree of homogeneity and organisational coherence. Leadership was spontaneous, actions were momentary and organisation was weak; what homogeneity there was developed through continued interaction. 'These were not like revolutionary crowds or lynch mobs, but, on the whole, a series of passive and uncertain groups waiting to be entertained' (Cohen, 1973, p. 149). Like the rock show, the soccer match and the punk concert, these rituals were occasions for positive exaltation produced by being away from home, from responsibilities and from routine.

The shared images were extremely important in mobilising crowds to uniform action; culturally sanctioned signs and symbols were always in evidence and could be used to justify or validate perceptions and actions. Symbols such as clothing, hairstyle, language and other stylistic attributes, created senses of group cohesion and propensities to act as a group and not simply as an aggregate of individuals. The coloured scarves of soccer supporters, the safety pins and torn clothing of punk rockers, the peculiar hairstyles of skinheads and Teddy Boys; all these functioned in a symbolic manner similar to the Rastafarian dreadlocks and coloured tams in generating a feeling of belongingness. But they also facilitated stigmatisation and the imputation of other negative characteristics. This crucial aspect of the mods and rockers and other phenomena is left somewhat under-developed by Cohen, but it is worth noting the role played by the media in diffusing and elaborating the symbols of certain groups at early stages in the emergence of folk devils. In making it widely known that, for example, skinheads adopted Doctor Marten brand boots, braces and cropped hair, and the greasers (or grebos) wore leather jackets, unwashed jeans and drove high-powered motorcycles, the media unwittingly created models for other interested youths to emulate. Previously unavailable knowledge was made available and youths were presented with ready-made and packaged symbols with which they could identify. The spread northwards of punk and skinhead, as well as mod symbols, after the incipient appearance of them in London owed much to the media's dissemination. The negative connotation applied to them by the wider audience heightened their attractiveness to youths not wishing to identify with parental cultures and therefore predisposed to accept alternative stances. An imitation effect went into motion and eventually the youth deliberately incorporated components of the type-cast role into his self-conception. In this process, the actor would indulge himself in the typified folk-devil role and simultaneously provide the empirical referent for media and public suspicions. The chants of 'we are the hooligans' from the terraces of English soccer grounds is illustrative of the self-conscious internalisation of the devil role, though the Sex Pistols' punk rock anthem captures the spirit equally well : 'We're pretty vacant; and we don't care.'

Cohen's work, then, as a sociological study of the creation of moral panic presents a plethora of processes operating at different levels: ambiguous crowd situations leading to unstructured rumours and suspicions of future events, media presentation of news and images lending a cognitive basis for a panic, public pressures determining the creation of a control culture, stereotypical packages being adopted and later internalised by actors, voyeuristic crowds contributing stimuli to activity. He provides a document of the internal dynamics of a panic-creation process and the formation of an object for that panic, the folk devil. (Some of his themes I have ignored, extracting only those features of interest to the present analysis.) Underlying the whole work in the paradox that reactions manifested as a response to certain events can unwittingly work to reproduce those events in greater volume and affect the participants to those events' self-conceptions as deviants.

The panic waned when other newsworthy phenomena pushed themselves into the public arena of discourse (long hair, drugs and, most strikingly, skinheads) and the pattern of events became all too familiar and predictable to be interesting. There was a trailing off of enthusiasm among mods; due perhaps to maturational reform and commercialisation; the mod style had inbuilt obsolescence. Rockers were more enduring but they were simply irrelevant without their adversaries and came back into the limelight as greasers (and later grebos) after the issue of the skinhead challenge to not only them, but to a whole range of diverse groups. Finally, but importantly, harassment by the police, raids on clubs and parties and refusal of service in cafes pushed groups to the extreme outer fringes of society and deterred new recruits from joining the culture.

Cohen concludes with the following observation: 'More moral panics will be generated and other, as yet nameless folk devils will be created' (1973, p. 204). The examples of the skinheads, the punk rockers and the Rastas bear out this suggestion and provide parallel cases of the effects of societal reaction. There is nothing quite as successful as a 'disaster', whether a war or just a scare, for stirring the upright conscience. The ritual denunciation and condemnation of some phenomenon, natural or social, individual or collective, brings together diverse bodies of people and unites them in the face of adversity. In this, panic stimulates collective consciousness and common awareness of threatening situations.

Inevitably, they are triggered off by a single event or isolated group of events which signify the advent of danger. The washed-up carcass of a mutilated victim may portend the coming of a shark panic for a small coastal community in which all members are affected, the 'Jaws' effect. Where media of communication are an important source of information, however, actors physically removed from an event, such as an assassination, may find themselves vicarious participants to panics of cataclysmic proportions; consider the death of John F. Kennedy. Even a totally fictitious event like Orson Welles' 'War of the Worlds' broadcast can result in the type of panic usually reserved for disaster anticipations. The panic which gripped Birmingham's district of Handsworth in 1977–8 and affected, in some measure, the whole black community, was triggered off by the publication of a document warning of the incipient menace of the Rastaman.

THE 'SHADES OF GREY' REPORT

For despite the fact that much contemporary discussion of the issues involved tends to stress particular race relations or political aspects, the issues themselves remain complex. In this sense, there are no blacks and whites in Handsworth. It is all shades of grey. (John Brown, 1977)

John Brown's study was instigated after pressure on the West Midlands Police from Claire Short, the then director of All Faiths for One Race (AFFOR), a community project based in Handsworth, Birmingham. Detecting that relations between the police and young blacks in the area were growing tenser, AFFOR requested an independent inquiry into the worsening situation with a view to implementing changes. Brown was called in to undertake the research which was financed by the Barrow and Geraldine S. Cadbury Trust. He had held positions at the University of the West Indies at the Leeward and Windward Islands and was head of the Department of European Languages and Institutions at the Cranfield Institute of Technology.

Brown began his research in July 1977 on the basis of four main criticisms levelled at the police from various quarters. They were:
(1) Harassment of black youth on the streets, particularly after dark by young police officers in Panda cars.
(2) Violence against persons and property during investigations and whilst making arrests.
(3) Indiscriminate use of police dogs against black youth.
(4) The futility of procedures for complaints against the police.

Without accepting the criticisms, the Chief Constable of the West Midlands Police Force, Philip Knights, CBE, QPM, conceded that 'myths and realities were now so woven together in Handsworth that dangers were growing of physical confrontation between police and black youth, and that the area needed new preventive initiatives' (Brown, 1977, p. 1).

Although Handsworth's subdivisional statistics in terms of recorded and detected crime were insignificant by comparison with other areas of the West Midlands, its high incidence of robbery and assaults with intent to rob merited attention. Additionally, local crime data showed 'firstly, that some 90% of the known assailants are youths of West

Indian origin or descent; secondly, that the great majority of the known victims are defenceless – mainly women and the elderly' (1977, p. 3). (Before proceeding I should enter a short caveat: these police statistics were of citations and arrests and not convictions.) The majority of crimes involving violence were committed in a particular area of Handsworth usually between dusk and the early hours of the morning and 'mainly by a particular group – some 200 youths of West Indian origin or descent who have taken on the appearance of followers of the Rastafarian faith by plaiting their hair in locks and wearing green, gold and red woollen hats.' But:

> The tragic irony is that whilst these youths claim identity as Rasta men, the nature of their criminality in fact represents a betrayal of the non-violent ideology of the Rastafarian faith; and in view of the concern expressed on this score by brothers of the Ethiopian Orthodox Church, it is appropriate to make distinctions between the true Rastafarians and the criminalised Dreadlock sub-culture in Handsworth. (Brown, 1977, pp. 3–7)

Again let me register a cautionary note: my own work in Handsworth revealed no basis for dichotomising 'true Rastafarians' and the 'criminalised Dreadlock sub-culture'. The picture I pieced together was far more complex with many differing factions of the movement holding to a variety of commitments, perspectives and assumptions. Few points of ideological or behavioural unity existed beyond the fundamental, underlying imperative to upgrade blackness by ascribing to it positive values, and the twin concepts of the centrality of Africa and the divinity of Ras Tafari. My impression was more of a kaleidoscopic array of beliefs and actions encased in a circumambience of Rastafarian concepts and categories. The association of Rastafarian squats with 'criminalised sub-cultures' is also a dubious generalisation and, as for the Ethiopian Orthodox Church, its concern was more with the way in which Brown's work had brought the whole Rastafarian community into disrepute (much of the trouble-making in Handsworth was dismissed by the EOC members as 'youthful overflows' or 'rascally behaviour').

One astute Rastaman opined: 'This report has been the most savage attack on the whole movement ever. Now all Ras Tafari is in mortal danger. I cannot even dream of the damage it has done.'

A point at which Brown's findings and my own do agree is that many of the Rastas he spoke to had suffered from the adjustment to English schools after moving from the West Indies and many had 'records of poor family relationships'. They also perceived themselves to be 'victims of white racist society'. That many Rastas did feel discomfort at school due to curricula and linguistic disjunctures is undeniable; though others progressed sufficiently through school to take up positions in institutes of further education. (Some were in employment and attended colleges of technology or further education on a part-time basis – electrical engineering being a popular line of study – while others were enrolled as full-time students, often studying for GCE qualifications. Most pertinently, in Handsworth the Handsworth Technical College at Goldshill Road had a number of full- and part-time Rastafarian students.)

If by 'poor family relationships' Brown meant that migration had exacerbated an already fragmented West Indian family structure and reduced the amount of parent–child contact, thus leaving the youth more amenable to peer group influences and opening up opportunities for conflict with parents (for example, about being involved with the movement) then I agree with him. In Handsworth, many Rastas explained how their allegiance with the movement had created frictions, or 'confrontations' as they preferred to put it, with parents, some of which led to their banishment. Others had left home before the drift to Ras Tafari and their affiliation simply attenuated family relationships. In the overwhelming majority of cases Rastas reckoned that their parents had chastised them for their pursuits (though I heard the occasional story of how involvement in the movement had enabled the member to appreciate the parents' beliefs – however 'misguided' – and gain greater understanding of their distress).

Though seeing themselves as 'victims of a white racist society' tends to dramatise somewhat, every Rastaman I encountered in Handsworth and elsewhere cited instances of racism and were pessimistic about their own life chances when confronted with the type of 'built-in racism' (as some called it) of British society. After this, however, Brown's scenario begins to deviate from my own:

> Many of the couple of hundred 'hard core' Dreadlocks who now form a criminalised sub-culture in the area live in squats. Almost all are unemployed. And apart from the specific crimes for which they are responsible, they constantly threaten the peace of individual citizens, black, brown and white, whilst making the police task both difficult and dangerous since every police contact with them involves the risk of confrontation or violence. (p. 8)

I found not a scintilla of evidence to suggest that a 200 'hard core' existed in Handsworth. There were a number of squats and the majority of the squatters were unemployed and not, I detected, averse to handbag-snatching, pickpocketing and sometimes more serious robberies. But they were in no sense a structured hard core: Handsworth's Rastafarian contingent formed a very loosely connected series of cells interacting with each other at intervals, sometimes only casually. They were certainly no constant threat to the complete community – though they were often seen as such after the publication of the report!

This so-called 'hard core' were allegedly exerting a growing influence on hundreds of other West Indians in the district and therefore having a noxious effect on the whole black community.

Having located the source of the problem, Brown concentrated on the response of police officers based at Handsworth's Thornhill Road station which he reckoned signified 'the brick and stone heart of Babylon' for the dreadlocked ones.

> And where the Rastas are involved, there's always a risk of violence. Then I usually send more than one car . . . Over-reacting? I don't think so. I've seen too many of the lads done over. And I've suffered myself. Look, there's the scar still on my arm where a Rasta bit me last year. Right through the uniform.

> They've [the Rastas] said they'll take a WPC, gangbang her and return the bits to Thornhill Road . . . I've been followed by groups of Rastas out on patrol, and involved in incidents that really frighten me. It's made me wonder how long I can continue.

> . . . the most vicious assault that night was almost certainly committed by a 6 foot 4 inch Dreadlock with a record of 14 previous convictions, including indecent assault, burglary, assault occasioning actual bodily harm, criminal damage and the possession of an offensive weapon. He stabbed a policeman in the knee with a 20 inch long knife, after which the policeman used his truncheon to ward off more blows. There are about twelve cuts across the truncheon, some of them quite deep . . . (pp. 9–10, 16 and 18)

Probably the most trenchant remark came from a Permanent Beat Officer who contrasted the older and younger blacks:

> The first generation, you could always humour them, laugh and joke. Even for serious offences you could use humour. But those days are gone. The new generation questions everything. These Rastas, they're boys trying to seek identity, hostile to everyone. (p. 22)

Of all the conflict-fraught relationships in Handsworth the Rastaman–CID officer encounter was cited as the most aggravated. The two groups were seen as mutually antagonistic with Rastas regarding the CID as 'crazy men' and 'animals' and the CID identifying the Rastas as the central cause of all their headaches. But no trace of racism was found among the CID; a concern with the victims of attacks and the direct, repetitious experience of apprehending the same offenders time after time shaped their attitudes towards the 'Dreadlocks'. Sympathy came down on the side of the CID – if only because of their anxiety about the human consequences of crime: 'This factor – police concern for the victims – is too slightly regarded, too lightly considered, by society; and will continue so whilst political, legal and academic concern remains so obstinately offender-centred' (p. 25).

The CID expressed concern not only about the Rastas' escalating use of offensive weapons and their increasingly high level of organisation in the execution of crime, but also about the effect the 'hard core' was having on younger black members of the community – particularly school children. Another difficulty cited was the reluctance of Rastas to co-operate after arrest: 'With the young Rastas you have to be prepared for aggro in one form or another – abuse, obstruction, lies, violence . . .'

Not that Brown is totally out of sympathy with the Rastafarian youth; he recognises that there are two parties to any conflict:

> On one side, the youth Dreads, brimful of unused energies, fear and resentment, aggression and ideological ardour, some with violence aching to be out of them: a short fuse for police sparks. On the other, the young coppers, understaffed, overworked, some on overtime . . . their noses constantly rubbed in the shit of human experience, the sufferings of Dreadlock victims, abuse, obstruction, lies: tense with expectations of meeting violence . . . (pp. 27–8)

And concedes that 'Almost inevitably – though still too hastily – police tend to identify Rastafarian appearance with unlawful force and criminality, despite the fact that the true adherents of the Rastafarian faith are often people of quietist disposition to whom crime is anathema.' (p. 28).

In Handsworth myths were seen to absorb reality and the polarisation offered few signs of hope for improvement: 'So that virtually every form of contact with young Dreads, however remote from criminal matters, has potential for conflict' and 'Even the most guarded optimism is something of a luxury here' (pp. 29 and 36).

Though Brown's loyalties lay with the police force that commissioned his study, he conceded that much of the conflict in Handsworth could be viewed from two perspectives:

> From the determinist angle of vision, the Dreadlocks are seen essentially as infected victims of a society that has condemned them to educational, social, racial and economic disadvantage, and whose injustices and tyranny drive them inevitably – and thus to some extent legitimately – to violence against that society. Other

community workers see the Dreads rather as sources of infection, dominating, indoctrinating and criminalising other West Indian youth, and thereby endangering the health and reputation of the West Indian community as a whole (p. 34).

But, as if to complicate its position even further, the police had to face the accusations of over-liberality from other sectors of the community: 'On the one hand they are denounced for harassing West Indian youth: on the other they are pressed – by West Indians – to take stronger action against West Indian youth' (p. 33).

Overall, Brown presented a sepulchral vision of Handsworth as a conflict-riven area bent on its own physical and social destruction. The perceived racialism of the police and the resentment this perpetuated among young blacks was seen as a malignant element, forcing police into awkward stances where they were attacked from all angles and could not hope to satisfy all factions. The absence of a well-structured leadership in the West Indian community exacerbated an already worsening situation and, unless collaborative links between West Indian organisations and the police could be formed, 'more and more youth will inevitably drift into the already established patterns of alienation and delinquency, thus reinforcing what has become, in effect, a local culture of disaffection' (p. 40).

Brown offered a number of policy directives, some commendable, but none of which affect the present analysis; more interesting was what the police actually did on the basis of the report. What is of central importance is not so much Brown's report but the way in which his thumbnail sketch of Handsworth as a crucible of racial ferment was reacted to by the police, the media and indeed the 'general public'. I hesitate to offer point-by-point criticisms of all Brown's findings by drawing on my own work; I feel that my disagreements are apparent in the whole of this book. But it is impossible to deny the impact the report made not only in Birmingham but nationally, galvanising the police to action and sending tremors of panic through the community. Brown had given a shape and definition to the menace stalking the streets of Handsworth. But residents of Brixton, Notting Hill, Leicester, Manchester and Bristol, as well as other parts of Birmingham, would have found the description very familiar.

As I have stated, Brown's study was in itself uninteresting; it was the way in which certain agencies reacted to its findings which made it a sociologically significant landmark in the Rastafarian movement's development; and it is to this independent variable of social reaction that I now turn.

AFTERMATH

Before late 1977 the *Birmingham Evening Mail*'s reportage of the
Rastas had been sporadic and with reference to particular events,
though its companion paper, the *Birmingham Post* had carried a short
article on the emergent movement in Handsworth (11 May 1976) and
a longer feature, headed 'Lost Tribes on the Warpath', which warned
of 'the Rastafarians, a black power movement which argues for their
repatriation and is growing in importance in the West Indian community (8 June 1976). Rumblings of loose rocks before the avalanche
came in the Autumn of 1977 when assaults and handbag snatches in
Handsworth were committed by 'two West Indians, aged 18 to 20
years with dreadlocks and wearing woolly hats' (27 August).

To coincide with the publication of Brown's report the *Birmingham
Evening Mail* (25 November 1977) published the first of a series of
articles which was provocatively entitled 'Terror Gangs Shock'. It
informed its readers that 'a hardcore of 200 young West Indians are
bringing terror to a three-mile area of a Birmingham suburb', a map
of which was provided and headed 'the centre for a reign of terror'.
The first article took as its starting point the *Shades of Grey* findings
and accordingly pinpointed the deviants as Rastas: 'The 200 troublemakers claim to be followers of the Rastafarian faith and wear their
hair in "dreadlocks" and dress in the traditional green, gold and red
colours.'

Such a description facilitated easy identification of the deviant for
those familiar with locks and colours, but without any real knowledge
of their relevance; now they were to be regarded as the trademarks of
troublemakers. Faithful to the Brown report, the article 'revealed' that
the majority of the 'hard core's' victims were 'defenceless white
women – although Asians are often targets'. In addition, it made
accusatory remarks about the housing associations such as Copec, New
Hestia and Midland Area, for making available property for legal
squats and, in so doing, 'creating problems' – presumably by
encouraging vagrants and runaways.

After an interval of ten days, the newspaper featured the second of
the articles, this time headlined 'Streets of Fear' and containing more
detailed examples of police encounters with Rastafarian members
given by young police officers at Thornhill Road police station (in
one notable instance an 18-year-old girl police officer tackled and
eventually subdued her six-foot Rastafarian assailant). It asked the
question, 'Who are "The Dreads", the 200 West Indian youngsters
who have brought terror to the streets of Handsworth?' And answered:

They are mostly unemployed youths who have broken away from
their families, and live in about 20 'squats' in empty houses. Their

name comes from the dreadlocks in which they plait their hair – like followers of the Rastafarian faith. They also adopt the traditional green, gold and red wool knitted 'tea cosy' hats of the Rasta men. (*Birmingham Evening Mail*, 6 December 1977)

Like the *Shades of Grey* report, it identified the 200 hardcore who claimed they were Rastafarian adherents but whose misdemeaning behaviour contradicted the tenets of the movement. Again, the reader was presented with a pre-processed image of the Rastaman as a distinguishable social type to which the blame for Handsworth's problems could be attributed.

The very name 'Handsworth' would be enough to evoke the feelings and interests of race relations students, for it has been popularly associated with all manner of problems connected with its high immigrant population over the fifteen or twenty years since 1950. Its very densely packed West Indian and Asian concentration makes it something of a microcosm. (Composition of Handsworth: Native whites – 22,900 (47·5%); West Indian (and West Indian descent) – 12,700 (26·5%); Asian (and Asian descent) – 12,400 (26%). Source: Birmingham Statistical Office.) In 1977 the area's problems took on a new dimension with a National Front rally staged in its environs in preparation for the Ladywood by-election. The confrontations involving police and an allegedly united front of Socialist Worker party members and young West Indians following the rally which climaxed at the Thornhill Road Station, prompted headlines of 'Race Riot' from the *Daily Mirror* (16 August). But it was not until the publication of *Shades of Grey* that the identity of a social group at the root of the various problems was revealed. Publicisation of the 'facts behind the wave of terror' (*Birmingham Evening Mail*, 6 December) gave a form and shape to an amorphous mass of loosely connected problems and disapproved of behaviours; it gave focus for orientation and, in its own words, spelt out publicly the 'frightening realities of a powder-keg situation'.

By the time of the third article on Handsworth (8 December) it had been announced that twenty extra policemen were to be drafted into the district for foot patrol duty in the first of a series of measures to deal with the troublemakers. A less hysterical feature this time but still emotive, it warned: 'Violent crime is mounting. The squatters, the "dreads" are still a menace.' It spoke of the moderate immigrant element in the district which was concerned with the growth in delinquency and, in some cases, anxious that police should take a tougher line with disaffected youth, leaving a situation in which 'on the one hand the police are denounced for harassing West Indian youth, on the other they are pressed – by West Indians – to take stronger action against West Indian youth'.

In the articles were all the seeds of an incipient local panic, including melodramatic headlines, the presentation of negatively valued typification, predictions of future trouble and exposures of inadequacies in existing security arrangements. But it was at a national level that the seeds were brought to flower. The *Guardian* (5 December) informed its readers that 'Extra police are to be drafted into the Handsworth suburb of Birmingham after a report which highlights increased crime in the area . . . The West Indians involved in violent crime, says the report, are now living in squats and are dressed like followers of the Rastafarian faith, plaiting their hair in locks. Many refer to themselves as the dreads and regularly attack elderly [*sic*] or defenceless people, almost always at night.' By the weekend the *Sunday Times* (11 December), in an article headed '20 bobbies lead race peace bid', spoke of 'The sudden change of policing style in a district which has been nationally infamous for 10 years as an example of inner-city deprivation.' The *Observer* on the same day opened its feature with a short scenario of police searching a Rastafarian squat for stolen goods or suspects: 'Knives were drawn, blood was spilt and a policeman was taken to hospital – several "dreads" are now in prison.'

The social reaction to phenomena is inevitably patterned by the nature of the information received about those phenomena. Individuals in society build up their common stock of knowledge through various channels, sometimes analysing and probing beneath superficial images, at other times accepting sets of ideas which serve as 'recipes' for everyday life. In other words, the individual employs a sense of practical rationality, at times inquiring whether the knowledge received does justice to the intricate components and processes of social reality; at other times addressing the world with a strictly pragmatic motive, pursuing only sufficient knowledge to get by and further immediate interests. In smaller-scale societies that knowledge would, in all probability, be transmitted and received first hand. Similarly, the ghetto, the university, the council estate etc., all serve to insulate their members and isolate relatively homogeneous groups and produce the possibility of first-hand knowledge. Reactions to deviant phenomena are structured by available knowledge and maybe confined to within that unit. An inner-ghetto protection racket, a campus prowler, or an estate wife-swapping circuit may all be reacted to on the basis of first-hand information which need not escape the boundaries of the particular unit.

The industrial society's mass media, however, opens up the possibilities for almost instantaneous communication of instances of deviance to areas remote from the original scene. The opportunities for the vicarious experience of deviant phenomena have been made available by the creation of networks of press, television and radio.

Whereas at other times, knowledge of fighting between youths on the beaches of Margate could have been encapsulated and confined to only residents, in 1964 it was made into common property and shaped accordingly. The mass media make plenty of capital out of reporting scandals, crime waves, bizarre events as well as natural deviant phenomena such as earthquakes, floods, hurricanes, and so on. Deviant phenomena are eminently newsworthy; they remind the rest of society about what is normal by dramatising the pathological.

In the current instance, a body of information was produced under the auspices of an agency of social control, the West Midlands Police, and transmitted, firstly at a local level and then at the national level, by newspapers – and later by television. Information on the Rastas in Handsworth, therefore, was filtered through two stages during which it acquired the clarity and definition of a social problem. Residents of Handsworth may have been anxious and concerned about the rising incidence of violent crime in the area for some time prior to the report (the police certainly were) but it was not until the documentation of the causes of the unrest and a set of images of who constituted the typical deviant by a socially accredited 'expert' that a clear conception of the problem could be gained – not only by residents of Handsworth but all of Birmingham and, later, all England. The hysterical reporting of the *Birmingham Evening Mail* and the more sobre treatment by the national press were sufficient to generate increased anxiety, concern and a widespread sense of panic. The object of this panic was the Rastaman and in the process of its creation he acquired for himself a new status: the folk devil.

In all the coverage afforded the Handsworth scares the hardcore thug was pictured in a highly typified fashion: masquerading as a follower of the Rastafarian faith, by adopting the symbols and emblems so as to make him indistinguishable from a 'true' Rasta: only his violent behaviour betrayed his true position. One of the effects of this was to introduce the distinction between the thug Rastafarian and the genuine article. As a Superintendent at Thornhill Road Station explained to me: 'The first thing you've got to do when you're talking about Rastafarians is distinguish between the real followers and those kids who stick a few posters of Haile Selassie on the wall, grow plaits and call themselves "Rastas". Most of them don't know what the hell they're going on about and they're the ones who cause all the trouble for us.'

Now, whilst objecting to the rigid dichotomisation, I concede that a number of Rastafarian adherents in the Handsworth area (and other areas of Birmingham) were prone to handbag snatching, pilfering and robberies of a more serious nature. (Though they would never admit this themselves, other brethren conceded the truth of this observation.) Some of this behaviour could have been facilitated, even commissioned, by their loss of recognition in the legitimacy of English Law and its enforcers; a Rasta expanded on his allegiance: 'I and I obey God's law, basic human truths and rights; not the law of the Queen of England.' Many unemployed Rastas supplemented their social security payments with the pickings from such endeavours. I also accept that the objects for such robberies were normally the more vulnerable women and Asians. I cannot, however, accept the view conveyed by Brown's report that the Rastas were consciously participating in an ongoing war with the Handsworth police force.

The report also neglected to point out that a great many Rastas in the district were not involved (except by implication) in any activity relating to violent robbery and were certainly not militantly anti-police – though many had allegedly experienced police harassment at some stage.

My purpose here is not to criticise Brown's study, but to show how its findings were severely consequential in promoting a new conception of the Rastaman, for, in failing to allow for the fact that a great many members did not participate in delinquency, the way was opened up for conceiving of all Rastas as 'hard core'. In other words, readers of the articles and reports who were not directly knowledgeable of the Rastas were nevertheless armed with a typified presentation of what constituted a hard core thug. For example, he had long plaited locks, wore the Ethiopian national colours and claimed to be Rastafarian. Effectively, all Rastas came to be associated with violence – if only because they all fitted the description. Expressed briefly: they were all tarred with the same brush.

The initial registration of the Rastafarian in the public consciousness as a new deviant social type worthy of attention by the media, the police and academics operated to estrange all Rastas from 'conventional' society. The knowledge of the Rastaman had been supplied and the sense of practical rationality precluded any further analytical excursions. Within weeks of the study, the cause of a disturbance in nearby Wolverhampton was attributed (by a Tory Councillor) to 'the Rastafarians (a West Indian sect)' who 'were planning to cause trouble in the town centre' (*Daily Mail*, 30 January 1978).

The generalised beliefs diffused through the media made their impact in a number of ways. First, the style and mode of presentation utilised by both Brown and the subsequent reports were rather lurid and drawn to exaggeration. In particular, the 'Streets of Terror' definition of Handsworth could almost have been designed to engender a sense of panic among Handsworth residents. What better choice of terminology to inject the community with sudden and infectious fear? 'Terror Gangs Shock' supplied a visible and comprehensible cause to the threat. The metaphors, headlines and vocabulary used in relation to Handsworth bore similarity to those used in the coverage of other folk devils: 'menace', 'thugs', 'violent confrontations', 'reign of terror', 'crime wave'; they had the effect of alarm bells and contributed to the highly emotionally charged climate in Handsworth in the immediate aftermath of the reports.

Additionally, some of the 'facts behind the wave of terror' were not exactly sound on examination. The 'gangs' and 'hard core 200' gave the impression of a structured and mobilised unit, geared for the terrorism of the community, whereas my research indicated that Rastafarian membership crystallised in loose collectivities, some more structured than others, but none displaying the features of a 'hard core' or a corresponding 'soft core'. Brown himself claimed that 'They [the Rastas] constantly threaten the peace of the individual citizen, black, brown and white, whilst making the police task both difficult and dangerous since every police contact with them involves the risk of confrontation or violence' (repeated in the *Birmingham Evening Mail*, 6 December 1976). The implication of this rather implausible statement is that no one, regardless of colour or office, was safe in Handsworth when members of the hard core were in evidence. By contrast, my work led me into situations of police contact with Rastas (who may not, of course, have been members of Brown's 'hard core') where relations did not involve even the slightest risk of violence. Brown's description would befit the Baader–Meinhoff gang better than Ras Tafari.

The cumulative effect of the language used to describe the problems of Handsworth to the Birmingham audience was to convey the image of geographical area plagued with day-to-day assaults and robberies where every resident was vulnerable to attack from the dreadlocked hard core whose destructive mission had rendered the district practically unfit for habitation.

If the language used in the reports conjured up a particular conception of Handsworth, the communication of the Rasta typification in a certain stylised way gave many Rastafarian symbols a new symbolic power unrelated to their original meaning. The words 'Rasta' and 'dread' had always been symbolic of a certain status to the Rastaman and the dreadlocks, coloured tams and prayer sticks were symbolic of the word 'Rasta' itself. A Rasta sighting another black wearing locks knew immediately that he was confronting a fellow member of the brotherhood. So, in turn, the locks, tams and sticks themselves became symbolic of the status (what some Rastas called 'the image of dread'). While for the Rastas these symbolisations were very positive and self-confirming, for readers of the Handsworth reports Rasta symbols, emblems and motifs became wholly negative in connotation. What might have been regarded as derivations of the Afro-look or peculiarities of the West Indian dress style, were, after the reports, transformed unambiguously into the trappings of the Rastafarian folk devil. This process, in which symbols and motifs came to take on a descriptive potential and provoke hostile reaction was also evident in the mods and rockers phase, when parkas and scooters evoked unfavourable feelings; no less so in the punk rock epoch in which safety pins and plastic clothing brought forth a punitive response from the wider society.

In every report or article on Handsworth the physical appearance of the Rastaman was mentioned, the most important aspect of which was the locks and this was critical in creating negative symbols and thus facilitating the labelling in terms of the typification. Rasta was removed from any previously neutral context and acquired a totally negative meaning for the wider society. Random questioning of Handsworth residents – of all colours – immediately after the report's release revealed a pronounced similarity (e.g., 'Oh, those muggers with the hair'; 'The woolly hat brigade you mean? Just a bunch of racist thugs'; 'There's nothing religious about that lot; it's an excuse to hide behind'; 'Vicious bastards with hair and all that bollocks about Africa'). The reason this particular attribution did not prove inimical to the movement was because, like militant North American blacks in the late 1960s, they accepted the negative connotations fully and turned them into positive forces. A Twelve Tribes Rasta put it to me: 'Them see that Rasta knows the truth and soon must come, must take his place in the world soon. Fear I? I thinks they must "cause that day is soon".'

In other words: if Babylon's agents thought they were bad, then that was simply an indication of their anxiety and concern about the movement's future. In the USA negroes used 'blackness' as a sign of value: 'The baddest motherfucker of them all' was a supreme status conferred on only extreme militants and campaigners. 'Badness' was used as an instrument for morally upgrading the self and morally downgrading outsiders. In a similar way, Rastas could wallow in the satisfaction that their hair and clothing was frowned upon and caused consternation and anxiety in the white community; they carried their 'dread': 'Babylon has seen the I man and must tremble in his presence; whosoever come up against I must fall.'

They could easily assimilate this effect of the panic, but they could not, on the other hand, deflect a third consequence. The apparently suppurating condition in Handsworth motivated the West Midlands Police to supplement their extant force with twenty additional foot patrol officers whose task would revolve around surveillance duties as opposed to reactive policing in which officers responded to each reported incident in cars. Brown had warned of the irreparable damage to police–community relations caused by the shortage of policemen in Handsworth, which he estimated at 20 per cent. The extra police officers in the district were experienced personnel, often moved from other beats for the new permanent foot-patrol duties.

This decision was arrived at after an emergency meeting of senior police officers to consider the report's conclusions. On the announcement of the proposal, a senior West Midlands Police spokesman was quoted as saying: 'The area is being given high priority although it is not a panic situation' (*Guardian*, 5 December 1977). Perhaps the change in policy was not the result of panic decisions, merely a clinical response in terms of certain images of the central deviant group in ways suggested by the Brown report. But it received almost instantaneous coverage by national and local newspapers, giving rise to a public awareness that Handsworth was having to cope with a highly potent threat: its police were directing control measures towards specific groups thought to be responsible for the rising crime – the hard-core Rastas. The point was not whether the Rastas presented any actual threat or not, nor whether the Handsworth police's decision to inflate its force was made under neutral or panic conditions but that the way the events – the publication of the report and the decision to increase police staff – slotted in with each other was highly suggestive of a strict causal relationship. Extra police were seen to be called in to combat the rising menace of the Rastaman, thus sensitising the public to expect more trouble from the deviant group. Headlines such as '20 Bobbies Lead Race Peace Bid' (*Sunday Times*, 11 December 1977) and 'Police Patrols Stepped Up To Combat Rising Crime' (*Guardian*, 5 December 1977) looked to consolidate the connection. The measures enacted by the West Midlands Police Force were for all intents and purposes part of the Rastafarian phenomenon. In effect, by addressing the perceived problem in this way, the police assured the magnification of the Rastafarian movement by prompting the media to create awarenesses.

Shortly after Christmas 1977, Birmingham City Council Urban Renewal Committee announced plans to introduce new, brighter street lighting in Handsworth so as to help police in their 'drive against crime' (*Birmingham Evening Mail*, 30 December 1977) and in the following January two police officers were sent to Jamaica in an effort to gain 'a better understanding between blacks and police' (*Birmingham Evening Mail*, 10 January 1978).

The police's reaction was organised within a framework of institutionalised procedures. So, although the switch to foot-patrol duty officers was a rather sudden reversal of policy, it was assimilable within existing forms of social control and could therefore be dismissed as a panic measure. Nevertheless, the meeting called after the reception of Brown's report and the decisions arising from it gave the strong impression that the new moves were adaptations to a particular deviant group. In this respect, the response can be understood as an

ment of what was called 'the societal control culture'. Similar
features were found in the way in which Jamaican agents of social
control responded to the perceived violent threat of Rastas after three
separate incidents by mobilising a total attack on both Rasta groups
and ganja crops in the name of the national good. Though not of the
same scale or intensity, the Handsworth measures reflected some
elements of the veritable emergency system erected in Jamaica to
rescue its population from the imminent disaster. Drawing in
additional officers was comparable to recruiting the help of the militia
to combat the Rastas. In both cases the capitulation to the deviance
had the effect of alerting the wider society to the scope and nature of
the danger. In Handsworth the measures were regarded as legitimate
and, in many cases, welcome; the negative symbolisation provided
the basis for this reception. The way the situation had been described
by Brown was highly permissive of a positive orientation to the
measures and afforded the police a mandate for their strategies. The
nearest to a quintessential mark of approval was: 'It's about time
they started doing something about this; the situation is serious nowadays. The more [police], the better, I say' (middle-aged man). Others
reflected a similar concern: 'It's terrible the way it's been let to
deteriorate . . . I live in Brecon Road, but you get the "litter" from
Heathfield Road'; 'This area is in a shocking state. I can't think the
extra police will help that much, but they might stop it from getting
much worse.'

As the front-line enforcers of social control, the police perform a
critical function in the designation of deviant statuses. Their practical
reasoning and everyday interpretations and decisions about phenomena
have effects on popular conceptions about deviance and how it should
be dealt with. A phenomenon which may at some historical period or
in some geographical area be regarded as inimical to the interests of
the community may at a different stage and in a different setting be
interpreted as harmless and unworthy of police attention (the movements of Bedward and Howell, for example). Determinants of such
changes are varied and embrace political and commercial spheres, as
well as the more parochial pressures exerted from within the community (see Chambliss, 1976; Turk, 1976). Sometimes legal innova-
tions result; often changes in police implemented by the police are
sufficient to deal with the deviance. Much of the stigma attached to
the Rastas in Jamaica was removed after the late seventies. Relaxation
of stringent policies relating to ganja and more lenient punishments
for offences, combined with the movement's escalating popularity
among more 'respectable' members of the island's middle class, contributed towards the removal of many negative evaluations placed on
the Rastaman. But the very opposite process was in operation in
England.

Stigma attribution, or 'branding', must be seen as a complex process, one of the key variables of which is police policy. As the officially designated agents of civil power they exert a keen influence on what the rest of society comes to view as noxious or innocuous, malignant or benignant. And in so doing, they can gear public expectations to impending dangers and thus engender panics. Handsworth's police force made it known in December 1977 that they were preparing themselves for trouble, the central cause of which would be the 'dreads'. It was a simple response to a series of situational pressures; effectively, a show of force through increasing the sheer volume of on-duty policemen. If the strategy was designed to alleviate the growing anxiety and concern among Handsworth's residents, it surely failed; for, given the emotionally charged atmosphere at the time, the reinforcements only served to solidify what might previously have been suspicions or hearsay, by publicly and officially confirming that there was indeed trouble in the district and there was going to be more in the future (otherwise, why the extra policemen?). In musical terms, the population of Handsworth had been 'cued in'! In one notable instance, I asked an unsuspecting white Handsworthian about the area's problems: 'Haven't you been reading the *Mail*? It's like Harlem around here nowadays with all these dreads; and its got to get worse for certain, you mark my words.' The events in Handsworth built up to a steady crescendo of panic leading to public misconceptions about the district, the polarisation of Rastas and the sensitisation of Handsworthians to expect future dangers from the deviants. Expectations arising after the police measures had an air of certainty rather than probability; the revelation of the new plans ostensibly warned the troublemakers that the police were intent on bringing pressure to bear on them, but also served to reassure the public that efforts were being made to curb the menace (though it also retroactively undermined previously existing arrangements in the area).

But by giving the impression that they were plunging themselves into a titanic struggle with the Rastas in an attempt to restore 'normality' the police gave sustenance to a reservoir of apprehension and anxiety. The unintended consequence of the move was to cultivate the growth of panic rather than curtail it, thereby promoting a social reaction which drove the Rastas to the extreme peripheries of the community. What might otherwise have remained an ambiguously problematic area was, after the 1977–8 events, a clearly defined problem territory characterised by the 'hard-core' Rastas.

As the culpable villains of the peace, Rastas were understandably concerned about the unfolding situation in which they were forced into deviant roles. Whilst acknowledging that many of the brethren were answerable for some of the police's (and Brown's) accusations, they grew anxious at the prospect of all Rastas being brought into further disrepute and subjected to intense police harassment as the result of Brown's contention. Their association (if only by similarity of appearance) placed them in a vulnerable position, for, as Paul Rock points out: 'Deviants who are recognisable as rule-breakers can stigmatise those with whom they associate' (1973, p. 29).

Though they did not react in any organised way, several self-appointed spokesmen articulated strong criticism at both the content and the reporting of the study. The problem facing every wearer of tams and dreadlocks – that of being identified as a member of the 'hard core' – was recognised as the single most deleterious consequence of the events for the Rastas themselves. The fear that type-casting would produce an adverse community reaction and the creation of conditions conducive to conflict was a constant one. A deviant role had been carved out for the 'dread'; the danger was that he might have been forced to play it. A Rasta expressed his apprehension: 'Shades of Grey has done much damage to the faith: people now look at a man of dreadlocks and think "there is a bad man, a threat". Now every I man with locks is thought of in this manner and we must feel pressure even harder.'

Exacerbating the apprehension was the lack of mechanisms through which sentiments of the black community could be routinely recorded. The control mobilisation system in Handsworth was geared to a central plan: that of encasing the Rastaman in the grip of the law. One of the keys in this plan was police initiative and Rastafarian brethren were mindful of the wide ranges of activity implied in this: 'We must feel the pressure even harder'; 'There is men around oppressing we because of the faith and because of what I stand for'.

The upshot of the Handsworth panic was that the series of loosely structured groups of blacks orienting themselves around the belief system of Ras Tafari were ascribed a deviant role which singled them out for purposes of elucidation, action and possibly the justification of action. The highly complementary parts of the police and the media in cultivating a public image for this role and its associations with violence contributed to the sense of panic and consternation informing the public reaction to the deviance. This assignment to the deviant role was based on the questionable wisdom of Brown's study, but the consequences of such an assignment were still of the highest import-ance to the Rastaman himself. From the moment of the report's release the Rasta became a fully fledged deviant in the eyes of the wider society, including the police whose response was to strengthen convictions about the deviant nature of the whole Rastafarian enter-prise. The image evoked hostility and judgements about its desirability.

Although I have been concerned with the transmission and diffusion of societal reaction through the mass media and the police, my use of this key variable has been confined to those institutions and not to a more generalised level. I take what the police do about and how the media treat deviant phenomena as reliable 'litmus tests' of what the wider society does and thinks about them. In any case, these control agencies determine the nature of the information available to the rest of society and, therefore, exert a powerful influence on the quality and tone of the reaction. The opinions, beliefs and themes presented by the police and the media may, of course, encounter resistance from the audience they reach, or at least some sectors, and for this reason it would be unwise to assume a complete homogeneity of reception and reaction. Such an assumption implies a conception of members of the receiving society sharing a set of common values and moral rules, the creation of which might be entrusted to an authoritative body; a substantial consensus about the moral world; and the possibility of complete and unrestricted absorption of ideas generated by external agencies. In England of the 1970s there existed a plurality of possibly critical groups which may have constituted a deviance-defining re-action contrary to those conceptions expressed by the police and the media; most particularly groups which were better informed about the Rastafarian movement than the media and the police. It would be invalid to exaggerate the universality of the effects of police manoeuvres and media presentation, the authoritative version. How-ever, there is, I contend, feasible ground for suggesting that the 'official' reaction articulated by the media and which informed the preactive control measures penetrated the public consciousness and affected what was thought and done about the Rastas. My reasons for suggesting this stem from two sources. First, the observation noted earlier that actors address the social world with a pragmatic motive, moved by a sense of practical rationality which dictates that the bulk of knowledge about the world will be taken secondhand and accepted as long as it serves a range of immediate purposes. Those members of society unable to test available information on the Rastas had little opportunity to dispute the contentions of the police and the media and would have had to assume the existence and characteristics of such groups (as, indeed, sections of society would have to about mods, drug addicts, paedophiles, Ku-Klux-Klansmen etc.). For the most part there is little time, need or, for that matter, inclination to investigate the validity and accuracy of the information. Themes and ideas offered by authoritative agents are assimilated with relative comfort into a stable background of understandings and definitions. As an EOC member astutely noticed: 'Who takes the trouble to find what Rasta is trying to say or do? They think him something like the Ku Klux Klan or something like that.'

Secondly, like many types of imputed deviance, the Rastafarian phenomenon was territorially confined; Handsworth being the main focus but many other urban centres also featuring. Where Rastas were stabilised and concentrated in specific areas the possibility of direct encounters with residents was considerably heightened, though, given Rastafarian postures, the maintenance of social distance was likely. Such a social gulf was likely to discourage exploration of the accuracy of police and media information and physical proximity would not have significantly reduced anonymity. My experience in the area at the time of the panic suggests that many white residents associated sights of Rastas with the *Birmingham Evening Mail* reports, progressively integrating the strange phenomenon into a background of expectancies and understandings. The appearance and actions of Rastas only validated the quality of the received information which in effect increased the social distance by accelerating the typifying processes of Handsworth residents (i.e. by providing typical schemes for interpretation). The imputation of deviance to the Rastas was documented by what John Kitsuse calls 'retrospective interpretations', 'a process by which the subject reinterprets the individual's past behaviour in the light of new information' (1964, p. 96). Knowledge of the Rastafarian movement, its history, development and meaning to West Indian youth in Britain, however sketchy or unfounded, furnished the items for a fresh perspective on the Rastas and what they allegedly stood for. Or, as Rock (1973, p. 33) puts it: 'The revelation that someone is deviant can bring about a total reformation of the significance of his past, present and future actions.' And a middle-aged Handsworth resident: 'I'd wondered what all this business was about; sticks and hats and all that. But, to be honest, it didn't dawn on me till I read the reports.' A by-product of this was the tendency to ostracise the wearers of locks and tams and place them apart as members of a menacing deviant group rather than merely a social curio. They were vivid reminders of a socially unacceptable element which needed to be eradicated. The reciprocal rejection fits in nicely with the Wilkins–Cohen cycle in which the polarisation of the deviant facilitates the description of him in increasingly abstract terms, eventually allowing him less and less freedom to play anything but the deviant role. Consolidation of the typification ensues.

The panic in Handsworth was precipitated by the focusing of police, press and public attention on an area of events which had, up to December 1977, escaped notice. The creation of alarm was a response to press reporting rather than to any statistical trend behind the 'wave of terror', for, as I have noted, the media coverage of the Rastafarian phenomenon created a conceptual reality in spite of any other social reality and it was the images portrayed in the media which were oriented to by the public. And, after all, when individuals are characterised in a particular way, they are already under pressure to fulfil the social type posited. Richard Quinney in his discussion of the efficacy of the media in producing public conceptions of crime and their consequences reminds us that 'social reality begins in the imagination' (1970, p. 291). Deviance does, indeed, begin in the imagination and this suggestion in no way denies the reality of Rastafarian people with their own particular ideas, ambitions, values and interpretations; nor does it imply an atomic conception of the Rasta in which he is propelled by exterior forces in some deterministic fashion. The theoretical advance of my approach is that it is the identifications, interpretations and inferences of certain groups about other groups (usually more vulnerable ones) which transform the reality of deviance.

In this application, the process worked as follows: the police's recognition of the 'dreads' as folk devils constituted the attribution of deviant status and the concomitant negative evaluations of group traits; this assignment, or labelling, was amplified and often distorted through media exposure; warnings and the introduction of new proactive control strategies further alerted the local and national press to the imminence of more trouble from the deviant group and sensitised the wider society to expect trouble; polarisation of the Rastas followed with general societal reaction and, in particular, police reaction ensuring a severe limitation on opportunities to escape the role model which had been constructed for them.

My treatment is open to question because I have left underdeveloped the extent to which the public branding affected the Rasta's self-image. Obviously, the acceptance of the label is never inevitable. My work revealed that some members who actively respected the moral and legal codes of society openly celebrated their deviant status in conjunction with the moral upgrading of blackness programme: 'Suspicious of I! Hah! Them ras suspicious. Let them be; Rastaman he no care. It is dread,' a Rasta told me. They rejoiced in the stigma and interpreted others' negative attributions positively (in terms of the Babylonian conspiracy): '. . . Babylon must tremble'. More cautious were those concerned with the unfavourable after-effects of the study and its by-products: 'We must feel the pressure even harder.' It is, perhaps, too early to assess the longer-term consequences on the Rastas' self-conceptions. Some may undergo personal transformations of identity and come to view themselves as committed deviants; some may feel the blunt edge of the police's punitive stance and be forced to reconceptualise their position, possibly dropping their faith or making their allegiance less obvious. What is certain is that no Rastafarian affiliate in England would remain unaffected by the Handsworth scare.

Chapter 11

Conclusion: The Spell of Africa

No one knows when the hour of Africa's redemption cometh. It is in the wind. It is coming. One day, like a storm, it will be here. When that day comes all Africa will stand together.

Marcus Garvey, 1967

THE SPARROW AND THE OAK

Ras Tafari was the second back-to-Africa movement to emerge in England, its predecessor being the brainchild of the abolitionist campaigner Granville Sharp, who in the 1780s conceived and executed a plan to repatriate thousands of Africans living in London (see Walvin, 1973, pp. 144–58). The two movements shared few common features and would defy mention in the same sentence were it not for the vision inspiring and energising both. For Sharp, himself a product of the Enlightenment thinking, Africa presented itself as a new Utopia, an experimental society where his own theories could be put into action. Utopian elements were also evident in the Rastafarian Africa where, it was contended, all blacks would find their own Zion; repatriation would herald the beginning of a 'new age' when black people would return to their rightful fatherland, Babylon would be destroyed and the social order would be transformed. In both instances, the vision of Africa was exactly that – a vision; it bore no necessary relationship to the bone-hard, practical reality of Africa replete with its political and economic complexities, and relied more on a simple mythology built around the image of a Golden Age.

Like practically every movement which sought to reunite black peoples with their original homeland, the Rastafarian movement in both Jamaica and England utilised what David Jenkins calls 'the Phantom land', (1975, p. 28), a symbolic Africa which contrasts with the geographical entity.

From the first day on which an African was captured then blessed by some swaggering fifteenth century Portuguese cleric and consigned to a terrible Atlantic crossing, there have been two distinct

Africas. There is the geographical entity, with its millions of social realities, and there is the Africa of the exiled Negro's mind, an Africa compounded of centuries of waning memories and vanquished hopes translated into myth. (Jenkins, 1975, p. 9)

The strain to return to Africa has existed since the earliest slave days: Jenkins (1975, p. 13) notes how slaves in the process of transportation to the Americas would throw themselves overboard still locked in their irons in vain attempts to swim home (see also H. O. Patterson, 1967, pp. 195-8). Africa has periodically recrudesced in one form or another ever since, whether as the new home to which all black people would ultimately gravitate, as in Garvey's philosophy; as the watchword for racial conflict, a tactic employed by black power leaders; or as an imaginary ancient land untouched and unspoiled until the attacks of the white 'devils' as used by the American Nation of Islam. Over a 400-year duration Africa has surfaced repeatedly to charge the hearts and minds of blacks in the Diaspora and inspire them to new ambitions and fresh modes of thought. Ras Tafari was no exception; participation in the movement linked its members with their fatherland and in so doing provided them with the nucleus of a new sense of selfhood or social identity based not on England or the West Indies but on Africa. Through proclaiming their distinctly African character, Rastas could emphasise and even exaggerate their cultural differences; they were an enlightened people set apart from the wider society and, in a great many ways, pure anomalies. Rastas thought that as uprooted Africans they had no right to be in England – or Jamaica for that matter – and, furthermore, were preparing for the exodus which would most assuredly arrive in the near future. The concept of Africa helped crystallise otherwise ambiguous or unknown and certainly unfocused ambitions by giving West Indian youths in England an objective around which to organise; it was the central dynamic of the whole movement.

But to view the Rastafarian movement as a straightforward attempt to repatriate blacks would be insensitive. The issue of Africa was far more complex; a Rasta expressed his version in the form of a short parable: 'I see Africa as my spiritual and material home. You see each little bird has a resting place. A sparrow might jump from an oak to a beech tree and yet he knows that his nest is in the oak tree; so he can travel from various places, but he knows when his work is done the oak is his tree. So I'm out here in the world professing my Father's word and when my work is over I'll know where my resting place is: Africa.'

The sparrow and the oak analogy is revealing because it suggests that Rastas could effectively retain their very intimate connections with their 'spiritual home in Africa', the oak, and yet pursue their

worldly existence physically separated from it, the implication being
that it was sufficient to recognise that the black man's rightful homeland was Africa and it was to this continent he would ultimately and
inevitably return; but at what stage remained unspecified, 'when my
work is over'.

It would be unfair to characterise the orientations of each and every
member with the sparrow and oak story, but there was sufficient
response along this line to suggest a pattern. The Rastafarian incorporation of the 'two Africas' into one objective gave rise to all manner
of complication, and disentangling the two was not, I felt, the most
fruitful analytic approach; for the Rastas themselves were never to be
drawn anywhere near an unambiguous statement of objective, the
closest approximation encountered being: 'Africa must hear our cry
one day and Africa must answer our cry one day because as I says
we are people of our ancestors and you know they must really
recognise our cry and seek to help us there. And by that I means we
will get back on the boat where we came from in the beginning and
just go back to Africa.' Another Rasta was equally insistent in his
claim: 'Africa is where all black men are descended from and so it's
back to Africa we must go.'

In other words, Africa the geographical entity would assist them in
their struggle to return to what they considered to be their true
homeland. But when asked whether the realisation of Africa was
possible in England (i.e. without physical repatriation) another Rasta
answered: 'Yes. Difficult but practical.' And the author of the
sparrow and the oak reminded me: 'My spirit is now in Africa but
my material soul is in Great Britain.'

The easiest synthesis of all perspectives on Africa would seem to be
as follows: the realisation that all black men are really Africans ('the
true self') stimulated the awareness that negroes must ultimately
return physically to the fatherland; in the meantime, however, it was
sufficient to proclaim their African identity and articulate their desire
to return but without actually pressing any practical programmes –
just wait for the millennium to take its course; when the hour of
redemption did arrive Africa would welcome back its lost children.
The interim period was to be spent, as one Rasta said, 'culturising
ourselves', growing aware of African cultures and promoting that
awareness among other blacks in England; what might be called
'counter-acculturation'. Despite their protestations to the contrary, the
Rastas' conception of Africa as a geographical entity owed more to
the 'phantom land' than to any other reality.

The relationship between the ultimate goal of redemption and the
precursory phase of 'culturisation' was never a comfortable one.
Garvey, in particular, never satisfactorily resolved the tensions introduced by tying together the two and, despite his repetitious insistence

on a physical return, made some recantations during his later life. His wife, Amy Jacques Garvey (1970, p. 135), reflected that the 'back-to-Africa' slogan was attributed to the UNIA in ridicule and she was quoted as saying:

> . . . after Marcus Garvey had returned millions to Africa *spiritually* he had done his work. It was finished in the real sense. I believe if Garvey had lived, he would have studied conditions in Africa even more than in the New World and he would have realised that the return to Africa had taken place . . . *There was no back-to-Africa movement except in a spiritual sense.* (Essien-Udom, 1962, p. 61, my italics.)

The tension between the two ideals had also run through the history of the Jamaican Ras Tafari. Writing of the millenarian enthusiasm at the start of the 1960s, H. Orlando Patterson asserted: 'That in fact, the last thing the cultist, in the depth of his being, would wish to happen is for the ships to come' (1964*b*, p. 17) – though, in view of the thousands who sold up or merely left their belongings in expectation of the transportation, I am at a loss to see how Patterson arrived at such a conclusion. Some thirteen years later Leonard Barrett was able to, rather blandly, state 'that close to 50 per cent of the movement's membership still holds to the doctrine of repatriation; that is the miraculous return to Ethiopia by the supernatural power of the king' (1977, p. 172). The newer members cultivated a posture around the phrase, 'liberation before repatriation'.

The reason for such a persistent diversity in objective within the movement can be attributed to the absence of any clearly defined locus of authority beyond the individual member. Roy Wallis (1976, p. 14) characterises this as 'epistemological individualism' and cites it as the fundamental criterion of the cult as opposed to the sect, a distinction which I find unexceptional. Unlike sectarian forms of religious organisation, Ras Tafari contained a belief system which was so fluid and open to differential interpretation that it yielded no source of legitimate attribution of heresy. So, for example, in Garvey's organisation where he was the final authority, the doctrine of 'Africa for the Africans' was cemented by his judgement and any wavering from his interpretation could be rejected as heretical. But in Ras Tafari the determination of what was to constitute the correct doctrine were largely matters for individual judgement. Apart from the original Rastafarian triangle of Howell, Hibbert and Dunkley (and, possibly, Ricketts), no leaders emerged who were capable of reducing the ideological diffuseness by imposing their own specific doctrinal inter-pretation. For this reason the Jamaican movement remained something of a hydra.

In the English context the movement was acephalous, spawning no effective head and developing without the aid of a strictly defined doctrine. The 'Africa for the Africans' doctrine, which was borrowed from early Garvey, was always amenable to reformulation, depending on which conception of 'Africa' was used; whether it was to mean a 'physical' or 'spiritual' return to Africa, or both, was to be decided by the individual brother. Hence ambivalence over ultimate ambition was shot throughout the whole belief system.

Presuming for the moment that a physical repatriation was the ultimate objective of every member – and not one Rasta would deny this – there arises the complicating factor of how this was to be achieved. The majority were defectors from the Garvey line, tending to side with the original Rastas in their belief in Haile Selassie's power and intention to effect the redemption: 'It is written in Revelations and so it is God's will.' Others were more hard-headed in their approach: 'We see this [the African redemption] happening on a governmental basis.' Still others saw the two as compatible, with God inspiring a pragmatically worked return but without actually intervening in the process itself: 'These are the last days . . . I and I are preparing for the new age when we shall return to our homeland . . . this is God's will.' But in all cases the redemption was regarded as sanctioned by Haile Selassie; even those politically aware members envisaged almost miraculous, rapid social changes in Africa which would enable the continent to accommodate the thousands upon thousands wishing to be repatriated. The movement did not lose its millenarian dimension in the transition from Jamaica; it remained guided by a vision of salvation.

But if the ultimate ambition of the African redemption was what Essien-Udom calls esoteric, 'centred upon eschatological and apocalyptic hopes (1962, p. 8), the exoteric components, 'the means for coping with the material, cultural, moral and psychological problems which are purported to impede the advancement of the Negro masses' (1962, p. 59) were equally, if not more important in impelling the members to fresh modes of thought and action.

This involved what has been called 'culturisation', roots-searching or plainly asserting the essential 'Africanness' of black peoples: 'It's for us to revive our true self and really know our ability by discovering our history and by discovering our history we know what we were capable of in the past and find a kind of terminus where we can look to the future; 'We try to get our culture back.'

RASTA AND NEGRITUDE

This exoteric aspect of the Rastafarian enterprise invites comparisons with another movement concerned with counter-acculturation and whose leaders were at pains to establish a truly black cultural tradition based on Africa. Although similar impulses had emanated from such diverse sources as the Mau Mau uprising (Barnett and Njama, 1960; Corfield, 1960), the Harlem renaissance (Vincent, 1976, sections 6 and 7), the Haitian revolution (James, 1938a) and the Afro-Cuban movement (Coulthard, 1962, ch. 2), it was given coherent artistic expression in the 1930s through the work of Aimé Césaire, a black poet from Martinique residing in Paris. He wrote:

> My *négritude* is not a tower nor a cathedral
> It delves into the red flesh of the soil
> it plunges into the burning flesh of the sky
> (in Coulthard, 1962, p. 60)

Césaire's poem in *Cahier d'un retour au pays natal* (1947) not only announced his personal discovery of the quality *négritude*, but outlined the various stages of this discovery beginning with an awareness of the abhorrence of the poverty and decay resulting from the French colonisation of Martinique, passing into a contempt for the white world and then an attack on Western conceptions of rationality or reason: 'We hate you and your reason.' In effect, the work signals a negation of European world views through the rejection of reason which underpins Western modes of thought (see Horton, 1967) and its substitution with what Coulthard calls 'a mystical oneness with the world' (1962, p. 59). The discovery of the negro modality is a total dissolution of the subject–object dualisms in an almost pantheistic embrace of nature and fellow blacks; as Leopold Senghor, who helped develop the concept into a social movement, declared: 'European reasoning is analytical, discursive by utilization; Negro–African reasoning is intuitive by participation' (1968, p. 74).

Rejection of Western modes of thought and the advocation of a new way of apprehending social reality was seen as peculiarly negro and therefore not available to whites. Resurrected were African traits of art, mysticism, communion and complete freedom of expression and these were elevated to positions of stature so that blacks could feel pride and dignity in their African heritage. In its broadest sense négritude became, as Senghor summarised it: 'the awareness, defence and development of African values' (quoted in Mazrui, 1978, p. 26).

Though principally a literary critique of Western society and its systematic suppression of negro potentiality by dissociating blacks from what were regarded as their real African modes of thought and subjecting them to acculturation, négritude took on a more programmatic complexion with the poet-President of Senegal Leopold Senghor. The impulse became the 'rediscovery of one's past, one's culture, one's ancestors and one's language' (L. V. Thomas, 1965, p. 115). Inspired by the African ethnographer and historian Leo Frobenius,

Senghor delved into African culture, to which he attributed the characteristic of being 'Ethiopian', as a way of coming to grips with the different sense of reality he presumed existed in ancient African societies (Ita, 1973). Noted by L. V. Thomas, the 'Senghorian path of socio-cultural development' was 'at once a question of finding what in the past makes possible a forecast of the future'.

Outside Senghor, négritude made little contribution at an active political level, affecting in the main French-speaking black artists, particularly those who were absorbed by the surrealistic implications of its imperative to irrationality; Frantz Fanon, himself influenced by négritude, confessed: 'I threw myself into the arms of the irrational. I became irrational up to my neck' (1952, p. 122). Its last major public manifestation as an organised movement was at its 1959 congress held in Rome.

The négritude movement elicits inescapable comparisons with the exoteric dimensions of Ras Tafari; comparisons that stem from its fundamental feature: the rejection of white impositions: 'Initially *négritude* developed as a reaction to white racism, as dialectical opposition to the cultural values imposed by whites' (L. Kuper, 1974, p. 92). The replacement of African thought for Western modes and the strain to excavate African culture by laying bare the Negro Arcadia which existed before the arrival of the Europeans were expressions of the rejection of white definitions of reality which assigned the black man to a position of inferiority. Followers of Ras Tafari refused to accept willingly conventional conceptions of reality and instead formulated new conceptual maps to follow in their subjective reconstructions; maps stimulated and sustained by a vision of Africa which bore no necessary resemblance to the continent itself. To follow Coulthard, it was an Africa 'not of African civilizations or African cultural values, but of Africa itself as a vague geographical region, and the imaginary and emotional fatherland of all the Negroes in the world' (1962, p. 71). Négritude never advocated a return to Africa in a physical sense, seeking only to make its presence urgently felt by the millions of 'exiled' blacks who had been sucked into Western ways of thinking and thus accepted racial categories. But the central counter-acculturative impulse informing the movement showed clear similarities to the exoteric component of Ras Tafari. Here was the attempt to create an African consciousness for blacks wherever they were; a return to Africa through realising its presence in the minds of negroes.

Building on this, proponents of négritude wanted to dissolve the subject–object distinction of Western thought and re-establish a 'mystical oneness with the world'. Rastas similarly rejected conventional dualisms: their expression of 'I and I' was, in a Rasta's own words, 'oneness of two persons'. Such a unity was the theoretical basis of the brotherhood which was believed to tie all blacks together in the face of the white world. The notion of brotherhood also finds expression in négritude, especially in the Haitian poet Jean Price-Mars, who asserted: 'We belong to Africa by our blood' (in Coulthard, 1962, p. 73). This awareness in itself could be interpreted as antithetical to Western thought, or, as the négritude student Abiola Irele puts it, 'the poles of *individual* consciousness for the whites, and of *collective* consciousness for the blacks' (1965, p. 341). The departure from dualism released a powerful bonding force which held together the membership of both movements.

Such a belief helped promote the sense of past and future which the Rastas used so effectively to spur their ambitions. Bob Marley's prophetic song 'Exodus' captured it: 'We know where we're going, we know where we're from. We're leaving Babylon, going into our father's land.' But also Senghor's programme was to find what in the past would make possible a forecast of the future. The idea was that by probing for clues about African history and achievement the black man would find his roots which would instil in him a new sense of pride and selfhood and in turn inspire him with confidence about his future. For the négritudinarian this was a transformation of black consciousness; for the Rastafarian it was a transformation of the social order.

Even at lower altitudes similarities occur. The Rastas' insistence that all African societies were part of Ethiopia until Babylon conspired to dissect the continent and atomise its population finds agreement with Senghor (1968, p. 11) who identified 'Ethiopia' with 'Black Africa' (though it seems he misunderstood Frobenius on this issue. See Ita, 1973).

Both movements were condemnatory of conventional Christianity as a tool of colonialism used to keep blacks in subjection and perpetuate their physical and mental enslavement. Négritude saw such religions as in 'hyprocritical connivance with colonialism and imperialism' (Coulthard, 1962, p. 66).

And, of course, the contributions of the Rastas in Jamaica to such fields as music, dance, sculpture and poetry (Barrett, 1977, pp. 185–97) indicates a similarity with the attempts of négritude artists to develop purely black cultural spheres. By inspiring higher levels of black creativity the movements tried to undermine the previously unquestioned prestige and superiority of white culture and so upgrade the achievements of blacks. (At the time of my research British Rastas' artistic projects were at the embryonic stage, but efforts were being made to cultivate this aspect of the movement, with painting, wood carving and poetry being popular pursuits.)

Both movements were fuelled by the recognition that colonialism had robbed blacks of their cultures. A Rastaman explained 'We have

seen how colonialism has stripped us completely of everything that
has identified us as a people over the centuries and it has degraded
us to the extent that we can no longer express ourselves as Africans.'
And so the effort was made to realise this past culture by erasing
from their minds the noxious influences of colonialism. The négritude
poet, Léon Damas, asserted:

> We have stripped off our European clothes . . .
> Our pride in being Negroes,
> The glory of being black.

Both thrusts were to upgrade the black man by excavating his past,
even exaggerating his primitiveness (what Rastas called 'the way of
the ancients') and using this to imbue him with a new-found pride
and dignity in being black, in being African.

Négritude has been criticised for being over-contemplative and it
would be fair to subject Ras Tafari to the same allegation (see
Adotevi, 1969). It was the Nigerian poet Wole Soyinka who jibed:
'A tiger does not go around proclaiming its tigritude – it just pounces'
(quoted in Lowenthal, 1972, p. 283). Much earlier Garvey had
warned: 'The tiger is already loose and he has been at large for so
long that there is no longer one tiger, but there are many tigers' (1967,
Vol. I, p. 80). The 'tiger' is the black man who has realised his 'true
self' as an African; for Rastas he had accepted Ras Tafari, for
négritudinarians he had recognised his négritude. But to wait for the
tiger to pounce, presuming Soyinka meant by this political activism,
is to misunderstand the nature of both enterprises. For the most part
négritude and Ras Tafari did not translate into political movements.
Their concerns were to upgrade the black man not through overt
political activity, but through instilling him with a sense of culture,
his own culture compounded of the distinctive qualities of what were
assumed to be elements of African culture. (For further reading on
négritude see Césaire, 1959; Skurnick, 1965; Berrian and Long,
1967; Depestre, 1969; Coulthard, 1969, 1970; Baxter and Sansom,
1972.)

EPILOGUE

Ras Tafari, like négritude, was a movement of counter-acculturation,
the process of trying to eliminate the influences of the dominant white
society and develop a distinct and separate culture. Its method for
achieving this was by creating a culture and, despite all the statements
to the contrary ('it's for us to revive our true self and really know our
ability'), Rastas were not engaged in the task of discovering or
recovering their past, but creating one anew on the basis of an

imaginary Africa. This is not to suggest that this Africa is in any way inferior to the geographical entity, for it has in its various manifestations over the centuries exerted a spell-like influence over black movements, impelling their members to new modes of thought and action.

As for the Rastas' particular conception, Africa was a paradise lost, the Zion which would be restored to them after centuries in the Diaspora. It was a vision inspired by Garvey but nurtured and elaborated by successive generations of Rastas believing themselves to be the true lost tribes of Israel. Such a belief was by no means the exclusive property of the Rastas; Africa and the Americas have abounded with black separatist movements stirred by the vision of a new Zion and sheltering their members with the conviction that they were the chosen few who would find salvation (see Fauset, 1944; Shepperson, 1953; Fernandez, 1965). The sociological importance lies not in the contents of the visions themselves but in the thoughts and actions they provoke amongst those individuals coming under their spell; the imperative to integrate an imagined heritage of the past with the exigencies of the present and the future, and the development of a sense of purpose and unity providing for meaning and motivation in the lives of the members.

The Rastas' concern to return to Africa and the 'way of the ancients' illustrated the strain to establish some continuity with the past, a continuity which they saw had been disrupted by the devastations of colonialism and migration. During the process their cultures had been appropriated and they had been left with nothing but remnants of a European culture which repeatedly depreciated blacks and any cultural contribution they had made. In the act of countering this perceived process the Rastas tried to reaffirm what they thought to be their traditional African culture; they proclaimed themselves as Africans (or Ethiopians) and made it known that they wished to return to Africa. But it was an Africa which they had created, an image on which to project their dreams and ambitions – it could function in any way they desired.

But importantly, it provided a cultural reference point or focus for their sense of culture and here is the key to understanding the enterprise. Black youths in Britain saw themselves as deprived, 'suffering' at the hands of the white man's Babylon, subjected to 'pressure'. Materially deprived certainly, but culturally lacking too. Their response was to invent for themselves a fictive culture based on the phantom land of Africa. The roots-searching thirst for knowledge of Africa, through reading and reasoning, was no esoteric exercise, but an attempt to link their own vacant lives with those of their ancestors and to use this as a projection for the perfect future. Once the link had been forged they approached 'insight', became liberated from old ways and saw themselves as parties in the apocalyptic struggle with the evil of Babylon.

It would be facile to conclude that because the expected millennium will not arrive and the Rastas will not be returned to their fatherland that the movement will fade into obscurity as dreams die and West Indian youth work out more appropriate recipes for long-term plans. The importance of Rasta was that blacks in the 1970s seized the initiative and, in an upsurge of religious zeal, plunged themselves into a quest for culture; and it was a quest which took place in England. It was the postures, perspectives and pre-dispositions the vision of Africa bred on British shores that had relevance. Whether the emergence and relatively rapid growth of the Rastafarian movement will eventually have any lasting effect on the fabric of British race relations is open to question. At the time of writing the defection rate was virtually non-existent (only a handful of EOC members conceded that Haile Selassie was not God) and the movement's impact was being felt at younger age levels with black schoolchildren adopting the colours without real conviction but still demonstrating an assonance with the movement. This development suggests a stylisation of Rasta whereby its basic impulses could be harnessed and converted into fashion and it would be unwise to dismiss such an idea. The reservoir of enthusiasm for Rasta was enormous, but whether this was to be translated into membership or peripheral attachment was to be largely decided by the amount and intensity of external attack or social criticism heaped on the move-ment. Such 'pressure' was anticipated for the Rastas by the man to whom every brother looked for inspiration and guidance. It seems fitting then to close, as I started, with his caution and prophecy.

To face the battle of human opposition is the duty of the courageous oppressed, and as four hundred million of us who suffer from the grinding heels of prejudice and injustice prepare ourselves the world over, the world may laugh, but surely by the character of our makeup we shall surprise them all, and lead our children into the light of freedom, that for which the noblest men of all ages have suffered. (Marcus Garvey, 1967. Vol. II, p. 226)

Figure 5   *Rastafarian Milestones: England*

1955	Attempt to form the United Afro-West Indian Brotherhood
1958	Rastas sighted in Brixton, London
1968	Formation of the Universal Black Improvement Organisa-tion and its political wing, the People's Democratic Party
1971	Fox and Adams (Wold) form local of the EWF in London
1972	Twelve Tribes of Israel is formed in London
	Haughton's activity in Birmingham

1973	Establishment of the EOC in England
	Grand Rastafarian Ball in London
1974	British release of Bob Marley and the Wailers' 'Natty Dread' album
1975	Death of Haile Selassie
	National tour of Marley and the Wailers
	Incipient spread starts in England
1976	EOC's Abba instructs members to discard belief in the divinity of Haile Selassie and remove locks
	Release of 'Rastaman Vibration' record
1977	Publication of the *Shades of Grey* report
1978	Broadcast of London Weekend Television programme, 'Credo', on the English movement

Statement of a Rastaman

The author of the following was one of the founder members of the English EWF. He claims to be at the political extreme of the Rastafarian movement, 'a true Garveyite' and admits to have been criticised by other brethren for his activist stance. After reading drafts of some sections of my work, he suggested that I might include a statement by him. Although he is a member of the Ethiopian Orthodox Church, his views are by no means representative of that body.

MARCUS GARVEY AND HAILE SELASSIE

First, I should say that I am not trying to prove the truth or falsity of the belief in the divinity of Haile Selassie I, a belief not recognised by any other religious organisation, but am simply attempting to explain why it is *possible* to believe such.

One has to understand that the 1930s was a period not long after the Emancipation. Many people still living in Jamaica might have been slaves themselves. Having seen no improvement in their situations, they came to realise that some kind of strength had to come from the African continent. They could not expect any meaningful freedom without a power base in Africa. This realisation was caused by Marcus Garvey who always said 'Africa for the Africans' and that blacks must look to Africa for their spiritual and political guidance. He also said that every black man should see God through his own spectacles and worship the God of Ethiopia. Without this he could not expect to find his own identity.

It is said that Garvey was the man who founded the Rastafarian movement but perhaps this is not entirely correct because Garvey never publicly acclaimed Haile Selassie as having divinity. And Garvey was alive *after* Haile Selassie's coronation. At first this struck me as strange, but when I looked more deeply at what Garvey did in fact say it became clearer – that when a black king is crowned this will mean our deliverance is near. Not a *God* but a *sign*. He did not even say it was Haile Selassie. A certain amount of people had eyes on Ethiopia, the only nation resisting European domination at the time. Europe was not far from its height of power and all Europeans had achievements they could point to with pride. So it was necessary for blacks to find somebody that could be elevated to a position where he could be worshipped in order to restore some pride and hope for black peoples. They thought Haile Selassie must be the man of which Garvey spoke. It appears not only Rastafarian brethren thought this but the considerable majority of people in Jamaica. And this to begin with was because of his numerous titles. Conquering Lion of the Tribe of Judah, Root of David, King of Kings etc. Also, bear in mind that black peoples the world over are very very religious – this is part of their nature, and there is always strong adherence to religious beliefs. So they equated their situations to those of the Israelites who experienced similar captivity and looked for inspiration from the Bible. The fulfilment of the prophecy of Revelations when the Kings of the earth gather to make war with the Lamb, the Rastafarian movement identified when the Italians invaded Abyssinia. Also, the prophecy said 'Behold, a white horse and he that sat thereon' and, because Haile Selassie sat on a white horse, this was thought to be a divine happening. Revelations also said the Lamb would overcome the kings of the earth because they would fight with each other and this is what happened. The Italians ended up fighting with the British who moved into Africa to drive out the Italians and Germans.

It may not seem tangible to say Haile Selassie is around today but spiritually he is around as much as Jesus Christ and Moses in the people's hearts and minds. If the Rastafarian doctrine is correct then Haile Selassie must be waiting somewhere for the annhilation of world powers, possibly World War III, so he can then take his role as ruler of the world. Quite possibly he can appear when he considers it necessary. Only history can decide this and one cannot ridicule and condemn people on the grounds of them believing this to be so any more than one can do so for believing in Jesus Christ or Allah.

POLITICS AND RAS TAFARI

The movement in this country is a minority within other minorities. It is also without a leader and therefore without a role. In Jamaica accepting Haile Selassie as divine has political implications and the only way they can realise themselves is to have their political power – and this, I feel, will happen with a Rastafarian government. But this is not conceivable in this country. In Jamaica Manley's socialism is a carbon copy of British politics and cannot work because it forgets the basic thing – people must have food to eat. This situation will deteriorate and Rastas are the only ones sufficiently outside the political arena to be above the corruptive influences of the system. They will get the total backing of the people when it is realised that the parliamentary system has failed them and their forefathers and their children. In England life is not tough enough for the movement to have any political impact and this is why Ras Tafari has an imbalance. Accepting Ras Tafari causes a lot of young guys to want to learn higher spiritual things before learning to live in a day-to-day fashion, i.e. they lack *discipline*. There are no leaders, therefore no discipline and no role for the movement. Unlike Moses we have no power over our former slaves, and let's face it that is what we are – slaves. I used to be attacked for trying to cultivate such discipline and political awareness. I tried to show that politics is what you eat, drink and where you sleep. Unless we have this element Rastas will continue to have the reputation of reggae singers and do nothing constructive. Looking different is only a beginning. Now progress must be made towards realising our full potential and making ourselves be accepted seriously. At the moment people look at Ras Tafari and think it is bad, something to be cut out of society. In time they will come to see the true benefits of the movement to black peoples, not only here, but in the world.

July, 1978

Bibliography

BOOKS AND ARTICLES

Aberle, David F. (1966) *The Peyote Religion among the Navaho*, Chicago: Aldine Publishing.

Adotevi, Stanislas (1969) 'Négritude is dead: the burial', *Journal of the New African Literature and the Arts*, parts 7–8 (July), pp. 70–81.

Argyle, Michael and Beit-Hallahmi, Benjamin (1975) *The Social Psychology of Religion*, London: Routledge & Kegan Paul.

Baldwin, James (1962) *Nobody Knows My Name*, New York: Dell.

Ballard, Roger and Ballard, Catherine (1977) 'The Sikhs: the development of South Asian settlements in England', in J. L. Watson (ed.), *Between Two Cultures*, Oxford: Blackwell, pp. 21–56.

Banbury, Thomas (1894) *Jamaican Superstitions; Or the Obeah Book*, Kingston: De Souza.

Banton, Michael (1967) *Race Relations*, London: Tavistock.

Banton, Michael (1977) *The Idea of Race*, London: Tavistock.

Barkun, Michael (1974) *Disaster and the Millennium*, London: Yale University Press.

Barnett, Donald L. and Njama, Karaj (1960) *Mau Mau from Within*, New York: Monthly Review Press.

Barrett, Leonard E. (1968) *The Rastafarians: A Study in Messianic Cultism*, Caribbean Monograph Series 6, Rio Piedras, Puerto Rico: Institute of Caribbean Studies.

Barrett, Leonard E. (1974) *Soul-Force: African Heritage in Afro-American Religion*, New York: Anchor Press/Doubleday.

Barrett, Leonard E. (1977) *The Rastafarians: the Dreadlocks of Jamaica*, London: Heinemann.

Baxter, Paul and Sansom, Basil (eds) (1972) *Race and Social Difference*, Harmondsworth: Penguin.

Becker, Howard S. (1963) *Outsiders: Studies in the Sociology of Deviance*, New York: Free Press.

Becker, Howard S. (1964) *The Other Side*, New York: Free Press.

Beckford, James (1975) *The Trumpet of Prophecy: A Sociological Study of Jehova's Witnesses*, Oxford: Blackwell.

Beckwith, Martha Warren (1923) 'Some religious cults in Jamaica', *American Journal of Psychology*, vol. 34, pp. 32–45.

Berger, Peter L. (1969) *The Social Reality of Religion*, London: Faber & Faber.

Berger, Peter L. and Luckmann, Thomas (1972) *The Social Construction of Reality*, Harmondsworth: Penguin.

Berlitz, Charles (1975) *The Bermuda Triangle*, St. Albans: Panther.

Berrian, Albert H. and Long, Richard A. (eds) (1967) *Négritude:*

Essays and Studies, Hampton, Virginia: Hampton Institute Press.

Bessell, M. J. (1938) 'Nyabingi', *Uganda Journal*, vol 1, no. 2 (October), pp. 73–86.

Bittner Egon (1967) 'The police on Skid Row: a study of peace keeping', *American Sociological Review*, vol. 32, no 5, pp. 699–715.

Bognador, Vernon and Skidelsky, Robert (eds) (1970) *The Age of Affluence,* London: Macmillan.

Boot, Adrian and Thomas, Michael (1976) *Jamaica: Babylon on a Thin Wire*, London: Thames & Hudson.

Bowen, W. Errol (1971) 'Rastafarism and the new society', *Savacou: A Journal of Caribbean Artists* (June), pp. 41–50.

Brazier, Chris (1977) 'On the link between reggae and new wave', *Melody Maker*, 26 November.

Brown, John (1977) *Shades of Grey: A Report on Police-West Indian Relations in Handsworth*, Cranfield: Cranfield Institute of Technology.

Burridge, Kenelm (1969) *New Heaven New Earth*, Oxford: Blackwell.

Calley, Malcolm J. C. (1965) *God's People: West Indian Pentecostal Sects in England*, London: Oxford University Press.

Carmichael, Stokely and Hamilton, Charles (1967) *Black Power: The Politics of Liberation in America*, New York: Random House.

Cashmore, Ernest (1977a) 'The Rastaman cometh', *New Society*, vol. 41, no. 777 (25 August), pp. 382–4.

Cashmore, Ernest (1977b) 'Jah people' (review of L. E. Barrett's *The Rastafarians*), *New Society*, vol. 42, no. 791 (1 December), pp. 479–80.

Cashmore, Ernest (1978) 'A sociological analysis of the history, development and current state of the Rastafarian movement in Jamaica and England', unpublished thesis, Department of Philosophy and Religion, Central Reference Library, Birmingham.

Cashmore, Ernest (1979) British Journal of Sociology, vol. 30, no. 3 (September) 'More than a version: a study of reality creation'.

Cassidy, Frederic G. (1961) *Jamaica Talk*, London: Macmillan.

Césaire, Aimé (1959) 'The man of culture and his responsibilities', *Présence Africaine*, vol. 24–25 (February–March) pp. 125–32.

Chambliss, William J. (1976) 'The State and criminal law', in William J. Chambliss and Milton Mankoff (eds), *Whose Law? What Order?*, New York: Wiley, pp. 66–106.

Chambliss, William J. and Seidman, Robert B. (1971) *Law, Order and Power*, Reading, Massachussetts: Addison-Wesley.

Chambre, Major (1858) *Recollections of West-End Life*, London: Hurst & Blackett.

Clarke, Edith (1974) *My Mother Who Fathered Me*, London: Allen & Unwin.

Clarke, John (1973) 'Skinheads and Youth Culture', Stencilled Paper 23, Centre for Contemporary Cultural Studies, University of Birmingham.

Clarke, John (1975) 'The skinheads and the magical recovery of community', *Cultural Studies*, vols. 7 and 8 (Summer), pp. 99–102.

Cohen, Abner (1974a) *Two-Dimensional Man*, London: Routledge & Kegan Paul.

Cohen, Abner (ed.) (1974b) *Urban Ethnicity*, London: Tavistock.

Cohen, Stanley (1973) *Folk Devils and Moral Panics*, St Albans: Paladin.

Cohn, Norman (1957) *The Pursuit of the Millennium*, London: Secker & Warburg.

Corfield, F. D. (1960) *Historical Survey of the Origins and Growth of Mau Mau*, London: HMSO.

Coulthard, G. R. (1962) *Race and Colour in Caribbean Literature*, London: Oxford University Press.

Coulthard, G. R. (1969) Review of A. H. Berrian and R. A. Long's *Négritude: Essays and Studies, Caribbean Studies*, vol. 9, no. 1 (April), pp. 81–3.

Coulthard, G. R. (1970) 'Négritude – reality and mystification', *Caribbean Studies*, vol. 10, no. 1 (April), pp. 42–51.

Cronon, E. David (ed.) (1973) *Marcus Garvey*, Englewood Cliffs: Prentice-Hall.

Cronon, E. David (ed.) (1974) *Black Moses: The Study of Marcus Garvey and the Universal Negro Improvement Association*, London: University of Wisconsin Press.

Dahya, Badr (1974) 'The nature of Pakistani ethnicity in the industrial cities in England', in A. Cohen (ed.), *Urban Ethnicity*, London: Tavistock, pp. 77–118.

Dallas, Robert C. (1803) *The History of the Maroons*, London: Strahan, Longman & Reese.

Dalrymple, Henderson (1976) *Bob Marley: Music, Myth and the Rastas*, London: Carib-Arawak.

Daniel, W. W. (1968) *Racial Discrimination in England*, Harmondsworth: Penguin.

Davison, R. B. (1966) *Black British: Immigrants to England*, London: Oxford University Press.

Depestre, René (1969) 'Le metamorphoses de la négritude en Amerique', *Présence Africaine*, vol. 75, no. 3, pp. 19–33.

Downes, David (1966) *The Delinquent Solution*, London: Routledge & Kegan Paul.

Edelman, Murray (1964) *The Symbolic Uses of Politics*, Urbana: University of Illinois Press.

Edwards, Adolph (1972) *Marcus Garvey, 1887–1940*, London: New Beacon Books.

Egbuna, Obi (1970) *Destroy This Temple*, London: MacGibbon & Kee.

Egbuna, Obi (1971) 'The "contradictions" of black power', *Race Today*, vol. 3 (August), pp. 266–8 and (September), pp. 298–9.

Elkins, Stanley M. (1963) *Slavery: A Problem in American Institutional and Intellectual Life*, New York: Grosset & Dunlap.

Essien-Udom, E. U. (1962) *Black Nationalism: A Search for Identity in America*, Chicago: University of Chicago Press.

Fanon, Frantz (1952) *Peau noire masques blancs*, Paris: Editions du Seuil.

Fauset, Arthur Huff (1944) *Black Gods of the Metropolis: Negro Religious Cults in the Urban North*, Philadelphia, Penn.: University of Pennsylvania Press.

Fernandez, James W. (1965) 'Politics and prophecy: African religious movements', *Practical Anthropology*, vol. 12, no. 2 (March–April), pp. 71–5.

Firth, Raymond (1953) 'Social changes in the western Pacific', *Journal of the Royal Society of Arts*, vol. 101, no. 4909, pp. 803–19.

Firth, Raymond (1973) *Symbols, Public and Private*, London: Allen & Unwin.

Fleming, Ian (1971) *The Man With Golden Gun*, London: Cape.

Foner, Nancy (1977) 'The Jamaicans: cultural and social change among migrants in Britain' in James L. Watson (ed.), *Between Two Cultures*, Oxford: Blackwell, pp. 120–50.

Galdstone, Iago and Zetterberg, Hans (eds) (1958) *Panic and Morale*, New York: International Universities Press.

Garvey, Amy Jacques (1968) *Black Power in America*, Kingston: United Printers.

Garvey, Amy Jacques (1970) *Garvey and Garveyism*, London: Macmillan.

Garvey, Marcus (1967) *Philosophy and Opinions*, 2 vols. (compiled, A. J. Garvey), London: Cass.

Goffman, Erving (1959), *The Presentation of Self in Everyday Life*, New York: Doubleday/Anchor.

Goffman, Erving (1970) *Strategic Interaction*, Oxford: Blackwell.

Goody, Esther N. and Groothues, Christine Muir (1977) 'The West Africans: the quest for education in London', in J. L. Watson (ed.), *Between Two Cultures*, Oxford: Blackwell, pp. 151–80.

Hall, Stuart (1976a) *Africa is Alive and Well in Diaspora*, Unesco Conference on 'Social structure, revolutionary change and culture in southern Africa', Mapuro, Mozambique.

Hall, Stuart (1976b) 'Violence and the media', in N. Tutt (ed.), *Violence*, London: HMSO, pp. 221–37.

Hebdige, Dick (1975) 'Reggae, rastas and rudies', *Cultural Studies*, vols. 7 and 8 (Summer), pp. 135–54.

Herskovits, Melville J. (1941) *The Myth of the Negro Past*, New York: Harper & Brothers.

Hill, Clifford (1970) 'Some aspects of race and religion in Britain', in D. Martin and M. Hill (eds), *A Sociological Yearbook of Religion in Britain*, vol. 3, London: SCM Press, pp. 30–44.

Hill, Clifford (1971) 'Pentecostalist growth – result of racialism?' *Race Today*, vol. 3, pp. 187–90.

Hiro, Dilip (1973) *Black British, White British*, London: Monthly Review Press.

Hiro, Dilip and Fay, Stephen (1967) 'Man it's beautiful – but does it work?' *Sunday Times*, 29 October, p. 8.

Horowitz, Irving Louis (ed.) (1978) *Science, Sin and Scholarship*, London: MIT Press.

Horton, Robin (1967) 'African traditional thought and western science', *Africa*, vol. 37, no. 1 (January), pp. 50–71 and vol. 37, no. 2 (April), pp. 155–87.

Irele, Abiola (1965) 'Négritude or black cultural nationalism', *Journal of Modern African Studies*, vol. 3, no. 3 pp. 321–48.

Ita, J. M. (1973) 'Frobenius, Senghor and the image of Africa', in R. Horton and R. Finnegan (eds), *Modes of Thought*, London: Faber & Faber, pp. 306–36.

James, C. L. R. (1938a) *The Black Jacobins*, London: Secker and Warburg.

James, C. L. R. (1938b) *History of Negro Revolt*, London: Fact.

Jarvie, Ian C. (1972) *Concepts and Society*, London: Routledge & Kegan Paul.

Jenkins, David (1975) *Black Zion: The Return of Afro-Americans and West Indians to Africa*, London: Wildwood.

Johnson, Linton Kwesi (1975) 'Roots and rock: the Marley enigma', *Race Today*, vol. 7, no. 10 (October), pp. 237–8.

Johnson, Linton Kwesi (1976a) 'Jamaican rebel music', *Race and Class*, vol. 17, no. 4 (Spring), pp. 397–412.

Johnson, Linton Kwesi (1976b) 'The reggae rebellion', *New Society*, vol. 36, no. 714 (10 June), p. 589.

Kallynder, Rolston and Dalrymple, Henderson (n.d.) *Reggae: A People's Music*, London: Carib-Arawak.

Kidel, Mark (1977) 'New wave', *The Listener*, vol. 97, no. 2515 (30 June), p. 862.

Kitsuse, John I. (1964) 'Societal reaction to deviant behaviour', in H. S. Becker (ed.), *The Other Side*, New York: Free Press, pp. 87–102.

Kitzinger, Sheila (1966) 'The Rastafarian brethren of Jamaica', *Comparative Studies in History and Society*, vol. 9, pp. 33–9.

Kitzinger, Sheila (1969) 'Protest and mysticism: the Rastafari cult of Jamaica', *Journal for the Scientific Study of Religion*, vol. 3, no. 2 (Fall), pp. 240–62.

Kuper, Adam (1976) *Changing Jamaica*, London: Routledge & Kegan Paul.

Kuper, Leo (1974) *Race, Class and Power*, London: Duckworth.

Lanternari, Vittorio (1963) *The Religions of the Oppressed*, London: MacGibbon & Kee.

Lawrence, Daniel (1974) *Black Migrants–White Natives: A Study of Race Relations in Nottingham*, London: Cambridge University Press.

Lemert, Edwin M. (1951) *Social Pathology: A Systematic Approach to the Study of Sociopathic Behaviour*, New York: McGraw-Hill.

Lemert, Edwin M. (1964) 'Social structure, social control and deviation', in M. B. Clinard (ed.), *Anomie and Deviant Behaviour*, New York: Free Press, pp. 57–97.

Lester, Julius (1971) 'Black Power and Colonialism', in O. E. Uya (ed.), *Black Brotherhood: Afro-Americans and Africa*, Lexington, Mass.: Heath, pp. 279–82.

Lincoln, C. Eric (1961) *The Black Muslims in America*, Boston,

Mass.: Beacon Press.

Llewellyn Watson, G. (1973) 'Social structure and social movements', *British Journal of Sociology*, vol. 24, no. 12, pp. 188–204.

Long, Edward (1774) *The History of Jamaica* (3 vols.), London: Lowndes.

Lowenthal, David (1972) *West Indian Societies*, London: Oxford University Press.

M., Ruby and Essien-Udom, E. U. (1971) 'Malcolm X: an international man', in O. E. Uya (ed.), *Black Brotherhood*, pp. 257–78.

McCormack, Ed. (1976) 'Bob Marley with a bullet', *Rolling Stone* (12 August), pp. 37–41.

McGlashen, Colin (1973) 'The sound system', *Sunday Times* Colour Magazine (4 February), pp. 12–21.

McKnight, Cathy and Tobler, John (1977) *Bob Marley and the Roots of Reggae*, London: Star.

Mandefro, Abba L. (1971) *The Ethiopian Orthodox Tewahedo Church and its Activities in the West*, Kingston: Mandefro.

Marsh, Peter (1977) 'Dole-queue rock', *New Society*, vol. 39, no. 746 (20 January), pp. 112–14.

Marsh, Peter, Rosser, Elisabeth and Harré, Rom (1978) *The Rules of Disorder*, London: Routledge & Kegan Paul.

Matza, David (1966) *Delinquency and Drift*, New York: Wiley.

Mazrui, Ali A. (1978) 'Négritude, the Talmudic tradition of blacks and Jews', *Ethnic and Racial Studies*, vol. 1, no. 1 (January), pp. 19–36.

Melly, George (1970) *Revolt into Style: The Pop Arts in Britain*, London: Allen Lane.

Mission to Africa (1961) *Report*, Kingston: Government Printer.

Moore, Joseph G. (1953) *Religions of Jamaican Negroes: A Study of Afro-Jamaican Acculturation*, Department of Anthropology, Evanston, Ill.: Northwestern University.

Morland, J. K. (1958) 'Racial recognition by nursery school children in Lynchburg, Virginia', *Social Forces*, vol. 37, pp. 132–7.

Nettleford, Rex (1970a) *Mirror, Mirror: Identity, Race and Protest in Jamaica*, Kingston: Sangster & Collins.

Nettleford, Rex (1970b) 'Poverty at the root of the race issue in Jamaica: a special report', *The Times*, 14 September.

Norris, Katrin (1962) *Jamaica: The Search for Identity*, London: Oxford University Press.

Owens, Joseph (1977) *Dread*, Kingston: Sangsters.

Patterson, H. Orlando (1964a) *The Children of Sisyphus*, London: Hutchinson.

Patterson, H. Orlando (1964b) 'Ras Tafari: the cult of outcasts', *New Society*, vol. 4, no. 111 (12 November), pp. 15–17.

Patterson, H. Orlando (1967) *The Sociology of Slavery*, London: MacGibbon & Kee.

Patterson, Sheila (1963) *Dark Strangers*, London: Tavistock.

Philipps, J. E. T. (1928) 'The Nabingi', *Congo: Revue Générale de la Colonie Belge*, vol. 1, no. 1 (January), pp. 310–21.

Phillips, Derek L. (1973) *Abandoning Method*, London: Jossey Bass.

Pirsig, Robert M. (1974) *Zen and the Art of Motorcycle Maintenance: An Inquiry into Values*, New York: Bantam.

Proshansky, Harold and Newton, Peggy (1973) 'Colour: the nature and meaning of negro self-identity' in P. Watson (ed.), *Psychology and Race*, Harmondsworth: Penguin, pp. 176–212.

Quinney, Richard (1970) *The Social Reality of Crime*, Boston, Mass.: Little, Brown.

Reckford, Mary (1969) 'The slave rebellion of 1831', *Jamaica Journal*, vol. 3, no. 2 (June): pp. 25–31.

Rex, John and Moore, Robert (1967) *Race, Community and Conflict: A Study of Sparkbrook*, London: Oxford University Press.

Rex, John (1970) *Race Relations in Sociological Theory*, London: Weidenfeld & Nicolson.

Robinson, Carey (1969) *The Fighting Maroons of Jamaica*, Kingston: Sangster & Collins.

Rock, Paul (1973) *Deviant Behaviour*, London: Hutchinson.

Rock, Paul and Cohen, Stanley (1970) 'The Teddy Boy', in V. Bognador and R. Skidelski (eds), *The Age of Affluence*, London: Macmillan, pp. 288–320.

Runciman, W. G. (1966) *Relative Deprivation and Social Justice*, London: Routledge & Kegan Paul.

Sanders, Ed (1971) *The Family: The Story of Charles Manson's Dune Buggy Attack Battalion*, London: Rupert Hart-Davis.

Semmel, Bernard (1962a) *The Governor Eyre Controversy*, London: MacGibbon & Kee.

Semmel, Bernard (1962b) 'The issue of "Race" in the British reaction to the Morant Bay uprising of 1865', *Caribbean Studies*, vol. 2, no. 3 (October), pp. 3–15.

Senghor, Leopold S. (1968) *Africa and the Germans*, Tübingen and Basel: Horst Erdmann Verlag.

Shepperson, George (1953) 'Ethiopianism and African nationalism', *Phylon*, vol. 14, no. 1, pp. 9–19.

Simpson, George Eaton (1955a) 'Political cultism in West Kingston, Jamaica', *Social and Economic Studies*, vol. 4, no. 2 (June), pp. 133–49.

Simpson, George Eaton (1955b) 'Culture change and reintegration found in the cults of West Kingston, Jamaica', *Proceedings of the American Philosophical Society*, vol. 99, no. 2 (April), pp. 89–92.

Simpson, George Eaton (1955c) 'The Rastafari movement in Kingston, Jamaica', *Social Forces*, vol. 4, no. 2, pp. 159–71.

Simpson, George Eaton (1962) 'The Ras Tafari movement in Jamaica in its millenial aspect', in S. Thrupp (ed.), *Millenial Dreams in Action*, The Hague: Mouton, pp. 160–5.

Skolnick, Jerome H. (1966) *Justice Without Trial*, New York: Wiley.

Skurnick, Walter A. E. (1965) 'Leopold Sedar Senghor and African socialism', *Journal of Modern African Studies*, vol. 3, no. 3, pp. 349–69.

Smith, M. G., Augier, Roy and Nettleford, Rex (1967) 'The Ras

Tafari movement in Kingston, Jamaica', *Caribbean Quarterly*, vol. 13, no. 3, pp. 3–29 and vol. 13, no. 4, pp. 3–14.

Steiger, Brad (1977) *Atlantic Rising*, London: Sphere.

Thomas, L. V. (1965) 'Senghor and négritude', *Présence Africaine*, vol. 26, no. 54, pp. 102–33.

Thomas, Michael (1973) 'The wild side of paradise', *Rolling Stone* (19 June), unnumbered.

Thomas, Michael (1976) 'The Rastas are coming, the Rastas are coming', *Rolling Stone* (12 August), pp. 32–7.

Torode, John A. (1965) 'Race moves in on the unions', *New Society*, vol. 5, no. 142 (17 June), pp. 5–7.

Troyna, Barry A. (1977a) 'The reggae war', *New Society*, vol. 39, no. 753 (10 March), pp. 491–2.

Troyna, Barry A. (1977b) 'Angry youngsters – a response to racism in Britain', *Youth In Society*, vol. 26 (December), pp. 13–15.

Troyna, Barry A. (1978) 'Race and streaming: a case study', *Educational Review*, vol. 30, no 1, pp. 59–65.

Turk, Austin T. (1976) 'Law, order and conflict: from theorizing towards theories', *Canadian Review of Sociology and Anthropology*, vol. 13, no. 3 (August), pp. 282–94.

Ullendorff, Edward (1973) *The Ethiopians: An Introduction to Country and People*, London: Oxford University Press.

Vincent, Theodore G. (1976) *Black Power and the Garvey Movement*, San Francisco: Ramparts.

Von Daniken, Erich (1971) *Chariot of the Gods*, London: Corgi.

Von Daniken, Erich (1972) *Return to the Stars*, London: Corgi.

Wallace, Anthony F. C. (1956a) 'Revitalization movements', *American Anthropologist*, vol. 58, pp. 264–81.

Wallace, Anthony F. C. (1956b) 'Stress and rapid personality change', *International Record of Medicine*, vol. 169, pp. 761–74.

Wallis, Roy (1976) *The Road to Total Freedom: A Sociological Analysis of Scientology*, London: Heinemann.

Walvin, James (1973) *Black and White: The Negro and English Society, 1555–1945*, London: Allen Lane.

White, Garth (1965) 'Rudie, Oh Rudie!' *Caribbean Quarterly*, vol. 13, no. 3, pp. 39–44.

Wilkins, Leslie T. (1964) *Social Deviance: Social Policy, Action and Research*, London: Tavistock.

Williams, Anthony J. (1974) 'The role of the prophet in millenial Cults', unpublished thesis, Exeter College, Oxford University.

Williams, Joseph J. (1938) 'The Maroons of Jamaica', *Anthropological Series*, vol. 3, no. 4, Boston, Mass.: Boston College Press.

Wilson, Bryan R. (1973) *Magic and the Millennium*, London: Heinemann.

Wilson, Bryan R. (1975) *The Noble Savages*, London: University of California Press.

Wilson, Colin (1973) *The Occult*, St. Albans: Mayflower.

X., Malcolm and Haley, Alex (1966) *The Autobiography of Malcolm X*, London: Hutchinson and Collins.

MUSIC

'Trench Town Rock' written by Bob Marley, by Bob Marley and The Wailers, B and C Music, Trojan Records, 1971.

'Slave Driver' written by Bob Marley, from *Catch A Fire* by The Wailers, Copyright Control, Island Records, 1973.

'400 Years' written by Bob Marley, from *Catch A Fire* by The Wailers, Tuff Gong Music, Island Records, 1973.

'Duppy Conqueror' written by Bob Marley *or* Lee Perry, from *Burnin'* by The Wailers, Tuff Gong Music, Island Records, 1973.

'Get Up, Stand Up' written by Bob Marley and Peter Tosh, from *Burnin'* by The Wailers, Tuff Gong Music, Island Records, 1973.

'Burnin' and Lootin'' written by Bob Marley from *Burnin'* by The Wailers, Tuff Gong Music, Island Records, 1973.

'Natty Dread' writer not credited, from *Natty Dread* by Bob Marley and The Wailers, Rondor Music, Island Records, 1974.

'Them Belly Full (But We Hungry)' written by Bob Marley *or* L. Coghile and C. Barrett (on *Live* album, Island Records), from *Natty Dread* by Bob Marley and the Wailers, Rondor Music, Island Records, 1974.

'Positive Vibration' written by V. Ford, from *Rastaman Vibration* by Bob Marley and The Wailers, Rondor Music, Island Records, 1976.

'Keep Your Dread' written by Manley Buchanan, from *Natty Cultural Dread* by Big Youth, New Town Sound, Trojan Records, 1976.

'Exodus' written by Bob Marley, from *Exodus: Movement of Jah People* by Bob Marley and The Wailers, Bob Marley Music BVI/ Rondor Music, Island Records, 1977.

'Anarchy in the UK' written by Jones, Matlock, Cook and Rotten from *Never Mind the Bollocks, Here's the Sex Pistols* by the Sex Pistols, Virgin Music, Virgin Records, 1977.

Index